The Directory of Humor Magazines and
and
Humor Organizations in America
(and Canada)
3rd Edition

The Directory of Humor Magazines and Humor Organizations in America (and Canada)
3rd Edition

Edited by Glenn C. Ellenbogen, Ph.D.

Wry-Bred Press, Inc.
New York, New York

Library of Congress Catalog Card Number: 91-68398
ISBN: 0-9606190-5-4

Published by

Wry-Bred Press, Inc.
P.O. Box 1454
Madison Square Station
New York, NY 10159-1454

Table of Contents

Introduction

Humor is a funny thing. It brings laughter, enjoyment, relief, and oftentimes even insight to millions of people (including the 2,446,567 people who subscribe to the humor periodicals listed in this directory), and yet humor doesn't seem to be taken seriously in our culture.

Perhaps nowhere in America can the lack of appreciation for humor be seen better than in that great microcosm of Society—the Library. Just walk into your local library and say to your librarian, "My toaster just broke, my wife has a headache, and the IRS just sent me a notice that they're auditing my 1990 tax return. You know what I could really use just about now?—A good humorous article on Psychology. Where do I look?...Or better yet—puns. Give me some good puns. No, no...give me some *bad* puns. Where should I go?" Most librarians would probably tell you where to go.

With the advent of *The Directory of Humor Magazines and Humor Organizations in America (and Canada)*, this scenario has been radically changed. Now, when your library stocks the directory, you can readily find what you are looking for in the psychology humor category by looking up Psychology in the Cross Index of Subject Areas section of the directory. Here, you will find, for instance, the *Journal of Polymorphous Perversity*. And for good and bad puns alike, look under Word Play and Puns to find The International Save the Pun Foundation and its publication—*The Pundit*.

So, the next time you ask your librarian, "Do you know where there's a good humorous article on Psychology?" only to be met with, "I don't know," you can respond, "Well, if you look up under Psychology in *The Directory of Humor Magazines and Humor Organizations in America (and Canada)*, you'll see that the *Journal of Polymorphous Perversity* publishes humorous Psychology articles!"

Now, read and enjoy!

Glenn C. Ellenbogen
New York, New York

How to Use This Directory

The *Directory of Humor Magazines and Humor Organizations in America (and Canada)* lists humor magazines (under which is included humor newsletters, humor newspapers, humor serial directories, and periodicals on the topic of humor) and humor organizations. In order to be listed in *The Directory*, a magazine (or other periodical) must be primarily devoted to humor and be issued on a periodic basis. A magazine such as *The New Yorker* would not be listed, although it may carry cartoons and humorous pieces, because it is *not primarily* devoted to humor. In order to be listed in *The Directory*, an organization must be primarily devoted to humor and must allow individuals to participate in some way within the organization, or must publish a periodical primarily devoted to humor.

The magazines and organizations listed provided all of the information in response to a detailed questionnaire. All listings provide the **name** of the organization or publication, name of **editor(s)**, name of the **publisher**, mailing **address**, and publication **format** (magazine, journal, newsletter, newspaper, etc.). Most of the listings also provide the **telephone number**, year that the organization or publication was **founded**, and a **description** of the organization and/or publication. Organizations generally present their purpose and aims, along with information about periodic events that they sponsor. Publications describe their periodical and often give titles for some of the recent articles that have appeared in print.

To find out how many issues are published a year, you would look at the **frequency** data. You would also look to see how many issues of the publication were **published in 1991**, are **to be published in 1992**, and are **to be published in 1993**. The **volume number for 1992** is listed in order to make ordering easier. **Subscription periods** vary from publication to publication. Many subscriptions are on a Calendar Year Basis, i.e., no matter whether you order a 1-year subscription on January 1, 1992 or December 31, 1992, you will receive *all* the issues for 1992. Other subscriptions are entered from the date the order is received, i.e., if your 1-year subscription order is received in October 1992, the subscription will run until October 1993. A few publications have their own unique subscription periods.

Membership dues for organizations usually include the price of the periodical(s) produced by the organization. Some organizations require that you be a member in order to receive their publication(s), while others allow non-members to order subscriptions. All of this information is noted in the listings. **Rates** are generally listed for Individual subscriptions, Canadian subscriptions, Foreign subscriptions (i.e., other than Canadian), Library subscriptions, and sample copies. When ordering a sample copy, the date of the issue you receive is generally at the discretion of the publisher.

Many of the organizations listed have provided information on the number of their members, while many publications have provided information on their **circulation rate**.

In order to help you to visualize the publications listed, information has been provided as to their physical dimension (**size**), the **average number of pages per issue**, **production method** (lettering and printing method), and **binding**. The average number of pages per issue varies widely. Publications generally fall into three categories of lettering. The first is "Typewritten/word processed," i.e., the publication in its finished form will reflect the quality of lettering that was produced either on a typewriter, word processor, or some combination. The second category is "Laserprinted," i.e., produced from a laser printer. The third category is "Typeset," the most professional of lettering, found in most books and widely circulated periodicals. Printing methods generally fall into three categories— mimeographed, xeroxed, and offset printed. Offset printing gives the most professional looking copy, although some good xerox copies can begin to approach the quality of offset printed work. **Bindings** fall into four categories—folded and loosely collated, stapled on the surface of the publication, saddle-stitched, and perfect bound. Four-page newsletters are usually folded and newspapers folded and loosely collated (i.e., their pages are not stapled on the edge or spine). Publications with very small circulations (and small budgets) are generally stapled on the surface of the publication, just as you would staple papers together in a corner. Most often, magazines are saddle-stitched, i.e., stapled professionally on the spine of the magazine like, for instance, *Time* magazine. Lastly, periodicals with many many pages are sometimes perfect bound, i.e., produced in paperback book format.

Most of the publications provide **information for authors**. Most of the publications accept **unsolicited manuscripts**, while others ask that you contact the editor first and **inquire** about the specific topic or article you have in mind before submitting your manuscript. A handful of publications do not accept manuscripts on an unsolicited basis. **Reporting time** is the amount of time it takes for a publication to respond to your submission. **Payment rates and terms** are also provided. Generally, only the magazines with very large circulations have large enough budgets to afford to pay for articles; the smaller magazines usually "pay" with free copies of the issue in which the article appears. Most of the publications are copyrighted. The **copyright arrangements between the author and publisher** are indicated. Again, these arrangements vary from "informal" to a formal contract. Some magazines allow the author to keep rights to the article, others require that the author assign all rights to the magazine, while still others require only 1st serial rights.

Advertising rates are presented. Many humor publications do not accept advertisements.

Excerpts from up to three **reviews** are reprinted for each of the publications listed.

Organizations and publications are **cross indexed by subject areas**. Each organization or publication chose those subject areas by which they would be cross indexed.

The **International Standard Serial Number** (ISSN) is listed for many of the publications. The ISSN is frequently used, particularly by libraries, in ordering periodicals.

All of the organizations and publications listed in this directory were given the opportunity to have a **"representative sample article"** or excerpt from an article reprinted next to their data listing. If a sample article was submitted by an organization or publication, you will find the article printed in a ruled box on the page following the data listing for that particular organization or publication. Bear in mind when looking at sample articles in this directory that, *although they may be typeset in this directory*, they may not have appeared in typeset form when appearing in the original publication. (Those humor magazines with small circulations oftentimes cannot afford the expensive typesetting process. Their sample articles, however, were often typeset to provide uniformity of format. *Even those magazines whose sample articles were originally typeset may have been re-typeset for this directory*.) In order to determine whether the magazine's articles typically appear in typeset format or whether the sample article was typeset especially for the directory, you would look at the data under "Production" in the data listing. The listing will indicate whether the magazine was originally "typeset" or produced by some other means (e.g., typewritten, word processed, laserprinted).

A Serious Note About College Humor Magazines

A Serious Note About College Humor Magazines

In his excellent review of the history of college humor magazines, George Test (1987) noted that college humor magazines have a long tradition of publishing satires and spoofs. *Harvard Lampoon*, for instance, has been publishing parodies since 1876. Having edited all three editions of *The Directory of Humor Magazines and Humor Organizations in America (and Canada)*, I can attest to another long tradition that college humor magazines have: they, by and large, do not respond to questionnaires about their magazines. For the first two editions of *The Directory of Humor Magazines*, not a single college humor magazine responded to our questionnaire. For this new, third edition, only a few responded.

Why is it that college humor magazines have proven to be so unresponsive to inquiries? Probably because they were not established to service the humor needs of the general public. They are staffed by unpaid student volunteers whose goal it is to have some fun while entertaining their fellow classmates. There is a high and quick turnover rate in staff; new editors come on board if not every semester then every new academic year. Editors are not greatly concerned with the business side of the magazine, with promoting the magazine and attempting to build circulation. Why should they be when they receive their financing from the university and distribute their magazines for free on campus? There is really little or no impetus, then, for college humor magazine editors and staff to be responsive to inquiries from the outside world.

How difficult, then, would it be for the reader to get his or her hands on a copy of a college humor magazine? Very difficult. Forget calling the telephone company's general information number to track down any given college humor magazine's telephone number. College magazines don't list their telephone numbers with the telephone company. While you might expect to fare better by simply calling the university switchboard, this is not always the case. For example, the switchboard operator at Harvard University had no idea how to reach the *Harvard Lampoon*. And even when you are rewarded by a university operator with the telephone extension for a college humor magazine, you're unlikely to have anyone pick up the ringing phone. After all, the staff may be in classes, on holiday break, on mid-winter break, on summer break, etc.

While from past experience I knew how responsive, or more accurately how unresponsive, college humor magazines could be when asked to complete and return questionnaires about their publications, I decided to conduct a short test of how responsive these magazines would be to fulfilling orders from the public. My empirical test was quite simple. After tracking down the addresses of the college magazines, I ordered *and prepaid* for a sample copy of each college's humor magazine. The results: 22% of the college humor magazines failed to fulfill the order. College humor magazines that did fulfill the orders certainly didn't break any speed records: On the average, the college humor magazines arrived via First Class Mail in about 8 weeks; one magazine (Emory University's *The Spoke*) arrived almost 12 weeks after it was ordered.

As a final (although, granted, limited-in-size) experiment, I journeyed to the campus of one college humor magazine (Columbia University's *Jester*) seeking out its office and staff. No one on campus seemed to have any idea where the magazine's office was located. I hit pay dirt in the student union building: the guard knew the office was somewhere in the building, but not exactly where. I finally found the office—unstaffed. I left a note asking that someone call me. No one ever did.

You will find the few college humor magazines that did respond to our questionnaire listed in the main section of this directory. The names, addresses, and telephone numbers for many of those college humor magazines that did not respond can be found in the Other Humor Magazines, Humor Organizations and Resources section of this directory.

It's a shame that college humor magazines are as unresponsive as they are to the public. After all, these magazines are often among the most irreverent, fresh, vibrant humor periodicals being published today. But, that's the way it is.

G. C. E.

References

Test, G. (1987). College humor magazines. In D. E. E. Sloane, *American humor magazines and comic periodicals* (pp. 531-539). Westport, CT: Greenwood.

Directory Listings

American Association for Therapeutic Humor

Founder: Alison L. Crane, B.S.N., R.N.
Publications: **Laugh It Up** and **Laugh It UpDate**
Publisher: American Association for Therapeutic Humor
              1163 Shermer Road
              Northbrook, IL 60062-4538
Format: **Laugh It Up** is a newsletter; **Laugh It UpDate** is a one-subject monograph
Editor: Karyn Buxman
Phone: (708) 291-0211
Founded: 1987
Description of Organization: The objectives and goals for the **American Association for Therapeutic Humor** are:
    1. To disseminate information about humor and laughter to its members through regular publications.
    2. To provide members with educational opportunities through lectures, seminars, and conferences.
    3. To function as an interdisciplinary network for its members.
    4. To be a clearinghouse of information on humor and laughter as they relate to well-being.
    5. To educate health care professionals and lay audiences about the values and therapeutic uses of humor and laughter.
    6. To develop, promote, conduct, and identify the need for research which further investigates the roles humor and laughter play in well-being.
    7. To encourage, support, and report on innovative programs which incorporate the therapeutic uses of humor.
Description of Publication: Objectives of **Laugh It Up** and **Laugh It UpDate**:
    1. To inform members about news, issues, developments, and trends relating to humor as a therapeutic intervention and laughter as a therapeutic process.
    2. To encourage, cultivate, and promote the professional and personal growth and development of members.
    3. To serve as a forum for opinions and perspectives in the area of therapeutic humor, its uses, values, weaknesses, etc.
    4. To recognize members' accomplishments, both individually and collectively.
    5. To provide news of association activities.
    6. To support, communicate, and foster understanding of association themes, policies, and objectives.
Frequency: 6 issues per year (3 issues of **Laugh It Up** and 3 issues of **Laugh It UpDate**, published on an alternating schedule)
# of issues published in 1991:   6
# of issues to be published in 1992: 6
# of issues to be published in 1993: 6
1992 volume: Volume #6
Subscription period: Subscriptions run from the date the order is received
Annual membership dues (includes newsletters and monographs):

Regular member:	$ 35
Student member/Retired member:	$ 25
Sustaining member:	$ 75
Organizational member:	$125

# of members: 350

Subscription rates (without membership):

	1 year	2 years	3 years
1 year/2 years/3 years:	$15.00	$30.00	$40.00
1 year/2 years/3 years (Canada):	US$20.00	US$40.00	US$55.00
1 year/2 years/3 years (Foreign):	US$20.00	US$40.00	US$55.00

        Sample copy: Free

Average # of pages per issue: 6 pages for **Laugh It Up**; 2 pages for **Laugh It UpDate**

Page size: 8 1/2" x 11"

Production: Laserprinted

Printing: Offset

Binding: Folded and collated loosely

Circulation: 600+

Author information:

        Newsletter and monograph accept unsolicited manuscripts but prospective authors should inquire first

        Reports in 3 weeks

        Author receives 10 complimentary copies of the issue in which the article is published as payment

        Newsletter and monograph own 1st serial rights and upon publication rights revert back to author

        Newsletter and monograph are copyrighted

Advertising rates:

        1/2 page black & white: $150

        Full page black & white: $300

Reviews:

        "Very informative and well written." (Fred F. Lighthall, Ph.D., Professor of Educational Psychology, University of Chicago)

        "**Laugh It Up** intelligently reports on the world of therapeutic humor: organizations, conferences, scientific research, and networking of the delightfully off-centered people involved." (Bruce M. Strombach, Hospital Consultant)

Cross-indexed:

        Business Humor

        Medicine Humor

        Dentistry Humor

        Nursing Humor

        Cartoons/Illustrations/Graphics

        Scholarly Reviews of Humor/Satire as a Subject for Study

        Research on Humor

        Summary of Conferences and Symposiums on Humor/Satire

        Education Humor

        Philosophy Humor

        Psychiatry Humor

        Psychology Humor

        Religion Humor

        Sociology Humor

Laughing All the Way to the Bank

The "Grantland" cartoon strip works. It works for universities, Fortune 500 companies, hospitals, insurance companies, and, yes, banks. Over 400 organizations and companies, with a total circulation of 1.7 million, now subscribe regularly to the concept that humor is a powerful—an extremely useful—communicator.

"'Grantland' touches on topics which would not otherwise by addressed in that company or group," said "Grantland"'s creator, W. Grant Brownrigg in an interview with us. "Briefly touching on a difficult subject through a cartoon can get the point across more effectively than a straight memo, because it doesn't usually threaten people as much as a direct confrontation does."

Yet there will always be some who are threatened by "Grantland"'s upside-down look at corporate culture. "I was in the corporate world for more than 20 years before I went off on my own with 'Grantland.' So, I'm intimately familiar with corporate culture, and it shows in my cartoons. Once in a while, someone will say, 'It's too true. We can't print it.'"

The flip-side of that, of course, is that he shows an uncanny understanding of the universal experiences in business. "The response to 'Grantland' has amazed me. With few exceptions, editors love the strip. One of my customers said to me, 'Are you sure you don't work here?' and another told me that 'Grantland' was the first business cartoon she wasn't ashamed to run."

Brownrigg also sees "Grantland" as a "permission slip" from the corporate powers, saying that "We're strong enough to have some fun at our expense. Let's not take ourselves too seriously. It's OK to laugh."

"Humor makes a statement about the corporation. It shows flexibility and strength at the same time. Without humor in a newsletter, the newsletter runs the risk of seeming like corporate propaganda, which is what my strip, 'This Draft is OK, But...' touches on."

"I work hard at keeping my strip gentle and understanding. It may be irreverent at times, but never savage. I want to be supportive of the corporate culture, not destructive of it."

"My strength is that I'm not a cartoonist trying to figure out what's going on in business in order to be funny. I'm a businessman with solid business experience who draws cartoons, and by doing so tries to explain what's really going on."

"Grantland" is available to use as infrequently as a one-time insert or as often as 52 weeks a year. Brownrigg also has a non-profit version of "Grantland" and can do a customized strip just for your company or group. If you'd like to get information about "Grantland," contact: W. Grant Brownrigg, 305 North Mountain Avenue, Upper Montclair, NJ 07043, or call him at 201/744-6866. He's easy to reach...and easy to talk to.

Therapeutic Clowning Opens Doors

Therapeutic clowning has helped many depressed, discouraged, and frightened people to cope with their tragedies a little more effectively. We recently received word from two different parts of the country about clowning making a real difference.

In one case, an older gentleman in Milwaukee refused to attend any activities in the extended care facility he called Home. He demanded that any visitors who were determined enough to keep visiting him not be allowed to sit down or touch anything during the five minutes he permitted them in his room. Developing any sort of relationship with him was difficult at best.

One persistent visitor was Cyndi Forbes, one of our Milwaukee members and a Remotivational Therapist. Cyndi visited him regularly over a period of several weeks, but his behavior was virtually unchanged. Then Cyndi decided her alter ego, Candy the Clown, should pay him a visit. After several visits, one day Candy asked him if he had ever been to the circus. Suddenly, and with great relish and detail, he described his feelings about the circus. He quickly moved on to discussing opera, musicals, theatre, and 45 minutes later, Candy left his room with him telling her the topics they would discuss at their next little chat.

"Although he still refuses most activities," Cyndi told AATH recently, "he now discusses a variety of topics, not just with Candy the Clown, but with Cyndi the Therapist and several other staff members."

"Consistency, understanding, patience, and sincerity blended with humor and clowning can open doors we are not aware exist or cannot otherwise break down."

At the Baby's Hospital in New York, a new clowning program has been well-received by their patients *and* the parents.

"It is not meant to be a program to introduce therapeutic humor per se," said Ginny Keim, one of the developers of this program and a Director there. "The focus of the clowning is to improve the quality of hospital life. That is particularly important when you not only have a lot of long-term hospitalization, as we do, but it is frequently a hospitalization of an entire family. Parents are here for very long hours, frequently overnight. Improving the hospital environment through these delightful and skilled entertainers is supportive of the healing process."

N.H. Humor Basket Filled With Care

Cathy A. S. Johnson, R.N., of Lyme N.H., started out by simply wanting to bring more light and laughter into her patients' lives, but in the process, has also tackled one of the U.S.'s biggest problems: the nursing shortage.

Cathy, a member of AATH since September, came up with the idea of The Humor Basket Program for her patients at Dartmouth-Hitchcock Medical Center a little over a year ago. The Humor Basket is literally a wicker basket filled with comic books, fragrant soaps, little games, and an obligatory rubber chicken. But the most popular item in the Basket is the book of crayoned drawings from local school children, filled with an abundance of color and intensity. And that's where Cathy bridged helping her patients with the nursing shortage.

Cathy designed a program where she goes into classrooms, grades K-8, and talks about The Humor Basket, her patients, and nursing. She effectively conveys to these children the wide range of opportunities available to nurses and presents herself as a role model through this project.

The initial proposal and subsequent implementation of The Humor Basket was so impressive, the Personnel Department of Dartmouth-Hitchcock MC has expressed great interest in helping financially, along with a grant Cathy has received from The Humor Project in Saratoga Springs, N.Y.

Cathy does all of this in her copious free time: her only responsibilities are rearing two children, working part-time as a staff nurse, helping her husband with his business, and running her household with humor. She deserves more than a pat on the back for her pioneering work—she deserves a vacation!

Association for the Promotion of Humor in International Affairs

Founders: Alfred E. Davidson, John E. Fobes, Richard E. Moore
Headquarters: **APHIA**   **APHIA**
               Box 357   5, rue de la Manutention
               Asheville, NC 28804   75116 Paris
                                                France
Phone: (704) 253-5383
Founded: 1973
Description: In these times of ever greater threat, the world needs even more humor. Through annual awards to humorists of world stature, **APHIA** promotes and values humor. **APHIA**'s award is the Noble prize. In order to be a fun organization and to avoid traditional struggles for control and administrative red tape, **APHIA** elects no officers and keeps no minutes or records. It is a non-organization. The Noble prize complements the Nobel prize. **APHIA**'s sole formal activity is a luncheon party each year, or almost each year, at which the Noble award is presented. The prize, although having tangible value, does not take the form of a check—**APHIA** numbers no munitions makers among its founders—but is chosen to fit the personality and the interest of each prize winner. For instance, 100,000 American pennies went to Art Buchwald in recognition of his passion for money. **APHIA** also awards a "Booby" prize—for which no fully satisfactory translation has ever been discovered. While the Noble prize is for those who try to be funny and succeed, the Booby goes to those who try to be serious and fail. Winners of the Booby include:

- President Nixon's press secretary, Ron Ziegler, for his repeated comment during Watergate, when it became impossible to defend a preposterous statement by his boss, that the statement "was no longer effective."
- U.S. Defense Secretary Caspar (Cap) Weinberger was awarded a Cap Pistol for disclaiming that his defense policy was limited to limited nuclear war.
- Who's Who in France, for substituting "Honor" with "Humor" in **APHIA**'s name—an elevation beyond our capacities. (An ink eradicator was the prize.)
- Senator Proxmire for his comment that most Americans living abroad spend their time in gambling casinos while their mink-clad wives frequented cafes and the like.
- Milton Friedman for his remark in 1974, "I would not worry about high oil prices, OPEC will promptly fall apart."

Cross-indexed:

General Humor
Social Sciences Humor
Humanities Humor
Political Humor

BALLAST Quarterly Review

Publisher: BALLAST Quarterly Review
2220 X Avenue
Dysart, IA 52224-9767

Format: Journal
Editor: Roy R. Behrens
Founded: 1985

Description: **BALLAST** is an acronym for Books Art Language Logic Ambiguity Science and Teaching. It is a journal devoted to wit, the contents of which are intended to be insightful, amusing, or thought-provoking.

Frequency: 4 per year (year runs from October through June)

\# of issues published in 1991:   4
\# of issues to be published in 1992:   4
\# of issues to be published in 1993:   4

1992 volume: Volume #7-8

Subscription period: Subscriptions run from the date the order is received

Subscription rates:

1 year:	Two first-class US postage stamps per year
1 year (Canada):	not available
1 year (Foreign):	not available
Sample copy:	Two first-class US postage stamps

Average # of pages: 16
Page size: 4 1/4" x 10"
Production: Typeset
Printing: Offset
Binding: Saddle stitched
Circulation: 600

Author information:
Journal does not accept unsolicited manuscripts

Advertising rates: Advertisements are not accepted

Reviews:
"An idiosyncratic dispatch of verbal illusions and visual anecdotes. Works like conceptual anti-freeze—keeps your inspiration unclogged." (*Whole Earth Review*)
"A charming quarterly diversion." (*Communication World*)
"A wonderful little journal." (*Journal of Graphic Design*)

Cross-indexed:

General Humor	Foreign Language Humor
Sciences Humor	History Humor
Social Sciences Humor	Library Sciences Humor
Humanities Humor	Literature Humor
Arts Humor	Limericks
Business Humor	Mathematics Humor
Regional/Local Humor	Philosophy Humor
Political Humor	Physics Humor
Cartoons/Illustrations/Graphics	Poetry Humor
Visual Satire	Psychiatry Humor
Anthropology Humor	Psychology Humor
Computer Sciences Humor	Sociology Humor
Education Humor	Word Play & Puns
English Humor	Zoology Humor
Film Media Humor	

While teaching at Black Mountain College, [Josef] Albers encouraged students to bring in any material they found, and on at least one occasion (this was later, in the mid-forties) was himself tested by the "solution." Several students hostile to Albers, and impatient of what they took to be the endless mechanics of the course, decided to do a three-dimensional construction out of a material not singular to Black Mountain but found there in plentiful supply: cow dung. That day in class, as always, the constructions were placed in front of the room, without names attached to them. Albers – again, as always – picked up each piece in turn, examining and criticizing it. "Ah (as he passed down the row), a good swindle: marbles made to look like fish eggs...and what's this one? Wonderful -- it looks exactly like muddy cow [excrement]! So real you want to pick it up and smell to be sure..." -- at which point he did; and was sure. But he never batted an eye. He simply put the [excrement] back down, omitted his usual comment on the "material's" color and form, and blandly proceeded on to the next construction.

Martin Duberman, *Black Mountain: An Exploration in Community* (New York: E.P. Dutton, 1972), pp. 68-69.

Three questions:

(1) Which craft was persecuted by the Puritans of New England?

(2) What was the name of the inventor of the steam engine?

(3) The name of the inventor of the sewing machine is pronounced how?

Interviewer: Do your own dogs do any Stupid Pet Tricks?
David Letterman: No. Well, actually, yeah. They each know one trick...We have two dogs, Bob and Stan. Bob and I sound the same when we eat potato chips. That's Bob's trick. And Stan's trick is that if you read him a list of TV commediennes he'll only get excited when you reach the name "Lucille Ball." The key word there is, of course, "ball." He loves to play ball.

David Letterman in an interview by Pat Hackett in the TV Cable Section of the *Milwaukee Journal*, Sunday, 9 June 1985, p. 3.

Below: Nine characters from a hypothetical alphabet by Debbie Gage.

My mother did the first terrible thing for which I never forgave her, y'know...my mother...She says to me, "Henry, I have a wart." I'm only four years old and I'm sitting in this little chair and she says, "Henry, what shall I do with this?" And I say, "Cut it off. With a scissors." Two days later she got blood poisoning and she says, "And you told me to cut it off!" and bang bang bang she slaps me, for telling her to do this. How do you like a mother who'd do that?

Henry Miller, quoted in Robert Snyder, ed., *This is Henry Miller, Henry Miller From Brooklyn* (Los Angeles: Nash Publishing, 1974), p. 25.

Von Neumann lived in this elegant house in Princeton. As I parked my car and walked in, there was this very large Great Dane dog bouncing around on the front lawn. I knocked on the door and von Neumann, who was a small, quiet, modest kind of a man, came to the door and bowed to me and said, "Bigelow, won't you come in," and so forth, and this dog brushed between our legs and went into the living room. He proceeded to lie down on the rug in front of everybody, and we had the entire interview -- whether I would come, what I knew, what the job was going to be like -- and this lasted maybe forty minutes, with the dog wandering all around the house. Towards the end of it, von Neumann asked me if I always traveled with the dog. But of course it wasn't my dog, and it wasn't his either, but von Neumann -- being a diplomatic, middle-European type person -- he kindly avoided mentioning it until the end.

Julian Bigelow [Princeton mathematician, recalling his job interview with John von Neumann], quoted in Ed Regis, *Who Got Einstein's Office?* (New York: Addison-Wesley, 1987), p. 110. Suggested by Joseph Podlesnik, a reader from Ithaca, New York.

Bits & Pieces

Publisher: The Economics Press, Inc.
               12 Daniel Road
               Fairfield, NJ 07004
Format: Magazine
Editor: Arthur F. Lenehan
Phone: (201) 227-1224
Founded: 1967
Description: **Bits & Pieces** is aimed at executives and management personnel. It contains brief,
               common-sense articles (100-350 words) about working with people, sandwiched
               between humorous anecdotes, epigrams, funny quotations, human interest stories, and
               an occasional bit of light verse.
Frequency: 12 issues per year
Issues per volume: 12
# of issues published in 1991:   12
# of issues to be published in 1992:   12
# of issues to be published in 1993:   12
1992 volume: Volume #25
Subscription period: Subscriptions run from the date the order is received
Subscription rates:
               1 year: $17.55
               Sample copy: Free
               Multiple subscriptions: Discounts available—see sample copy order form
Average # of pages per issue: 24
Page size: 4" x 6 1/2"
Production: Typeset
Printing: Offset
Binding: Saddle stitched
Circulation: 330,000
Author information:
               Magazine does not accepted unsolicited manuscripts
Advertising rates: Advertisements are not accepted
Cross-indexed:
               General Humor
               Business Humor

If you find a path with no obstacles on it, the chances are that it doesn't lead anywhere.

Those running for the office of President of the United States are looking for a platform that's different from their opponent's. It must be large enough for people to see, yet not large enough to allow an opponent to get on with them.

Tact is the art of making a point without making an enemy.

When O. Henry was a popular short-story writer during the early years of this century, he made a contract with a publisher to supply a story every week. Even O. Henry, genius that he was, sometimes ran into a dry spell, and a story just would not be written on time.

Once after he failed his editor two weeks in a row, he got this note:

"My dear O. Henry: If I do not receive that story from you by noon tomorrow, I'm going to put on my heaviest-soled shoes, come down to your rooms, and kick you downstairs. I always keep my promises."

Immediately, O. Henry wrote a characteristic reply: "Dear Sirs: I, too, would always keep my promises if I could fulfill them with my feet."

The biggest room in the world is the room for improvement.

A YOUNG MAN had been seeing a girl for several months. He wanted to ask her to marry him but he couldn't get up the nerve. Finally, he asked his father. "Dad," he said," "I want to marry Jane but I haven't the slightest idea of the right way to ask her."

"Son," said his father, "just ask her. There isn't any wrong way."

Hospitality is making your guests feel at home, even though you wish they were.

GRANDMOTHER was headed out the door to go to church one Sunday when she got a call from her daughter. Would Grandma like to have her three little grandchildren visit while daughter and son-in-law took a five-day holiday trip?

Grandma was so delighted she put $5 in the collection basket at church and thanked the Lord.

The Sunday after the grandchildren had returned home, she put $20 in the collection.

An American was on a walking tour of Ireland. He became lost and stopped to ask a native how far it was to a certain town. "Oh, only about a half mile down the road," said the Irishman, "and God speed you."

The American walked the half mile-no town. Once more he stopped and asked how far? Again he was told a half mile farther. He walked the half mile. No town. After the scene was repeated several times, he reached town.

A week later, on the return trip, he encountered the first Irishman who had given him the misinformation. "What was the idea?" he asked. "You told me that town was only a half mile from here."

"Well," was the reply," you poor man, I didn't want to knock the heart out of you-you looking so tired in the morning. In Ireland we do be always wanting to soften the journey of a stranger by giving him little dribbles of encouragement. Sure, there'd be nobody going anyplace on a hot day if people knew how far they had to go to get there."

"But," protested the other, "In America they take care to give you the exact information."

"Ah," said the Irishman, "that's the trouble with Americans. They don't think enough of you to tell you a lie."

WHEN "Bunky" Knudsen, son of General Motor's one-time president, William S. Knudsen, was 14, his father told him he could have a new (1927) Chevrolet if he would stop at the plant. Thrilled at the prospect, the boy hurried over. The car was waiting for him–in several thousand pieces. "It took me a couple of months to assemble the darn thing," he says, "but I finally got it running."

"Who hit you the hardest during your ring career?" a reporter once asked Joe Louis.

"Uncle Sam," replied the heavyweight champ.

the Blab

Publisher: the Blab
              3073 Rio Bonita Street
              Indialantic, FL 32903
Format: Newspaper
Editor: Varies with issue
Founded: 1989
Description: **[T]he Blab** varies from issue to issue. Sometimes a holiday is lampooned. Usually man's inhumanity and fathomless capacity for stupidity is illustrated, often with news clippings and articles culled from mainstream and underground publications.
Frequency: 10 issues per year
# of issues published in 1991:   10
# of issues to be published in 1992: 10
# of issues to be published in 1993: 10
1992 volume: Volume #4
Subscription period: Subscriptions run from the date the order is received
Subscription rates:

1 year/2 years/3 years:	$10.00	$20.00*	$30.00*
1 year (Canada):	US$15.00		
1 year (Foreign):	US$15.00		
Sample copy:	$ 1.00	(*depending on postal rate changes)	

Average # of pages per issue: 2
Page size: 11" x 17"
Printing: Offset
Binding: Folded
Circulation: 200+
Author information:

        Newspaper accepts unsolicited manuscripts
        Newspaper makes no payments for articles accepted
        Does not deal with issue of copyright of individual articles
        Newspaper is not copyrighted

Advertising rates: Inquire
Reviews:

        "You're too good at what you do to be on the sidelines." (Chuck Shepherd, co-editor, *News of the Weird*)
        "You've taken weird news clipping to a new height." (John J. Kohut, co-editor, *News of the Weird*)
        "Nice issue..." (Reverend Ivan Stang, co-editor, *The Stark Fist of Removal*)

Cross-indexed:

        Anthropology Humor
        Film Media Humor
        Religion Humor
        Sociology Humor

PRICE: 25c

the Blab

VOL. 2 NO. 5

THURSDAY, NOVEMBER 22, 1990

THANKSGIVING DAY ISSUE

EDITORIAL

Lately people have been asking me how I come by these news clippings. "Do I get them from a book?", they ask. No. The contents herein, do not emanate from a single source. "Where do you find all of these articles?". The Secret, at least for this and the previous issue, is to delve into the pages of the New York Times Index, wade through yards of entries, go blind staring at miles of microfilm on an infernal machine, after having made volumes of notes, and then take about a hundred photocopies. In addition to this, rake the encyclopedias, dictionaries and diaries of various reputable sources. Last, people generously contribute articles—alas, not nearly as frequently as I'd like. Each issue is different. For this issue I expected sparse findings. Yet, I managed to reap a crop rich enough to fill yet another fun-filled Blab. Well, now you know.

As with the Halloween issue, I did not plan to delve into a genealogy of this holiday. So, before I divulge the strange coincidences that emerged as I dug through the pages of the past, a brief history clearing up some popular misconceptions about this traditional holiday.

The origin of Thanksgiving predates the Puritan landing at Plymouth Rock by a few millennia. As far as anyone can tell (historians, archeologist and anthropologist) thanksgiving is as old as religion itself. The thanksgiving the Pilgrims celebrated is an adaptation of Lammas Day, formerly celebrated the first day of August, in England. Originally, this was only observed if there was an abundant crop of wheat, in this case, the first baked loaf of bread from each household was brought to church for consecration at Mass, as a token of thanks to god. Hence, the name, Loaf MASS). The first

Virginians Again Claim The First Thanksgiving
1962

RICHMOND, Va., Nov. 10 (UPI)—A lawyer has called on President Kennedy to concede, as "a matter of fairness," that Virginia settlers held the first Thanksgiving, not the Pilgrims.

John J. Wicker complained in a telegram to the President yesterday that the annual White House Thanksgiving proclamation, as usual, had placed too much stress on the role the Pilgrims of Plymouth, Mass., played in establishing the observance.

Virginians cite historical documents to support their case. They contend that the first Thanksgiving in America was observed on the shores of the James River, about 35 miles from here, more than a year before the Pilgrims reached the New World.

1936

Recall Thanksgiving of 1605

PORTLAND, Me., Nov. 25 (AP).—Maine folk will carry on tomorrow a Thanksgiving tradition dating back more than 330 years. Nearly a score of years before Governor Bradford of the Plymouth Colony issued his first Thanksgiving Day proclamation in 1621, a crew of English seafarers, under Captain George Waymouth, disembarked at Allen's Island, off the Maine Coast, to give thanks for a safe voyage. Thus in 1605, says the Maine Historical Society, Waymouth held the first Thanksgiving observance in the New World.

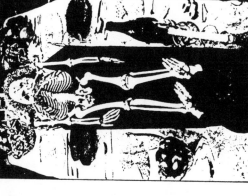

1936

ZOO TURKEY IS SAFE AFTER DAY IN HOSPITAL

A turkey among a million—perhaps it might be called a Scheherazade among turkeys, as that happens to be what they call it—clucked and preened itself yesterday in the animal hospital at the Bronx Zoo.

Behind steel bars as strong as those of the lions cage, removed far from the gaze of hungry visitors, this veritable turkey-in-the-straw had never even heard, so keepers say, of the sorrow Thanksgiving Day brings to its kind.

It must have known there was something different about the day, however. For it was taken to the hospital for safe-keeping, because, said Lee S. Crandall, bird curator, "we have missed a turkey or two on past Thanksgivings".

The birds, in previous years, disappeared mysteriously from the open bird sanctuary, which they share ordinarily with the wild ducks, geese, flamingoes and other avians with no special associations.

The present turkey, official zoo representative of the species melagris gallopavo sylvestris, or native American wild turkey, is a member of the old turkey family which assuaged the rugged Thanksgiving of the Mayflower Pilgrims. It was born three years ago on the Kellogg Sanctuary near Battle Creek.

Under the badge of diplomatic immunity the Park Department uniform, the keepers in the early morning hustled the turkey out of the open sanctuary, where a wire-netting fence alone protected it from the clutches of marauders, into its more substantial associations.

Later in the day John Toomey, head keeper, issued an official statement covering the oddest turkey dinner in New York.

Joey Skaggs interview, by Andrea Juno, RE/Search #11: Pranks! 1987

In 1981 I did a World Hunger Performance on Thanksgiving Day.

■ AJ: *How was this received?*

■ JS: I had the Abyssinian Baptist Choir sing *a capella*. I sculpted a coffin...cooked a turkey dinner and had a real articulated skeleton of a child as a centerpiece. I blew up giant photographs of starving children which I placed on easels. It was a very horrific visual; it was not a sweet Thanksgiving Day. *how many shopping days left 'til Christmas?* It was a horrific visual, and it did get *some* media attention, though not much, because it was a stark contrast to the Macy's Day Parade. The Macy's Day Parade is pure commercialism, and that's what the press wants to feed us. That's what the media *is* in many instances.

Reprinted from **the Blab** by permission of the publisher.

Capitol Comedy

Publisher: E. R. Partners
               P.O. Box 25605
               Washington, DC 20007
Format: Newsletter
Editor: Elaine Bole
Phone: (301) 881-8717
Founded: 1989
Description: Topical humor, largely political humor but also in-the-news humor.
Frequency: 12 issues per year
# of issues published in 1991:   12
# of issues to be published in 1992: 12
# of issues to be published in 1993: 12
Subscription period: Subscription runs from the date the order is received
Subscription rates:
               1 year: $105.00
               1 year (Canada):   US$105.00
               Sample copy: Free
Average # of pages: 4
Page size: 8 1/2" x 11"
Production: Word processed
Printing: Offset
Binding: Folded
Author information:
               Newsletter accepts unsolicited manuscripts
               Reports in 1 month
               Pays $5.00 per line accepted
               Pays $25.00 per cartoon accepted
               Newsletter owns all rights to the article
               Newsletter is copyrighted
Cross-indexed:
               Political Humor
               History Humor
               Limericks
               Joke Service Humor

VOLUME II ISSUE 12   SEPTEMBER 1991

CAPITOL COMEDY

A Monthly Collection   *of Quotable Quips*

Good-Bye Gorby, Hello Yeltsy . . .

Recent events have moved so quickly they've been breathtaking. Who would have thought that a major movement with such a long history of strength and stability would suddenly collapse under the weight of its own bankrupt ideas? But I'm sure the Democratic Party will someday bounce back.

The Soviet coup was over so fast, Bernard Shaw barely had time to dive under a desk.

It took a lot of people by surprise that the Soviet vice president was at the forefront of a coup that struck against Mikhail Gorbachev while he was on vacation. President Bush returned to Kennebunkport, but he ordered a closer watch kept on Dan Quayle.

> *I had a hunch the coup was in trouble when I heard its three top planners were named Curly, Larry and Moeski.*

When Gorbachev looked out a window of his summer house and saw troops approaching, he said, "I can't believe anything so repugnant would show up at our door," and Raisa said, "You mean Nancy Reagan's here?"

One of the plotters threatened to send Raisa's loved-one to Siberia. She said, "You leave Mikhail here with me," and the coupster said, "He's staying here — I'm referring to your American Express card."

A Soviet Report

The way the "Committee of Eight" screwed up, they should be named honorary congressmen.

The real reason some of the plotters have killed themselves is because someone told them the alternative was to flee to America and join the Democratic Party.

That best-selling book about suicide, "Final Exit," has now become the official handbook of the Communist Party.

Well, I guess Boris Yeltsin taught Mike Dukakis a lesson. You don't sit in a tank, you stand on a tank.

A couple of years ago, Boris Yeltsin was the butt of jokes, a man considered a clown and a buffoon. Are you listening, Dan Quayle?

Carolina Health & Humor Association

Founder: Ruth Hamilton
Publication: **Carolina HaHa Newsletter**
Publisher: Carolina Health & Humor Association
              5223 Revere Road
              Durham, NC 27713
Format: Newsletter
Editor: Ruth Hamilton
Phone: (919) 544-2370
Organization founded: 1986
Publication founded: 1987
Description of organization: The **Carolina Health & Humor Association** is a nonprofit educational service foundation dedicated to promoting humor systems in health care, business, and the community. **CHHA** offers humor techniques and training classes—"Certified Humor Presenter"— 3 phases of training completed over 18 months.
Description of publication: The **Carolina HaHa Newsletter** offers at least 3 articles per issue on a theme like Marriage and Family Humor. An upcoming issue (December 1991) is on Humor and Self Promotion.
Frequency: 4 issues per year
# of issues published in 1991: 4
Subscription period: Subscriptions run from the date the order is received
Annual membership rates (newsletter is included in the price of membership):
        Regular member: $20.00
Subscription rates (without membership):
        1 year: $20.00
Page size: 8 1/2" x 11"
Production: Typeset
Printing: Xeroxed
Author information:
        Newsletter accepts unsolicited manuscripts
        Reports in 2 weeks
        Author receives complimentary copies of the issue in which the article is published as payment
        Newsletter owns 1st serial rights
        Newsletter is not copyrighted
Advertising rates:
        1/2-page black & white: $50
Cross-indexed:

General Humor	Education Humor
Sciences Humor	English Humor
Social Sciences Humor	Medical Humor
Humanities Humor	Philosophy Humor
Arts Humor	Psychology Humor
Business Humor	Religion Humor
Regional/Local Humor	Word Play & Puns
Political Humor	
Cartoons/Illustrations/Graphics	
Visual Satire	
Scholarly Reviews of Humor as a Subject of Study	
Research on Humor	
Summary of Conferences and/or Symposiums on Humor	

Humoring Your Relationships

"How do you use humor in your marriage and do you have any specific funny moments?" Armed with this question, I surveyed several dozen couples. At first, I received little response. Couples were especially stumped on specific humor incidence. Then I got explanations like, "We have inside jokes that are only funny to us" or "You wouldn't want to print our humor." The folks that immediately responded were quick to say that humor is not something they set out to perform, but rather it is more of a survival mechanism. They reported that their humor came out of a previous seriousness syndrome. Here are the results:

Avery Henderson, a humor presenter, was quick to respond. He relayed a scene at his family reunion when, as all his relatives were leaving, he and his immediate family all donned Groucho glasses and blew the car horn as they pulled away. At anniversary time, he set the stage for a very romantic dinner, complete with a beautiful card. He proceeded to read the message aloud in a tender moment to his lovely wife. "You have given me the hardest time of my life this week!" he read with a twinkle in his eye.

One of our Carolina HaHa clowns, Joe Crane, reports that pets and a new kitten are great ways to involve the entire family in big guffaws. Joe happily recalled the time the entire family laughed uproariously as the new kitten danced to a flashlight beam. He'd move the flashlight right and the kitten would chase the beam, then to the left and the kitten would quickstep left.

Joe suggested ways he wished he and his wife could humorously solve some challenges. In the area of finance, he suggests that monthly, at bill time, he could play the part of the financial analyst who is called in to look at the cash outflow of "Mr. and Mrs. Smith." Therefore by acquiring comic perspective on this "other couple," he could objectively make suggestions for pruning the budget.

Ownership of property in marriage can make for a difficult situation. A friend reports that one time his wife became very upset when he delved into *her* jar of peanuts. Just to make a gentle suggestion, he went to the corner drugstore and bought 50 jars of peanuts and lined them up on the kitchen counter. But the joke was on him for he had bought salted peanuts and she only ate the unsalted variety. As we all know, love is worth more than a mound of peanuts.

Chinese fortune cookies are fun for another veteran couple of twenty years. When they go out to eat and are finishing up their meal with the cookie fortune, they add their own touch to the message. "You will come into a great sum of money *in bed*." Fortunes become great fun when "in bed" is added. They also get to enjoy the predictable comment of their teenage daughter who says, "That is *so* stupid."

The answerphone can become another humor communicator. I love one doctor's family phone message. "This is the Blum family...I'll save you some time. If you're calling to solicit, we don't want any. If you're calling to ask us to take on another job, we don't have any more time."

Sometimes the humor in marriage gets out of hand. One CaHaHa board member, Ginny Dudek, reports that her family liked practical jokes for awhile. But her husband had to call a truce when she sewed up the flap on all his underwear.

When I was married, there were many funny moments, often related to having or raising children. One such occasion was the birth of my fourth baby. By that time, I was somewhat of a pro at the procedure. My husband and I were laboring away in the birthing room at the local hospital. I was determined to get this over with and get home in a few hours for it was starting to snow. In walks my obstetrician, the man who is well schooled in all the techniques to make birthing more fun. He seriously asked, "Are you Lamaze?" And I quickly recanted, "No, I'm Zen Buddhist." He looked quizzically at my husband, the Methodist minister, and turned to walk away. My husband and I then laughed so uproariously that it was only seconds before another son emerged.

We had our pet stories also. My oldest son loved exotic pets but we could only afford a hermit crab at that time. (This is one pet that is best left in the ocean.) A fright occurred one night when I awoke to the sound of a tap tap tapping on my toe. It seems the hermit crab had lumbered from his aquarium in the still of the night, climbed a flight of stairs, and gotten into bed.

Maybe I've activated your memory buttons about the humor that is inherent in your marriage or relationship. Whether it's the planned humor of practical jokes, Groucho glasses or spontaneous birthing humor, we've all laughed to lighten trying situations and to survive our exotic budget pets!

—**Ruth Hamilton, M. Ed.,** ©1991
Ruth Hamilton is Director of Carolina Health and Humor Association, editor of the newsletter and is a humor presenter and program designer from Durham, NC.

Cartoon World

Publisher: George Hartman
P.O. Box 30367
Lincoln, NE 68503
Format: Newsletter
Editor: George Hartman
Phone: (402) 435-3191
Founded: 1936
Description: **Cartoon World** is a newsletter for cartoonists, gagwriters, hobbyists in cartooning, those interested in it, etc. Contains market news, hints, articles, essays, etc. We contact publishers, get new cartoon markets, and haven't missed an issue where we didn't have at least 10 brand new cartoon markets. Some have made $500 just from reading one issue of new markets.
Frequency: 12 issues per year
# of issues published in 1991:   12
# of issues to be published in 1992:   12
# of issues to be published in 1993:   12
Subscription period: Subscriptions run from the date the order is received
Subscription rates:

1 year/2 years:	$45.00	$85.00
1 year/2 years (Canada):	US$50.00	US$95.00
1 year/2 years (Foreign):	US$50.00	US$95.00
Sample copy: $5.00		

Average # of pages per issue: 26
Page size: 8 1/2" x 11"
Production: Typewritten/word processed
Printing: Xeroxed
Binding: Folded and loosely collated
Circulation: 300
Author information:

     Newsletter accepts unsolicited manuscripts
     Acknowledges receipt of unsolicited manuscripts
     Newsletter pays based upon length of manuscript (most manuscripts are contributed free to publisher)
     Newsletter owns all rights to the article
     Newsletter is not copyrighted

Advertising rates:

1/2 page black & white:	$ 50.00
Cover 2 black & white:	$100.00

Cross-indexed:

     General Humor
     Cartoons/Illustrations/Graphics
     Economics Humor
     Education Humor

Comedy Performers Association

Founder: Robert Makinson
Publication: **Latest Jokes**
Publisher: Robert Makinson
              P.O. Box 023304
              Brooklyn, NY 11202-0066
Format: Newsletter
Editor: Robert Makinson
Description: **Latest Jokes** is a collection of jokes for tv and radio personalities, comedians, and professional speakers. (You also receive the booklet "Being a Comedian.")
Membership dues (newsletter is included in price): $24.00
# of members: 55
Frequency: 12 issues per year
# of issues published in 1991:   12
# of issues to be published in 1992: 12
# of issues to be published in 1993: 12
Subscription period: Subscriptions run from the date the order is received
Subscription rates (*make check payable to Robert Makinson*):

1 year/2 years:	$24.00	$48.00
1 year/2 years (Canada):	US$24.00	US$48.00
1 year/2 years (Foreign):	US$24.00	US$48.00
1 year/2 years (Library):	20% discount	20% discount
Sample copy: $3.00		

Average # of pages per issue: 3
Page size: 8 1/2" x 11"
Production: Typed
Printing: Offset and xeroxed
Binding: Stapled
Author information:
              Prospective authors should inquire first before submitting manuscripts
              Reports in 3 weeks
              Newsletter pays $1-$3 per joke
              Newsletter owns all rights to articles
              Newsletter is copyrighted
Advertising rates:

1/2 page black & white:	$ 50.00
Full page black & white:	$100.00
Classified:	.50 per word

Cross-indexed:
              General Humor
              Social Sciences Humor
              Arts Humor
              Political Humor
              History Humor
              Philosophy Humor
              Poetry Humor
              Political Sciences Humor
              Psychiatry Humor
              Psychology Humor
              Religion Humor
              Joke Service Humor
ISSN: 0887-6991

I hear Russia has a new Ivan the Terrible. He just wrote a "Kiss and Tell" book about Gorbachev.

January 20th 1989 will be a great day for Ronald and Nancy to leave office. Not only do the stars say it, but the Constitution says it.

They say Dukakis doesn't know too much about foreign policy. Maybe that's why he wants to be President. The White House is a good place to really find out about that stuff.

If they elect me, we'll go back to the penny post card. Who can afford 15 cents nowadays?

Talk about your modern marriage. The ceremony was held in the maternity ward.

Just send $19.95 to Box 20, Ashcan, New Jersey. We fill all orders within forty-eight years.

Safe sex? He dirty dances with himself in front of a full length mirror.

The Reagans kept America moving. Astrology got a big boost, and condom production is at an all time high.

No man ever got a Broadway Parade for anything he ever did in the area of sex. But maybe that could be changed if we write enough letters to Mayor Koch.

Mayor Koch is worried about the Williamsburg Bridge and the Manhattan Bridge. If he were smart, he'd go to Washington and ask Nancy how long she and her astrologer think those bridges will last?

Poetry time: If this astrology
Is here to stay,
Reagan's hair
May soon turn gray.

We've got enough Elvis impersonators. We need more Rambo impersonators. The Ayatollah isn't afraid of Elvis.

In Iran, there's a few of them. Instead of killing people, they think about love. They're called "Born again Moslems."

Now here's the $64,000 question—If Nancy is in charge of Reagan, and the astrologer is in charge of Nancy...who's in charge of the astrologer?

Does God tell jokes?—He told one when He created the world. And He's still telling it. And we're all waiting for the punch line.

Comedy USA Industry Guide

Publisher: Comedy USA Industry Guide
                P.O. Box 20214
                New York, NY 10028
Format: Annual directory
Editors: Leslie Orlovsky, Donna Coe
Phone: (212) 628-2850
Founded: 1987
Description: **Comedy USA Industry Guide** is a comprehensive 280-page paperback directory containing contact information on comedians, comedy writers, agents, managers, publicists, comedy clubs, talent brokers/coordinators, production companies, plus more.
Frequency: 1 per year (published in January)
# of issues published in 1991:   1
# of issues to be published in 1992:   1
# of issues to be published in 1993:   1
Subscription rates:
          Annual (1 book): $60.00 (includes shipping)
Average number of pages per issue: 280
Page size: 8 1/2" x 11"
Binding: Perfect bound
Author information:
          Directory lists comedy writers, comedians, etc., for free
Advertising: Accepts advertising—inquire for rates

Comedy USA Newswire

Publisher: Comedy USA Newswire
              P.O. Box 20214
              New York, NY 10028
Format: Newsletter
Editor: Donna Coe
Phone: (212) 628-2850
Founded: 1985
Description: **Comedy USA Newswire** is a comedy trade publication covering business within the comedy industry. In the past, issues have covered new comedy clubs that have opened, polled comedy club owners on who they feel to be the best comedians to pull in an audience, and highlighted the Just For Laughs comedy competition held each year in Montreal.
Frequency: The number of issues published per year has varied in the past, but will become 10 issues per year starting in Summer 1992
# of issues to be published in 1993: 10
Subscription period: Subscriptions run from the date the order is received
Subscription rates:
              To be determined for the 10-issues-per-year subscription—Inquire
Page size: 8 1/2" x 11"
Author information:
              Newsletter does not accept unsolicited manuscripts
Advertising rates: Newsletter accepts advertising—Inquire for rate card

Comedy Writers Association

Founder: Robert Makinson
Publication: **Comedy Writers Association Newsletter**
Publisher: Robert Makinson
              P.O. Box 023304
              Brooklyn, NY 11202-0066
Phone: (718) 855-5057
Founded: 1977
Description: The purpose of the **Comedy Writers Association** is to discover comedy writers and to assist them in creating and selling comedy material. Members receive the current issue of *Latest Jokes* [see separate listing for this newsletter under Comedy Performers Association].
Frequency: 4 issues per year
Annual membership dues (*make check payable to Robert Makinson*): $18.00 (includes subscription to newsletter)

Subscription rates:
              Sample copy: $4.00
# of members: 110

COMIC HIGHLIGHTS

Publisher: Tom Adams Productions
P.O. Box 25989
Honolulu, HI 96825
Format: Magazine
Editor: Tom Adams
Phone: (808) 395-7500 [FAX: (808) 395-7502]
Founded: 1970 [Previously published under the names *The Electric Weenie* and *Zoo Keeper*]
Description: **COMIC HIGHLIGHTS** is a 15-page monthly, with 14 pages of one- and two-liners a la Carson/Leno and a 1-page newsletter, with a mostly conservative bent.
Frequency: 12 issues per year
# of issues published in 1991:   12
# of issues to be published in 1992:   12
# of issues to be published in 1993:   12
Subscription period: Subscriptions run from the date the order is received
Subscription rates:

1 year/2 years:	$125.00	$235.00
1 year/ 2 years (Canada):	US$125.00	US$235.00
1 year/2 years (Foreign):	US$135.00	US$259.00
Sample copy: US$10.00		

Page size: 8" x 7"
Production: Laserprinted
Printing: Offset
Binding: Folded and loosely collated
Circulation: 1,200
Author information:

   Magazine does not accept unsolicited manuscripts
   Magazine owns all rights to articles
   Magazine is copyrighted

Advertising rates:

   Magazine accepts 8 1/2" x 11" mailers at a cost of $500 per mailing

Reviews:

   "Thanks for making us sound: funny/topical/intelligent/wonderful/like we had a staff of writers (we don't)." (Bob Decarlo, WLOL Radio, Tampa, FL [Bob & Judd AM team])
   "You really ARE the best! I look forward to the day your gags arrive! Such a shot in the arm to our Morning Crew." (Rick Dees, AM DJ, KIIS, Los Angeles, CA)
   "You deserve a LOT of credit for having the success to last TWO giant decades in a business that is indeed a revolving door avocation. Congratulations." (Gary Owens, star of Laugh-In)

Cross-indexed:

   General Humor
   Joke Service Humor

Lady had personalized plates. "PMS." **No** one cut her off.

Authentic Mex. restaurant. Busboy pours you water & warns you not to drink it.

Pee Wee has this fantasy while making love, that he's with someone.

In the news...Columbian plane crashes. Looters arrested for snorting the debris.

Roseanne changes her name from Barr to Arnold. Because her favorite buffet serves people alphabetically.

New to the airways. Arab Air. Terrorists under 12 fly free.

Soon we'll find steam engines in cars. Now instead of emphysema we'll have frizzy hair.

Tragedy in the news. 28 clowns in a VW when the airbag accidently opened.

The Dr. asked him if he were schizo. He said, "Yes and no."

In the Mid East they cut your hands off for stealing. And throw away your fingerprint files.

Illinois, "Land of Lincoln." Chicago. Where he still votes.

Secret documents show if something had happened to Nancy, Ron would have assumed the Office.

On Donahue...a transsexual who sings, "I left my parts in San Francisco."

CRACKED®

Publisher: Globe Communications Corporation
              441 Lexington Avenue
              2nd Floor
              New York, NY 10017
Format: Magazine
Editors: Lou Silverstone, Jerry De Fuccio
Phone: (212) 949-4040
Founded: 1958
Description: **CRACKED®** is a general humor and satire magazine.
Frequency: 9 issues per year
# of issues published in 1991:   9
# of issues to be published in 1992:   9
# of issues to be published in 1993:   9
Subscription period: Subscriptions run from the date the order is received
Subscription rates:

1 year/2 years/3 years:	$14.40	$26.75	$33.75
1 year/2 years/3 years (Canada):	US$18.40	US$35.75	US$46.75
1 year/2 years/3 years (Foreign):	US$18.40	US$35.75	US$46.75
Sample copy: $1.75			

Average # of pages per issue: 52
Page size: 8" x 10 1/2"
Production: Typeset
Printing: Offset
Binding: Saddle stitched
Circulation: 300,000-500,000
Author information:
              Magazine accepts unsolicited manuscripts
              Reports in 3 weeks
              Magazine pays $75+ per page for writers
              Magazine pays $150+ per page for artists
              Magazine owns 1st serial rights
              Magazine is copyrighted
Advertising rates: Advertisements are not accepted
Cross-indexed:
              General Humor
              Cartoons/Illustrations/Graphics
              Visual Satire
              Film Media Humor
ISSN: 0883-6361

Current Comedy

Publisher: The Comedy Center
              700 Orange Street
              Wilmington, DE 19801
Format: Newsletter
Editor: Gary Apple
Phone: (302) 656-2209
Founded: 1958
Description: **Current Comedy** provides topical humor for public speakers.
Frequency: 24 issues per year
# of issues published in 1991:   24
# of issues to be published in 1992:   24
# of issues to be published in 1993:   24
1992 volume: Volume #35
Subscription period: Subscriptions run from the date the order is received
Subscription rates:
              1 year: $90.00
              Sample copy: $ 2.50
Average # of pages per issue: 5
Page size: 8 1/2" x 11"
Production: Typeset
Printing: Offset
Binding: Folded and loosely collated
Circulation: 5,000
Author information:
              Prospective authors should inquire first before making submissions
              Reports in 30 days
              Newsletter pays $15.00 per article
              Newsletter owns all rights to articles accepted
              Newsletter is copyrighted
Advertising rates: Advertisements are not accepted
Cross-indexed:
              General Humor
              Social Sciences Humor
              Business Humor
              Political Humor
              Joke Service Humor
ISSN: 0048-2102

I've designed an automobile that can run on ordinary tap water. I haven't gotten all the bugs out yet. So far, it will only run downhill.

If Helen Hayes is a national treasure, is 2 Live Crew a gross national product?

Pete Rose just got some more bad news. Pete Rose Boulevard in Cincinnati will be renamed Cooperstown Bypass.

In my neighborhood, they just opened a 24-hour religious convenience store— Heaven Eleven.

Isn't democracy wonderful? Under what other system can you vote to elect a politician, then sit on the jury that convicts him?

A seven-day waiting period for a handgun is a great idea. Think how well the nine-month waiting period to have a baby worked out.

If Moses were alive today, instead of climbing Mt. Sinai, he would ask God to use voice mail.

At this firm we make money the old-fashioned way—but we lose it using the latest technology.

My idea of the perfect vacation is a quaint little cabin in the woods, in walking distance to a babbling brook and a casino.

These days, everything seems to be a franchise. I needed an operation, and went to a guy called "Doctor Goodscalpel."

Political candidates are becoming more honest. I heard one say, "Ask not what your country can do for you, ask what you can do for me."

This hasn't been the best year. It's summer time and the living *still* hasn't gotten easy.

Call me old-fashioned, but it bothers me that "Victoria's Secret" is having a Back to School Sale.

Should our schools give more attention to math literacy or not? Well, to me it's seven of one and a half dozen of the other.

Money isn't everything. For instance, it isn't poverty.

Norman Schwartzkopf will receive $4,000,000 for writing an autobiography. The pen is mightier than the sword—and more lucrative.

Funny Stuff Comedy Almanac

Publisher: Funny Stuff
                2501 Astral Drive
                Los Angeles, CA 90046
Format: Newsletter
Editors: Howard Albrecht, Sheldon Keller
Phone: (213) 876-8098
Description: **Funny Stuff Comedy Almanac** contains authentic facts and birthdays—with unauthorized comments.
Frequency: 12 issues per year
# of issues to be published in 1992:   12
# of issues to be published in 1993:   12
Price: $12.50 per issue
# of pages per issue: 12
Page size: 8 1/2" x 11"
Production: Word processed
Printing: Offset
Binding: Saddle stitched
Advertising rates: Advertisements are not accepted
Cross-indexed:
                General Humor
                Joke Service Humor

Ann Landers ... 73 ... Columnist who dispenses counsel to the lovelorn and forlorn ... Along with her sister who writes "Dear Abby", they have cornered the market on advice -- In fact, every time someone in the world has a problem, the girls get a royalty of 2 cents.

JUL

5

Fri

PHINEAS T. BARNUM: BIRTH ANNIVERSARY ... 1810 ... Circus genius and promoter of the bizarre and unusual ...Some of his brilliant discoveries include the "Siamese Twins" -(he wanted to date one of them, but she couldn't get away) ... He also found General Tom Thumb who was so tiny he could chew gum - while it was still on the sidewalk - But his greatest and saddest find was "Spong-o The Rubber Man" - At the peak of his career, Sponge-o developed a severe itch and before they could get him to a hospital, he erased himself to death.

OLIVER NORTH SENTENCED FOR ROLE IN IRAN-CONTRA SCANDAL ... 1989 ... The retired Marine Lt. Colonel was convicted for falsifying and destroying documents - accepting an illegal gratuity -- and using the gap in his front teeth to impersonate David Letterman. - His wife had no idea **what** was going on -- She thought Fawn Hall was his college dorm.

TURKEY-RAMA ... McMinville, Oregon .. In 1962 this city was crowned the turkey capital of the world -- and if you've ever spent a night in McMinville, you'll know what a turkey it is ... Proud of its turkey-cultivating heritage, its motto is "If it's meat we got it - if it's fish we got it - if it's fowl we had it too long."

BIRTHDAYS

Katherine Helmond ... 57 ... Actress ... On the popular TV series, "Who's The Boss?", she plays glamorous Mona, the sexiest grandma in showbusiness ... In fact, she's so sexy, she was 45 before she discovered that cars also have **front** seats.

Robbie Robertson ... 47 ... Lead guitarist of "The Band." They were Bob Dylan's backup musicians before they went out on their own ... It was with Dylan that they played such hits as "Lay, Lady Lay" - "Mr. Tambourine Man" -- and one night after a sumptous Cinco De Mayo banquet of tostados, enchildas and bean burritos, they were inspired to compose what would become Dylan's greatest hit of them all -- "Blowing In The Wind."

JUL

6

Sat

FIRST AIRSHIP CROSSING OF THE ATLANTIC: ANNIVERSARY ... 1919 ... A British dirigible landed at New York's Roosevelt Field from England - Not wanting to risk the return trip, the outer skin was deflated and sent back to London as a raincoat worn by Orson Welles ... Believe it or not!

THE FIRST SUCCESSFUL ANTI-RABIES INNOCULATION ... In 1885, Louis Pasteur gave the treatment to a boy who had been bitten by a mad dog ... To this day it has saved the lives of countless victims -- including several of David Soul's ex-wives.

INTERNATIONAL CHERRY PIT SPITTING CONTEST ... It takes place on the "Tree-Mendus Fruit Farm" in Eau Claire, Michigan ... Entrants eat cherries and then spit the pits as far as possible on a black top surface -- It's events like this that have made Eau Claire the culture capital of the Midwest.

BIRTHDAYS

Merv Griffin ... 66 ... TV Host, business executive and the subject of the latest episode of "Lifestyles Of The Rich And Chubby."

Nancy Reagan ... 70 ... Former First Lady ... A public spirited woman who is now involved in a new campaign. She goes from bookstore to bookstore with the slogan, "Just Say No To Kitty Kelley."

JUL

7

Sun

BE NICE TO NEW JERSEY WEEK ... June 7th to the 13th ... A time to emphasize the good things about the state most maligned by American comedians ... And if you ever visit New Jersey, be sure to try one of their finest wines "Cabernet Nunzio" -- It has no cork - they stick a dead mobster's toe in the bottle.

Funny Stuff From the Gags Gang

Publisher: Funny Stuff
               2501 Astral Drive
               Los Angeles, CA 90046
Format: Newsletter
Editors: Howard Albrecht, Sheldon Keller
Phone: (213) 876-8098
Founded: 1988
Description: **Funny Stuff From the Gags Gang** is a 4-page, almost 100 jokes, publication, both timely and timeless for radio personalities, comics, and those who need humor in their speeches, written by the nation's top comedy writers.
Frequency: 24 issues per year
# of issues published in 1991:   24
# of issues to be published in 1992: 24
# of issues to be published in 1993: 24
1992 volume: Volume #4
Subscription period: Subscriptions run from the date the order is received
Subscription rates:

          1 year: $125.00 ($250.00 in major radio markets)
          1 year (Canada):   US$125.00
          1 year (Foreign): US$250.00
          Sample copy: Free

Average # of pages: 4
Page size: 8 1/2" x 11"
Production: Word processed
Printing: Offset
Binding: Folded
Circulation: 300+
Author information:

          Newsletter accepts unsolicited jokes
          Reports "immediately"
          Newsletter pays $5.00 per joke
          Newsletter does not deal with issue of copyright of individual jokes
          Newsletter is copyrighted

Advertising rates: Advertisements are not accepted
Cross-indexed:

          General Humor
          Sciences Humor
          Social Sciences Humor
          Humanities Humor
          Arts Humor
          Business Humor
          Regional/Local Humor
          Political Humor
          Cartoons/Illustrations/Graphics
          Joke Service Humor

Are there any mothers with tattoos on their arms that say "son?"

Which came first - the "chicken salad" or the "egg salad?"

If you eat at a diner called "Mom's", do you have to finish your vegetables before you can order dessert?

MARRIAGE FORUM

You know your honeymoon night is not going to be too swell when your wife has multiple yawns.

WHAT'S YOUR BUSINESS?

- The magazine business is very slow, so many publications are merging -- like "**AUDUBON**" and "**PSYCHOLOGY TODAY**" will merge to form a new magazine called "BIRDBRAIN."

- "**CATHOLIC DIGEST**" and "**PREVENTION**" have merged to become "RHYTHM."

- "**PENTHOUSE**" and "**NEW YORK**" have joined to form "NAKED CITY."

- "**GOURMET**" and "**HUSTLER**" have merged into "EAT SOME OF THIS."

QUAYLE QUOTES!

- "Quite frankly, a civil war is the best kind to have - because when you fight yourself, you always win."

- Have you heard of the new QUAYLE BONDS? ... No interest - no principle - no maturity - they just lay there and do nothing.

YOU KNOW HE'S CHEAP

... when he orders a Tupperware coffin.

... when he opens his wallet and a moth flies out.

... when he's got a suit that's 30 years old - and the pockets are new.

ACCIDENT REPORT

Last week on US Route 15, a truck suddenly exploded - and the fire destroyed its entire cargo of 350 thousand copies of Roget's Thesaurus -- Winesses were shocked - thunderstruck - aghast - dumbfounded - flabbergasted - astounded - bewitched, bothered and bewildered.

SHE'S SO UGLY

... you can't get spare parts for her anymore.

LITERARY PREVIEW
"Scarlett -- The Sequel To Gone With The Wind"

- RHETT BUTLER buys the patent for Eli Whitney's Cotton Gin - but is heartbroken when he learns you can't get gin out of cotton.

- SCARLETT O'HARA, desperate for funds, converts her beloved plantation, "TARA" into a resort for Confederate Soldiers -- called "CLUB REB."

- ASHLEY WILKES returns from the war a casualty - It seems that during the battle of Gettysburg he was run over by a wagon load of peanuts and became "Shell Shocked" ... He then buys TARA and turns it into a thriving leather bar and brokerage firm - where he sells stocks and bondage -- He also hires Jeb Stewart Feinstein to sing show tunes.

- Meanwhile, HATTIE McDANIEL, refusing to be called "MAMMY" one minute longer, slims down on Optifast - then balloons up again and gets her own talk show.

- Gentle MELANIE tearfully apologizes for burning Atlanta to the ground during a severe bout with PMS.

- BUTTERFLY McQUEEN goes to medical school and becomes an obstetrician - She is immediately sued for malpractice, because she **still** "don't know nothin' 'bout birthin' no babies."

- And the book ends when they all realize that the only thing that hurt the South more than Appomattox -- was **Lester** Mattox.

OVERHEARD IN A NEWLYWED'S KITCHEN

HUSBAND: "Honey, there's something missing from this gravy."

BRIDE: "What's that?"

HUSBAND: "The wallpaper."

Gag Re-Cap

Publisher: Gag Re-Cap Publications
            P.O. Box 774
            Bensalem, PA 19020
Format: Newsletter
Editor: Al Gottlieb
Phone: (215) 750-6848
Founded: 1954
Description: **Gag Re-Cap** describes cartoons published in leading magazines. It includes cartoonist's name, address of magazine, price paid for cartoon, cartoon editor, editorials, new markets, etc.

Issues per volume: 12
# of issues published in 1991: ·   12
# of issues to be published in 1992:   12
# of issues to be published in 1993:   12
Subscription period: Subscriptions run from the date the order is received
Subscription rates:

	3 months	6 months	1 year
3 months/6 months/1 year:	$16.00	$30.00	$50.00
3 months/6 months/1 year (Canada):	US$19.00	US$35.00	US$60.00
3 months/6 months/1 year (Foreign):	US$19.00	US$35.00	US$60.00

          Sample copy (current issue): $6.00
          Sample copy (back issue): $3.00
Average # of pages per issue: 15
Page size: 8 1/2" x 11"
Production: Typed
Printing: Mimeoed
Binding: Stapled in corner or on edge
Author information:
          Newsletter does not accept unsolicited manuscripts
          Newsletter is not copyrighted
Advertising rates: Advertisements are not accepted
Reviews:
          "Professional guides like Al Gottlieb's **Gag Re-Cap** Publications...are excellent aids to discovering a magazine's cartoon tastes." (Mort Gerberg, *Book of Cartooning*)
          "Notice the contents of **Gag Re-Cap** magazine and how all the markets are covered. This terrific publication will keep you busy!" (Ken Muse, *The Total Cartoonist*)
          "Thanks to you and your fine publications (which have always been so helpful to me), my sales for cartoons and short humor items are better than ever!" (Dominic Procopio)
Cross-indexed:
          General Humor
          Business Humor
          Regional/Local Humor
          Political Humor
          Cartoons/Illustrations/Graphics
          Joke Service Humor

COMPLETE WOMAN (BM)(FEB) Bonnie Kruger, 1165 N Clark St., Chicago, IL 60610 $20
(Glasbergen) MD to fat dame: "The best exercise to reduce your hips? Try this isometric exercise: lock your fingers together and place them firmly over your mouth, hold that position from the time you get home until you go to bed."

COSMOPOLITAN (M)(MAR) Parker Reilly, 224 W. 57th St., NY, NY 10019 $225
(Harbaugh) Sign near Quick Cash slot: "The credit card you just inserted has requested asylum."

FAMILY CIRCLE (17x, 3/15) Christopher Cavanagh, 110 Fifth Ave., NY, NY 10011 $250
(Polston) Man who's installed a basketball hoop on front door: "It's to give the paperboy more incentive to hit the porch."

NATIONAL ENQUIRER (W) Michele Cooke, Lantan FL 33464 $300
(Phelps) Parents to tot: "Now that our divorce is final, we discovered that our lawyer is the only one who can afford to bring you up!"

NEW YORKER (W) Lee Lorenz, 25 W. 43 St., NY, NY 10036 $500
(Cline) Man to man: "I've amounted to a hill of beans."

OMNI (M)(MAR) 1965 Broadway, NY, NY 10023 $150
(Vey) Researcher at maze: "If it were up to me, I'd give him the damn cheese and go home!"

PLAYBOY (M)(MAR) Michele Urry, 919 N. Michigan Ave., Chicago, IL 60611 $350
(Savage) Gal's dad, to her date facing document: "Nothing to be concerned about, John, it's simply our standard predating agreement."

READERS DIGEST (M)(MAR) Reprints $125
(Busino)(C) Kangaroo mom to offspring near porcupine: "No, your new friend may NOT stay overnight."

SATURDAY EVENING POST (9x)(MAR) Steven Pettinga, Box 567, Indianapolis, IN 46202 $125
(Carpenter) Receptionist to man with dog at Obedience School: "Your pet may go in, but you 'sit.'"

WALL STREET JOURNAL (Pepper & Salt) C. Preston, Cartoon Features Syndicate, Box A, Boston, MA 02123 $65
(Lowe) Boss: "Do me a favor, Stanley—make a career move."

Reprinted from **The Gag Re-Cap** by permission of the publisher.

Gene Perret's Round Table

Publisher: Gene Perret
                P.O. Box 1415
                South Pasadena, CA 91031
Format: Newspaper
Editor: Linda Perret
Founded: 1981
Description: **Gene Perret's Round Table** is a gathering place for comedy writers and humorists, a how-to publication for those interested in a career in comedy.
Frequency: 12 issues per year
# of issues published in 1991:   12
# of issues to be published in 1992:   12
# of issues to be published in 1993:   12
1992 volume: Volume #12
Subscription period: Subscriptions run from the date the order is received
Subscription rate:

          1 year: $49.95
          1 year (Canada):   US$49.95
          1 year (Foreign):   US$55.00 (surface mail) or US$62.00 (air mail)
          Sample copy: $ 2.00

Average # of pages per issue: 10
Page size: 8 1/2" x 11"
Production: Laserprinted
Printing: Xeroxed
Binding: Subscribers are provided with a vinyl binder in which to place the loose pages
Circulation: 200
Author information:

          Newspaper accepts guest articles from subscribers and authors receive no form of compensation
          Newspaper does not deal with the issue of copyright of individual articles
          Newspaper is copyrighted

Advertising rates: Advertisements are generally not accepted; however, ads are accepted free of cost for items that would be helpful to readers
Cross-indexed:

          General Humor
          Business Humor

RT

Gene Perret's ROUND TABLE

COMEDY NEWSLETTER

Vol. 10, No. 10

October 1990

"It's Not My Problem!"

Let's fantasize for a minute. You're in a fight for the Heavyweight Championship of the World. You speak to your opponent privately before the bell sounds beginning the first round. You sincerely tell him how you need this championship money because you're working at a job you dislike. What's worse, your boss hates your guts and refuses to approve any promotions or pay increases. Also, your wife dislikes your boxing so there's a definite strain on your marriage -- in fact, it may not survive. You ask if your opponent can keep all of that in mind as the boxing match progresses.

Then the fight begins. If you have a solid jab, a powerful hook, and solid defensive maneuvers, you might do well, maybe even win. If you don't, this guy's going to splatter you.

None of your pleading matters in the middle of the ring.

Now imagine that instead of fighting for the Championship Belt, you're trying to land a job as a writer. You're asking a comic, a producer, a publisher to read your latest submission. Does any of the pleading mean anything? Of course, not.

In the boxing ring, your punch carries the message. In the writing world, what you put on paper determines your success. Nothing else.

All of us need help in progressing to the next level of our career. We need a publisher, a producer, or a comic to read and respond to our writing. We need a booking agent to listen to our routines and hire us for some club. We need a talent coordinator to see our performance and put us on the Carson or Letterman show. So we do have to write query letters or make phone calls asking people to consider our talent. But that's all we can expect them to consider -- OUR TALENT. The rest is neither here nor there.

The people we are asking to help us also have to help themselves. They have a job to do, and in doing that job they have their own headaches, heartaches, and dilemmas. They're not interested in your problems of health, finances, or marital relations. They don't care that your spouse is tired of you spending so much money pursuing a comedy career. It doesn't impress them at all that you've been toiling at this for 17 years without a "break." They don't care that you sent some material to someone and they not only didn't return it, but they kept the stamps. Those are YOUR problems. Their problem is that the boss wants results and he hasn't been getting any.

You have every right to query anyone in the business. You're entitled to write or call and present your case. But do present your case. Present only that which shows your abilities and lists your credentials and experience.

It's to your benefit, though, to be professional and considerate. Don't take up the person's time with irrelevant material. Stick to the point of the inquiry. For the time being it's the only thing you two have in common.

Above all, avoid laying guilt. Believe me, whoever you're contacting already has enough of that. Don't say things like, "You're my last chance. If you don't respond favorably, I'm giving up." It's unfair, and it usually won't work.

I have found most of the people in the comedy profession to be generous and helpful — within reason. There are certain things they can't do, and certain things they won't do. They usually won't do anything you can do yourself.

And...they won't be bullied.

...by Gene Perret

The Harvard Lampoon

Publisher: Harvard Lampoon, Inc.
44 Bow Street
Cambridge, MA 02138
Format: Magazine
Editor: Elmer W. Green
Phone: (617) 495-7801
Founded: 1876
Description: **The Harvard Lampoon** is the nation's oldest humor magazine, specializing in humor that others would merely find offensive.
Frequency: 5 issues per year
# of issues published in 1991:   5
# of issues to be published in 1992:   5
# of issues to be published in 1993:   5
Subscription period: Subscription runs for 5 issues
Subscription rates:

1 year/2 years/3 years:	$15.00	$30.00	$45.00
1 year/2 years/3 years (Canada):	US$17.00	US$32.00	US$50.00
1 year/2 years/3 years (Foreign):	US$20.00	US$35.00	US$55.00
Sample copy: $3.00			

Average # of pages per issue: 48
Page size: 8" x 11 1/2"
Production: Typeset
Printing: Offset
Binding: Saddle stitched
Circulation: 10,000
Author information:
Authors should inquire first before submitting manuscripts
Reporting time varies
Magazine makes no payment for articles
Magazine acquires all rights
Magazine is copyrighted
Advertising rates:

1/2 page black & white:	$ 350
1/2 page color:	not available
Full page black & white:	$ 600
Full page color:	$1,000
Cover 2 black & white:	$ 800
Cover 3 black & white:	$ 800
Cover 4 black & white:	$1,100
Cover 2 color:	$1,400
Cover 3 color:	$1,400
Cover 4 color:	$1,750

Reviews:
"An American institution! But who wants to read an institution?!" (Dr. Kenneth Keeler, *The Harvard Advocate*)
Cross-indexed:

General Humor	Foreign Language Humor
Humanities Humor	Limericks
Arts Humor	Poetry Humor
Business Humor	Political Science Humor
Cartoons/Illustrations/Graphics	Word Play & Puns
Film Media Humor	Zoology Humor

Memoirs of Willie Pitt— Men's Room Attendant

When people find out what I do, the first thing they ask me is, without fail, "You ever heard any stars?"

Yeah, I've heard stars. A lot of stars. And let me tell you something, right here and right now: Nobody pisses like a star. Nobody. Not today, at any rate.

Now I'm not saying all stars are great pissers. Or even good ones. Tyrone Power had a bladder like a woman— like a *woman*. I might see him seven times a night, squirting off six seconds of juice at a time. Pathetic.

But the superstars. They know how to tank it up. Orson Welles, God rest his soul, had a bladder like some men have abdomens. I used to see him a couple times a year, and never did he once perform for less than a minute. I got some in-action polaroids of him if you ever want to see them. Amazing. And this is over a forty year span. I don't think anyone is ever going to be able to beat that record for consistency.

Now if Jimmy Dean had settled down he might have done it. But he was wild. You could see it in his eye when he unbuttoned his fly. He was going for a record every time out. He cut corners, took chances no sane man would even consider. That kid had guts. And I loved him for it. If the road hadn't killed him, his bladder surely would've. That dumb, crazy kid.

Of course the all time best is Sinatra. Without a doubt. Welles might have him on consistency; I can remember back in the early forties when you could squeeze more juice out of a booger than you could out of Frankie. But as the years passed, he matured into a fine pisser. And then an incredible pisser. And then— the best.

Once a year. I never know when, he hunts me down in whatever club I'm working in, and gives me a show. Never less than three minutes of pure full stream action. Never. The man knows how to please a crowd.

Out of nowhere I'll here this voice—"Hello, Willie." I'll look up and it's old blue eyes himself striding up to urinal number two—only he's so full of piss I could swear those eyes are green.

Sometimes he goes on for so long, I don't

think he's ever gonna quit. I think maybe he's been storing up the pish inside all fucking year, that what he's giving me here is the piss of a lifetime.

Once, a couple of years ago, as he passed the four minute mark, the grandeur of his tinkling fury dazed me, and I imagined for a moment that I could hear my own sweet mother once again singing me lullabies.

Oh Frankie, you're the greatest.

But these kids today, you think they care? Hell no. I tell them about Sinatra and Welles. They think I'm lying. Or worse yet, they're not impressed. Honor, Tradition, Bladder Control—mean nothing to these kids. And these were the words men *lived* by.

One time that Jud Nelson punk was in my place. He walks past, tosses me a quarter, and says, "I really had to piss, huh?"

He'd gone all ot twenty-two seconds.

Maybe.

He wants me to pat him on the fucking back.

Well I wasn't going to stand for that, I grabbed his arm, looked him in the eye, and told him, "Yeah, you had to piss alright. But you didn't really have to piss. Now when Humphrey Bogart sat at the same bar stool for thirteen consecutive hours—he really had to piss. When Jimmy Durante tied his wang in a knot for an entire night—he really had to piss. And when that little midget Billy Barty had his bladder poke out of his navel, gasping for a little air—Good God, Boy! That was pissing!"

At that point the kid tried to slip away. Lucky I had him in a ju-jitsu grip. I figured I was the only chance this kid had for a man's education.

"Listen," I said, "you're still young. You've got plenty of urinals in your future. Start training now. You could be a star."

Then I gave him my clincher. "Dare to be great," I said, "Dare to be great."

But it was no go. Nelson was too chicken-shit to even contemplate it. I could look right up those cavernous nostrils of his and watch his brains quiver. Pathetic. I let him go in disgust.

About the only people you can rely on for a good piss nowadays is the Japanese. Now, being a purist, I don't approve of all the fancy gadgets they use to enhance output. And they don't tip for shit. But they really get into it. Sometimes a whole team from a company will get together after work to see who's going to give in first. They'll wait by the faucets, swilling beer, eyeing the porcelain for hours. Then as soon as somebody gives up, they all jump in there and release themselves simultaneously. It's a beautiful sight. All that real yellow piss gushing into the gaping white mouths, and those japs looking to heaven and crying out to some fat god.

I can't wait til they take over the whole fucking joint. Swear to God.

—JBL

Reprinted from **The Harvard Lampoon** by permission of the treasurer.

HUMERUS

Publisher: Foolscap Press
                Box 222
                Piermont, NY 10968
Format: Magazine
Editor: William Stanley Wyatt
Phone: (914) 358-2371
Founded: 1988
Description: **HUMERUS** is a humor magazine, largely involving visual humor, art history satire, arts humor, general humor, political humor, and cartoons.
Frequency: 3 issues per year
# of issues published in 1991:   2
# of issues to be published in 1992:   3
# of issues to be published in 1993:   3
1992 volume: Volume #4
Subscription rates:
        Sample copy: $5.00 (no subscriptions are presently offered)
Average # of pages per issue: 78
Page size: 8 1/2" x 11"
Production: Laserprinted
Printing: Offset
Binding: Saddle stitched
Circulation: 2,500
Author information:
        Magazine accepts unsolicited manuscripts
        Reports in 3-6 months
        Magazine barters with author as payment: Author receives 2 complimentary copies of the issue in which the article is published and may receive artists's proofs, etc.
        Magazine owns 1st serial rights
        Magazine is copyrighted
Advertising rates:
        1/2 page black & white: $250
        Cover 2 black & white: $400
        Cover 3 black & white: $400
Reviews:

        "Thank you very much for sending a copy of **HUMERUS**...A quick scan reveals it as quite impressive and tantalizingly inviting." (Sister Adele Meyers, Thorpe Intermedia Gallery)
        "[**HUMERUS**] has real originality; every page with a surprise. Provocative as well as entertaining." (Dr. William Reese, Director, Rockland Camerata)
        "The latest **HUMERUS** is a gas from start to finish. You're nuttier than I ever supposed." (James C. Katz, Editor, *Columbia College Today*)
Cross-indexed:
        General Humor
        Arts Humor
        Political Humor
        Cartoons/Illustrations/Graphics
        Visual Satire

WALL STREET, 1866, looking west toward Trinity Church on Broadway.

Humor Correspondence Club

Founder: Robert Makinson
Publication: **HCC Membership List**
Publisher: Robert Makinson
              P.O. Box 023304
              Brooklyn, NY 11202-0066
Phone: (718) 855-5057
Founded: 1978
Description: The **Humor Correspondence Club** promotes communication between members by publishing a list of its members, who are humor enthusiasts, humor performers, or humor writers, and encouraging members to write to one another, leading to friendship and personal growth through a common interest in humor and its expression.
Frequency: Updated every 3 months
Annual membership dues (price includes membership list): $8.00
# of members: 80
Subscription rates (*make check payable to Robert Makinson*):

1 year/2 years:	$8.00	$16.00
1 year/2 years (Canada):	US$8.00	US$16.00
1 year/2 years (Foreign):	US$8.00	US$16.00
1 year/2 years (Library):	20% discount	20% discount

Page size: 8 1/2" x 11"
Production: Typed
Printing: Xeroxed
Binding: Stapled

Humor, Hypnosis and Health Quarterly

Publisher: Chuckle Institute
              P.O. Box 15462
              Long Beach, CA 90815
Format: Newsletter
Editor: Chuck Durham, Ph.D. (Director), Mary Durham, M.S. (Not Yet Co-director)
Phone: (213) 494-3173
Founded: 1987
Description: A quarterly humor newsletter.
Frequency: 4 issues per year
# of issues published in 1991:   4
# of issues to be published in 1992: 4
# of issues to be published in 1993: 4
1992 volume: Volume #6
Subscription period: Subscriptions run from the date the order is received
Subscription rates:

1 year:	$12.00
1 year (Canada):	US$14.00
1 year (Foreign):	US$16.00

Average # of pages per issue: 10
Page size: 8 1/2" x 11"
Production: Laserprinted and word processed
Printing: Offset
Binding: Folded and loosely collated
Circulation: 2,000
Author information:
    Newsletter accepts unsolicited manuscripts
    Reports in 1 month
    Author receives 30 complimentary copies of the issue in which the article is published
      (on request) as payment
    Newsletter owns 1st serial rights
    Newsletter is copyrighted
Advertising rates: Advertisements are not accepted
Reviews:
    "I am writing to let you know how much I enjoy your newsletter. Each issue I find new
      information. I also want to congratulate you on the Emergency Laughter Kit. What a
      great idea. I wish I had thought of it first. Keep up the fine funny work." (Allen Klein,
      Jollytologist)
    "I like the down-to-smirth quality of your work." (L. Gerald Buchan, Ed.D., School
      Psychologist)
Cross-indexed:

General Humor	Nursing Humor
Social Sciences Humor	Philosophy Humor
Humanities Humor	Psychiatry Humor
Business Humor	Psychology Humor
Scholarly Reviews of Humor/Satire	Word Play & Puns
as a Subject of Study	
Research on Humor	
Summary of Conferences and/or	
Symposiums on Humor	
Medical Humor	

Humor Stamp Club

Founder: Robert Makinson
Publication: **Humor Stamp Directory**
Publisher: Robert Makinson
             P.O. Box 023304
             Brooklyn, NY 11202-0066
Format: Serial Yearbook
Editor: Robert Makinson
Phone: (718) 855-5057
Founded: 1985
Description: The **Humor Stamp Club** provides members with information on U.S. and worldwide postage stamps relating to humor.
Annual membership dues (includes humor stamp directory): $8.00
# of members: 40
Subscription rates (*make check payable to Robert Makinson*):

1 year/2 years:	$8.00	$16.00
1 year/2 years (Canada):	US$8.00	US$16.00
1 year/2 years (Foreign):	US$8.00	US$16.00
1 year/2 years (Library):	20% discount	20% discount

Production: Typed
Printing: Xeroxed
Binding: Stapled
Advertising rates:

1/2 page black & white:	$ 50.00
Full page black & white:	$100.00
Classified:	.50 per word

Cross-indexed:
         Philately Humor

Humor Stamp Directory (1988)

What is a Humor Stamp?

- Commemorates a humorist

- Commemorates a humor writer

- Commemorates a serious personality who was also noted for humor

- Depicts children in a mirthful way

- Depicts animals in a mirthful way

- Is designed by children and is mirthful

- Depicts Santa Claus, as he is famous for his "Ho, Ho, Ho!"

- Depicts a clown or a caricature

- Has an unusual or exaggerated quality which is humorous

- Shows a person with a wide grin

[Scott Catalog Numbers are indicated for each stamp.]

Samuel Clemens 863 (Mark Twain—Most famous American humorist)

Will Rogers 975 & 1801 (Second most famous American humorist)

W. C. Fields 1803 (Movie comedian)

The Institute of Totally Useless Skills

Founder: Rick Davis
            The Institute of Totally Useless Skills
            20 Richmond Street
            Dover, NH 03820
Phone: (603) 742-6096
Description of organization: **The Institute of Totally Useless Skills (ITUS)** is an organization
            devoted to compiling and teaching skills that add nothing directly to society, but that in-
            directly promote self-esteem, coordination, concentration, social interaction, and FUN.
            Among the topics taught are: Juggling, Spoon Playing, The Best Paper Airplane, Palm
            Reading, Body Tricks, Advanced Eye-Crossing, Disappearing Body Parts, Spoon
            Hanging, Yo-Yo, Flyback, Hambones, Balances, Hand Gymnastics, Yodeling, Funny
            Faces, Bandannaning, Mime, Arm and Finger Stretching, The Longest Word, String
            Figures, Challenges, The Sound of One Hand Clapping, Pencil Tricks, Mouth Sounds,
            Odd Finger Snapping, and Weird Feelings. Our goal is to bring instant talent to the
            untalented, to teach everything you should have learned as a kid but didn't, and to boldly
            go where no curriculum has gone before. **ITUS** offers performances, workshops, books,
            and videotapes.
Annual membership dues:
            1 year: Free (diplomas, membership cards, and information can be received in exchange
                     for a S.A.S.E.)
# of members: 358

International Banana Club®

Founder: L. Ken Bannister
Publication: **Woddis News**
Publisher: International Banana Club
           2534 N. El Molino Avenue
           Altadena, CA 91001
Format: Newsletter
Editor: Paul Farber
Phone: (818) 798-2272 [FAX: (818) 446-0220]
Organization founded: 1972
Publication founded: 1976
Description of organization: Since 1972, our purpose has been to "keep people smiling and exercising the sense of humor daily." All members can earn a M.B. or Ph.B. (Masters or Doctorate) of Bananistry. The "Bananister Award" is presented to one person annually. The **International Banana Club** also holds an annual picnic and games (site announced) and an annual conference.
Description of publication: **Woddis News** is a quarterly newsletter available only to members. It includes hints on maintaining a sense of humor, recipes, legal tips, insurance tips, and how to get discounts.
Frequency: 4 issues per year
# of issues published in 1991:   2
# of issues to be published in 1992:   4
# of issues to be published in 1993:   12
Subscription period: Calendar year (i.e., all subscription orders received within the calendar year automatically begin with the first issue of that year)
Annual membership dues (newsletter is *not* included in the price):
          1 year: $10.00
Subscription rates:
          1 year: $12.00
          1 year (Canada):   US$20.00
          1 year (Foreign):   US$35.00
          Sample copy: $10.00
Average # of pages per issue: 6
Page size: 8 1/2" x 11"
Production: Word processed
Printing: Offset
Binding: Folded and loosely collated
Circulation: 8,000+
Author information:
          Prospective authors should inquire first before submitting manuscripts
          Newsletter makes no payment for articles accepted
Advertising rates:
          1/2 page black & white: $250
          Full page black & white: $450
Cross-indexed:
          General Humor
          Business Humor
          Cartoons/Illustrations/Graphics
          Limericks

THE INTERNATIONAL BANANA CLUB®

WODDIS NEWS

VOLUME I, NUMBER I, — NOVEMBER, 1977 | Published by The International Banana Club, Inc. 2524 N. El Molino Ave., Altadena, CA 92201 | Editor — Dave Curran   Circulation — 7,200

WE WANT TO HEAR YOUR IDEAS!

MESSAGE FROM THE T.B.

Woddis!, for crying out soft! We proudly present to you the very first edition of the I.B.C. "Woddis News". Keep it, read it, use it, show it to all your friends, all your relatives and the bunch you work with.

Our purpose is to influence more people to smile more often. We've received publicity in all parts of the country informing folks of our organization. (A reprint of one article is enclosed which tells the story from a reporter's viewpoint.)

To date 26 members have reached the yellow B.C. Hall of Fame, 20 with M.B. Degrees and 7 with P.H.B. (Doctorate Degrees). My sincere congratulations to all M.B.'s and P.H.B.'s. Remember it takes only 100 B.M.'s for your masters and 500 for the doctorate.

We encourage members of all ages and all titles anywhere and everywhere to organize B.A.'s (Banana Activities). Send a brief story along with a black and white glossy and we'll try and work it in the next newsletter scheduled for February. We need ad support too!

You'll all be bananalated to learn that we received official U.S. registration for the Banana Club® . Now, it's straight ahead, Woddis! **Everyone** needs written permission to use these words.

Cont.

Reprinted from **Woddis News** by permission of the publisher.

ONCE UPON A TIME . . . .

Far, far away in a distant land known as Southern California is the small village of Altadena. It's a pleasant community with streets, buildings, trees and even a stop light or two. A large town it's not for near the city gates there reads a sign: Welcome to Altadena — Come Again, all on the same sign! But this doesn't worry the fair people for they have what not another village does, a Banana Club! It's said that on clear days one can even see across the street if there's no smog.

Each eve the old T.B. proprietor of the now famous Banana Club®, races like a madman up the hills through the smog to the B.C., beginning his duty of spreading smiles and happiness across the land. Three speeding tickets later he makes it only to park in a red zone, but luckily the Police Department is next door so no one notices. Across the street are the good guys in our Fire Department. Fires aren't very common in Altadena so to keep the men smiling old T.B. tosses an incendiary bomb across every so often. The firemen know the T.B., a lot of people do. In fact, if the eviction petition hadn't been lost when some madman drove up the sidewalk where it was being signed, a lot more people would know about the old T.B. He's a good guy.

The Banana Club® itself is not exactly the largest office, it's said it's so small the mice are even hunchbacked, but it's there. The T.B. works behind his desk, the T.B.S. (Top Banana's Secretary) has hers and I even have my desk. If you like pretending you're Abe Lincoln in front of a fire it's great!

Each eve is a busy one, the T.B. answers letters, talks to people, makes plans and most of all spreads smiles to all those that visit the B.C. — even that group of people with the petition visited last night. The firemen liked it, they got to put out a real fire!

We of the Banana Club® are proud to work there. We know the good we are doing, we meet people every day and in fact we get a lot of interesting waves from the fair villagers of Altadena.

T.B. ANNOUNCES "GO BANANAS" PHOTO CONTEST, Altadena, California

Ken Bannister, T.B. has made it official that the B.C. Photo Contest will be conducted over the next two months. Open to all official members of the B.C.; get your stacamera out and remember- Rules are as follows:

— Theme: Anything to do with Bananas (in good taste).

— 8x10 or larger prints only. Either black and white or color accepted, preferably mounted on art board (except Polaroid). Fine material!

— Categories: Open Polaroid — Open anything in good taste goes; on instant film, portrait, commercial, industrial and banana candid.

Special interest and treatment will be given to early entries and all entries must be submitted in good taste. It should be understood that all photographs become property of the I.B.C. museum subject to display. Woddis! "Do it now, with a grin."

Rewards for winners will be announced. J. J. Allen, S.H.D. of Georgia is bound to win a few B.M.'s here!

PHOTO BY J. J. ALLEN

OPENING NOTE . . . . . .

Welcome to all new Banana Club® members who officially became "one of the bunch" and a big WODDIS from the Banana Club® staff.

International Brotherhood of Old Bastards

Founder: Brother Cozen P. Bantling, O.B.
Publication: **Ye Olde Bastards Bulletin**
Publisher: International Brotherhood of Old Bastards, Inc.
             2330 South Brentwood Boulevard
             St. Louis, MO 63144-2096
Format: Newsletter
Editor: Brother Solomon O. Sciuridae, O.B.
Phone: (314) 961-2300 [FAX: (314) 961-9828]
Founded: 1406 in Spain, moved to England in 1684, moved to NY in 1861, moved to St. Louis, MO
             in 1924
Description: The **International Brotherhood of Old Bastards** (**IBOB**) offers you everything a busy
             Old Bastard wants in a fraternal organization—no meetings, no committees, no assess-
             ments, no officers, no responsibilities, no annual dues, etc.! Just a membership card,
             newsletters, and the opportunity to brag you can prove you're a real bastard! **IBOB** is
             in compliance with the Civil Rights Acts (and recognizing that some of the biggest OB's
             around are women) we have opened our doors to members of the fairer sex. All the
             Supreme Archbastard requires is that the prospective member acknowledge that she is
             an Old Bastardette. It you are a Ms., you receive a special pink membership card. General
             membership requirements:
             •Age: Old enough to know better, but young enough to try.
             •Drinking Habits: Hearty
             •Motto: Do unto others before they would do unto you.
             •Pledge: To continue bastardly deeds in solemn hope of someday achieving the highest
                 honor of them all—the title of Supreme Archbastard (he's selected each year on
                 April 1st—Founder's Day).
Frequency: 12 issues per year
# of issues published in 1991:   12
# of issues to be published in 1992:   12
# of issues to be published in 1993:   12
Subscription period: Lifetime
Annual membership dues (newsletter is included in price of membership): Offering of $5.00, $25.00,
                                                                         or $500.00

Average # of pages per issue: 4-16
Page size: 8 1/2" x 11"
Production: Word processed
Printing: Offset
Binding: Folded
Author information:
             Newsletter does not accept unsolicited manuscripts
             Newsletter is not copyrighted
Advertising rates: Advertisements are not accepted
Cross-indexed:
             General Humor   Psychiatry Humor
             Medical Humor
             Dentistry Humor
             Nursing Humor
             Political Humor
             Cartoons/Illustrations/Graphics
             Law Humor

International Brotherhood of Old Bastards, Inc.

"Illegitimus Non Carborundum"

Office of the
Supreme Archbastard

2330 South Brentwood Boulevard
St. Louis, Missouri 63144

EMERGENCY BULLETIN—NEW BUSINESS IDEA

We have been looking for a supplemental or collateral source of income to sustain this organization. We have been relying exclusively on "free will offerings" and have usually operated at a deficit, subsidized by the Supreme Archbastard.

We are going to open a Cat Ranch and start a fashion fad for Cat Caps (replace Coonskin Caps since they have adverse ethnic connotations), Catskin Capes, Cat Fur Coats, Cat Fur Rugs, etc., etc., etc. As a result, we will require 100,000 cats for breeding stock. Each cat will average 12 kittens a year and the cat pelts will sell for $1.00 each (compare this with Mink for a real bargain). We get our breeding stock free by merely running ads in the paper, "Cats Wanted for New Business." Most people have trouble giving away cats, so we will relieve them of this burden.

As far as labor goes—we have got that figured out, too. We will hire unemployed disabled members of minority and ethnic groups so that we will be able to get grants from the Federal Government to subsidize a sheltered workshop, grants from the Ford Foundation, Rockefeller Foundation, etc. We will need 100 men to skin 5,000 cats a day after we get into full production.

Now, what will we need to feed the cats? We will start a Rat Ranch next door. We will need 1,000,000 rats as breeding stock. Any metropolitan area will gladly let us trap rats free of charge until we accumulate our full breeding stock. The rats breed 12 times faster than the cats, so we will have an average of 4 rats per day to feed each cat. Now, what will we feed the rats? We will feed the rats the carcasses and all remains of the skinned cats.

NOW, GET THIS: We feed the rats to the cats, and we feed the cats to the rats—we get the skins for nothing. Possibilities are unlimited—we may even franchise the business as Chinchilla and Mink ranches have so successfully done.

How can you help????? Send a free-will offering to help sustain I.B.O.B. while research is being completed, Government grants are being obtained, and "cat skinners" are being trained. Your suggestions are always welcome.

International Maledicta Society

Founder: Reinhold Aman
Publication: **Maledicta: International Journal of Verbal Aggression**
Publisher: Maledicta Press
           P.O. Box 14123
           Santa Rosa, CA 95402-6123
Format: Serial Yearbook
Editor: Reinhold Aman
Phone: (707) 523-4761
Founded: .1976
Description: The **International Maledicta Society** collects and publishes insults, curses, threats, nicknames, stereotypes, slurs, and other verbal aggression in all languages. All material is uncensored, including glossaries and essays. Topics published in **Maledicta** include: Medical Slang, Twisted Proverbs, Teenage Jokes, Gay Insults, Spoonerisms, Ethnic Slurs, Foreign Blasphemies, Sexual Slang, and Prison Slang. **Maledicta** is not primarily a humor publication, but much of the offensive material is humorous. Meetings of the **International Maledicta Society** are held in the U.S. and abroad irregularly.

Frequency: 1 issue every 2 years
# of issues published in 1991:   0
# of issues to be published in 1992: 1
# of issues to be published in 1993: 0
1992 volume: Volume #11
Subscription period: Subscriptions begin with current volume
Subscription rates (includes memebership dues):

1 year:	$22.00
1 year (Library/Institutional):	$26.00
1 year (Foreign):	US$27.00
Sample copy:	$22.00

Average # of pages per issue: 320
Page size: 5 1/2" x 8 1/2"
Production: Typeset
Printing: Offset
Binding: Perfect bound (sewn)
Circulation: 4,000
Author information:
           Inquire first before submitting materials for consideration
           Reports in 1 week
           Author receives 20 gratis offprints in lieu of payment
           Serial yearbook is copyrighted
           Publisher copyrights entire book but author may reprint elsewhere
Advertising rates: Advertisements not accepted
Reviews:
           "A bit shocking, very funny and virtually unputdownable." (*Washington Post*)
           "**Maledicta**'s ribald wit is so nicely matched with scholarship that the journal is by way of a real find." (*Library Journal*)
           "A clearinghouse for connoisseurs of profanity and cuss words." (*New York Times Book Review*)
Cross-indexed:

General Humor	Sciences Humor
Social Sciences Humor	Humanities Humor
Arts Humor	Regional/Local Humor
Political Humor	Cartoons/Illustrations/Graphics

Research on Humor
Business Humor
Anthropology Humor
Economics Humor
English Humor
Foreign Languages Humor
History Humor
Limerick
Mathematics Humor
Poetry Humor
Religion Humor
Word Paly & Puns
Joke Service Humor

Scholarly Reviews of Humor
  as a Subject for Study
Computer Sciences Humor
Education Humor
Film Media Humor
Geology Humor
Law Humor
Literature Humor
Medical Humor
Psychiatry Humor
Sociology Humor
Zoology Humor

ISSN: 0363-3659

The Moving Spray Can:
A Collection of Some Contemporary English Graffiti

Venetia Newall

The vast majority of graffiti in England that I have seen, especially those in rest rooms, are of a sexual nature: **Life is a sexually transmitted disease; Monogamy leaves a lot to be desired; Rugby is a game played by gentlemen with odd-shaped balls; Be security conscious—80% of people are caused by accidents; An erection is like the theory of relativity—the more you think about it, the harder it gets; Is a castrated pig disgruntled?; Sex is bad for one, but it's very good for two; Christmas comes but once a year—thank God I'm not Christmas;** on the back of a truck: **Make Love not War—see driver for details; Conserve energy-make love more slowly; Does the lateral coital position mean having a bit on the side?; Safeguard your health—don't sleep with any damp women; Y-fronts prevent fallout** (a tight jockey-style men's underpants with a Y-shaped front); **Genitals prefer blondes; The only difference between a stick-up and a hold-up is age; Girls are made of sugar and spice, so how come they all taste of anchovies?; Hello, I'm from outer space. My sex organs are in my thumb. Congratulations. You've just been screwed; Eunuchs unite—you have nothing to lose; Sex was bad until Snow White discovered 7-Up.** Written at about five feet above the floor: **Sex stunts your growth** (underneath, one foot above the floor:) *Now you tell me!*; **Join the Abbey Habit: Fuck a monk** (the Abbey is a well-known building society), and in a ladies' rest room: **If the cap fits, wear it.**

Contraceptive vending machines in a men's rest room are a prolific source of data: **My dad says they don't work; Don't buy this chewing gum. It tastes of rubber; New shape! New sensitivity! But the same old feeling!; Go gay—it's cheaper!; Place 50p in slot, wait for coin to drop, pull handle out, push back firmly. If this is sex, it sounds very boring; Buy me and stop one.**

French letter is a slang expression for a male contraceptive; again on vending machines: **Not for sale during the French postal strike; If the French won't buy our lamb, don't buy their French letters. Be patriotic: If this machine is out of order see the landlord. And if it's in order, see the barmaid.** Some of these vending machines say *Made in the U.K. Absolutely safe and reliable* and it is traditional to add **So was the Titanic.** A cold-water tank had written on it: **This is not a contraceptive machine.**

Sexual graffiti are very broad-based: **Buggery is boring, incest is relatively boring, necrophilia is dead boring; Cunnilingus is not an Irish airline; Oral sex is all a matter of taste; Cunnilingus—a taste of things to come; A fertile imagination is no compensation for vasectomy; Let's keep incest in the family; One thing about masturbation—you don't have to look your best;** *Another thing about masturbation—you meet a better class of person*; **Sado-masochism means not having to say you're sorry; Bisexuality—the best of both worlds; I'm into necrophilia, bestiality and sadism. Am I flogging a dead horse?; My mother made me a homosexual** (underneath:) *If I give her the wool, will she make me one?*; **Homos are a pain in the arse.**

Graffiti can appear anywhere, but the most usual place is in the public rest room, especially in establishments where they sell liquor: **Drink wet cement and get really stoned; You don't buy beer, you rent it; Reality is an illusion caused by a lack of alcohol; Do you have a drink problem?** *Yes, I can afford it*; **Drink problem? I drink, I fall over. No problem; God says "Alcohol is thine enemy."** *God also says "Love thine enemy,"* and in a ladies' rest room: **Every time I think I know where it's at, someone moves it.**

Inevitably, in rest rooms a percentage of the graffiti are scatological: **Testimony to Ed: Ed is the contemporary Manifestation of all the shit there's ever been; Life is like a shit sandwich: the more bread you have, the better it is; Eat shit! 500 billion flies can't be wrong; Eat bran and the world will fall out of your bottom; Constipation is the thief of time. Diarrhoea waits for no man.** British Rail trains have the following notice in their rest rooms: *Passengers are requested not to use the toilet whilst the train is standing at a station* (someone added:) **Except at Aldershot** (a town in Hampshire); **Life is like a pubic hair on a toilet seat—sometimes you just get pissed off; It's no use standing on the seat, the crabs in here can jump ten feet.** In very small letters two feet to the right in a men's rest room: **If you can read this, you're pissing in your right shoe. Drink Harpic. It sends you clean round the bend** (Harpic is a well-known brand of lavatory cleaner). A sign on a road passing a farm reads *Pick your own strawberries*, altered to read **Pick your own nose.**

English insularity is reflected in **Keep Britain tidy: kill a tourist** and **Cleanliness is next to Godliness, but only in an Irish dictionary.** Police brutality underlies **Save the Police a job. Beat yourself up.** British Rail and the public transport system in general are well-deserved targets of abuse: **God made things that creep and crawl/But British Rail, it beat them all**; on a British Rail poster: **It's quicker by snail**; a sign: *British Rail advise that this Right of Way is not Dedicated to the Public* (added:) *Neither is British Rail!* **Come the Revolution, British Rail will be the first to go—if they arrive on time; Keep this bus tidy. Throw your tickets out of the window!; Keep Death off the Roads—drive on the sidewalk.** Other emendations include (outside a school:) **Drive carefully. Don't kill a child. Wait for a teacher.** A British Airways poster: **Breakfast in London, Lunch in New York, Baggage in Bermuda; Indian driver—smoke signals only**; *Kindly pass along the bus/And so make room for all of us* (added:) **That's all right, without a doubt/But how the hell do we get out**; *Assist the conductor, give the right change* (altered to:) **Amaze the conductor, give the right change**; on a bus timetable: **Take no notice. They are all wrong times**, and an advertisement for a Fiat car: **Designed by a computer, silenced by laser, built by robot, driven by moron.**

We are also interested in the environment: **Clean air smells funny; Save trees—eat a beaver** (this is an American import, for we don't have beavers). On a dirty car: **Don't clean me. Plant something; Christ did not say "Kill Trees for Christmas." Keep London tidy—eat a pigeon every day; Preserve Britain's wildlife—pickle a squirrel; Stop air pollution. Stop breathing!** and **Save water. Bath with a friend.**

The International Save the Pun Foundation

Founder: John S. Crosbie, Chairman of the Bored
Publication: **The Pundit**
Publisher: John S. Crosbie Ltd.
                Box 5040, Station A
                Toronto, Ontario M5W 1N4
                CANADA
Format: Newsletter
Editor: John S. Crosbie
Phone: (416) 922-1100 [same number for FAX]
Founded: 1978
Description: **The International Save the Pun Foundation** is the world's largest apocryphal society, fighting illiteracy by encouraging people to have fun with words. The **Foundation**'s motto is, "A Day Without Puns Is Like a Day Without Sunshine — There is Gloom For Improvement." **The Pundit** is a monthly newsletter, airmailed worldwide and containing the best examples of word-play (puns) received from **Foundation** members. Each year, the **Foundation** selects and releases to the press "The Ten Best-Stressed Puns of the Year."
Frequency: 12 issues per year
Issues per volume: 12
# of issues published in 1991:   12
# of issues to be published in 1992: 12
# of issues to be published in 1993: 12
1992 volume: Volume #12
Subscription period: Subscriptions run from the date the order is received
Subscription rates (includes membership fee and newsletter):
                1 year/2 years: $ 20.00 $40.00
                1 year/2 years (Foreign):   US$ 20.00   US$40.00
                Lifetime membership: $100.00
Average # of pages per issue: 4
Page size: 8 1/2" x 11"
Production: Typewritten/word processed
Printing: Offset
Binding: Folded
Author information:
                Newsletter accepts unsolicited manuscripts
                Reports in 1 week
                Authors receive no payment for articles
                No formal arrangements are made with authors for copyright of individual articles
                Newsletter is copyrighted
Advertising rates: Advertisements are not accepted
Reviews:
                "...Members don't have to worry about a shortage of puns, because they share their best each month in the group's newsletter, **The Pundit**..." (*Chicago Sun*)
                "...[The **Foundation**'s members are] people who enjoy wordplay. Full members (those who have eaten recently) receive the foundation's newsletter, which lists a collection of selected puns. Sponsors competitions: presents prizes for best puns..." (*Boston Globe*)
                "...Though the **Foundation** is a light-hearted enterprise, there is a serious side to it:

[Chairman] Crosbie says, 'Language is vital to the ability of the English-language world to continue. We can't use words well if we aren't comfortable enough with them to play with them.'" (*The San Bernardino Sun*)

Cross-indexed:

    English Humor
    Literature Humor
    Research on Humor
    Word Play, Puns, and Limericks

ISSN: 0712-1318

The Ten Best-Stressed Puns of 1990

One of the stories chosen from [**The Pundit**] for the Ten Best-Stressed Puns of the Year list concerns the famous "Indy 500" race in Indianapolis, Indiana. This year, residents near the track plan to file suit because of the foul-smelling exhaust fumes. They are seeking damages for Indy scent exposure.

In another part of the United States, after the wife of a well-known swindler had had her kitchen remodelled and asked her husband how to pay the contractor, he said, "Give him some of that new money I've just printed. After all, he's a counter fitter."

Last summer, frozen food companies had trouble finding good-quality vegetables for processing because of the dry weather. As a result, many were culled but few were frozen.

The little grandson asked his grandfather if he could croak like a frog.
"Sure," said Grandpa, who then issued a great frog-like sound.
The grandson jumped up and down with glee. "Goody, goody!" he exclaimed. "Mama said, 'When Grandpa croaks we're all going to Disneyland!'"

When Scrooge died and the town dog catcher was sent to pick up his dog, it attacked him so fiercely that he cried, "The cur is worse than the deceased!"

Most people know the legend of William Tell, but not many know that he and his family were championship bowlers whose team was sponsored eagerly by local merchants. Even now, to be able to claim that the Tells once represented your family business would be of great advertising value. Unfortunately, the old records have been lost and today we can't be sure for whom the Tells bowl.

The origin of a famous Disney movie cry can be found in Disneyland itself. When the park first opened, Mr. Disney had an apartment over its fire hall with windows that opened above the dock at the rear where the park's supplies were delivered.
Every morning, the crew on the dock had to wait until Disney was awake before going to work. But as soon as he was up, his secretary would call out of his window, "Walt's up, dock!"

Jack was sitting in the school auditorium eating some cheese when his friend Sam came in and grabbed a piece.
"Good cheese!" Sam exclaimed. "What kind is it?"
"Nacho," Jack replied.
"But I thought Nacho was the runny kind."
"Well, I know this is Nacho," Jack responded, "because when I swiped it off the tray in the cafeteria the counter man yelled, 'Hey! That's Nacho cheese!'"

Did you know that Paul Revere had an English barber who used to visit him secretly at night? One evening, Paul's wife got suspicious. She listened at his study door and finally called out, "What's going on in there?"
"It's all right, my dear," Paul called back. "The British are combing."

When the King of Kale first took his young son out to view their great expanse of vegetables and herbs the lad was impressed and strode on in awe through what was soon to be his very own vast ptomaine.
On his father's return from the fields, the Queen asked, "Where is our son?" To which the King replied proudly, "I have left my food-prince in the stands of thyme!"

Excerpted from **The Pundit** by permission of the publisher.

International Society for Humor Studies

Founder: Don L. F. Nilsen
Publication: **HUMOR: International Journal of Humor Research**
Publisher: International Society for Humor Studies
             Don L. F. Nilsen, Exec. Sec.
             English Department
             Arizona State University
             Tempe, AZ 85287-0302
Format: Journal
Editor: Victor Raskin
Phone: (317) 494-3782
Founded: 1988

Description of organization: **The International Society for Humor Studies** promotes all aspects of humor research. It sponsors a quarterly journal—**HUMOR**—which contains a newsletter. It sponsors annual international conferences. The 1992 conference will be in Paris, France; the 1993 conference will be in Luxembourg; and the 1994 conference will be in Ithaca, New York. It also sponsors the Julia-Moore good-bad poetry competition. Humor bibliographies are also available from ISHS. There are more than 100 bibliographies on humor as it relates to every conceivable subject, ranging from Africa to Western America. The subjects include all genres, times, geographical areas, and disciplines.

Description of publication: **HUMOR: International Journal of Humor Research** is a quarterly scholarly international and interdisciplinary journal for the publication of high-quality research papers on humor as an important and universal human faculty. Humor research draws from such academic disciplines as anthropology, biology, computer sciences, education, family science, film studies, history, linguistics, literature, mathematics, medicine, philosophy, physiology, psychology, and sociology. The Editorial Board and the Board of Consulting Editors are composed of prominent humor researchers who specialize in these disciplines.

Frequency: 4 issues per year
Issues per volume: 4
# of issues published in 1991:   4
# of issues to be published in 1992:   4
# of issues to be published in 1993:   4
1992 volume: Volume #5
Subscription period: Calendar year (i.e., all subscriptions received in 1992 automatically begin with the first issue of 1992)
Annual membership dues (members receive the journal for free):

      1 year (Regular member): $ 45.00
      1 year (Student member): $ 35.00
      1 year (Libraries): $108.00 + postage
      Sample copy: $21.50 regularly (however those requesting sample copies can receive a copy of Vol. 1 No. 4 for free *while supplies last*)

# of members: 550
Average # of pages per issue: 120
Page size: 6" x 9"
Production: Typeset
Printing: Offset
Binding: Perfect bound
Circulation: 550

Author information:
> Journal accepts unsolicited manuscripts
> Submit manuscripts in quadruplicate along with a 200-word abstract
> Reports in 3 months
> Author receives 5 complimentary copies of issue in which article appears as payment
> Journal owns all rights to articles
> Journal is copyrighted
> Submit manuscripts to: Victor Raskin, Editor-in-Chief
>   Department of English
>   Purdue University
>   West Lafayette, IN 47907
>
> Submit books for review to: John S. Morreall
>   College of Liberal Arts
>   Rochester Institute of Technology
>   Rochester, NY 14623
>
> Submit newsworthy items to: Don L. F. Nilsen
>   English Department
>   Arizona State University
>   Tempe, AZ 85287-0302

Advertising rates: Accepts advertisements. For rate card, contact:
                               Walter de Gruyter & Co.
                               Postfach 110240
                               D-1000 Berlin 11
                               Germany
Cross-indexed:
> Anthropology Humor
> Computer Sciences Humor
> Dentistry Humor
> History Humor
> Linguistics Humor
> Literature Humor
> Mathematics Humor
> Medicine Humor
> Nursing Humor
> Philosophy Humor
> Psychology Humor
> Sociology Humor
> Scholarly Reviews of Humor
>   as a Subject for Study
> Research on Humor

ISSN: 0933-1719

Introduction

AVNER ZIV

Jewish humor is the humor created by Jews, reflecting special aspects of Jewish life. This broad definition includes popular verbal humor, such as jokes, or anecdotes (collected generally by folklorists), as well as humor created by professionals. Therefore, popular Jewish jokes collected by folklorists, Shalom Aleichem's writings, and parts of Neil Simon's plays and Woody Allen's movies are all examples of Jewish humor. Since humor reflects a people's life, it changes and varies accordingly. Thus, one can talk about East European, Sepharadic, American, or Israeli Jewish humor. In spite of the great differences in the life conditions of these different communities, Jewish humor has certain characteristics which make it unique. What is generally identified in the professional literature as Jewish humor originated in the nineteenth century, mainly, but not exclusively, in Eastern Europe. Today in the USA, Jewish humor is considered one of the mainstreams of American humor, and a couple of decades ago 80 percent of the most successful humorists were Jewish (Janus, 1975). At the beginning of the nineteenth century, however, a sense of humor was not at all associated with Jewishness. Herman Adler, the chief rabbi of London, wrote an article in 1893 in which he argued against the view that Jews have no sense of humor. It is perhaps interesting to note that not only Jews but non-Jews as well today consider "a good sense of humor" as one of the notable characteristics of Jews.

There is much discussion about what Jewish humor is and in what ways it is different from other cultures' humor. Academics from many disciplines argue among themselves, proposing many definitions and not agreeing on any of them. As an example, Ben-Amo's article entitled "The myth of Jewish humor" (1973) argues that there is not such thing as Jewish humor. Another article by Oring (1983), "The people of the joke: On the conceptualization of Jewish humor," demonstrates that it exists and is very much alive. You have probably guessed my bias since I am in the process of organizing the Fourth International Conference on Jewish Humor. In my view the main characteristics of Jewish humor are the following:

1. An intellectual dimension: a desire to distort the reality, to alter it and make it laughable (and thus less frightening and threatening). Reducing the awful reality into absurdity is a cognitive process by which one tries to make life more tolerable.

2. A social dimension: trying to maintain internal cohesiveness and identity. By comparing "us" with "them" it is possible to show that even if in reality "they" are strong, "we" can still win, mainly by using our wits.

3. An emotional aspect: helping one to see oneself as one is, namely far from perfect. Making fun of some unsavory aspects of one's behavior and personality might help in accepting them. It can even show that they are not so terrible: the proof—I can even laugh at them. Another emotional aspect related to self-disparagement is the sympathy one earns from others, and being accepted is, and was for two thousand years, a serious problem for a wandering people.

These aspects of Jewish humor reflect a psychologist's view. From other disciplines, the point of view is different. Some views are presented in this issue. The articles in this special issue were selected from the 36 papers presented at The Third International Conference on Jewish Humor (Tel Aviv, 1988). The First International Conference on Jewish Humor was held in Tel Aviv in 1984, the second in New York in 1986.

The topics of the articles in this issue represent three disciplines: literature, sociology, and psychology. The "literary papers" deal with Jewish "characteristics" in writing. Stora-Sandor in her paper presents some general stylistic traits apparent in Jewish writing. The roots of these traits are deep in the Jewish culture, mixing several registers of language, the trivial and the sublime, an ironical and skeptic view of the world. Doubting is one way to seek the truth. When one believes that things are not what they seem to be, humor is not far away. The paper by Marie-Christine Pauwels de la Ronciere on Saul Bellow's humor illustrates some aspects of the previously mentioned paper. However, it enlarges the stylistic view, illustrating it with a review of the visual ironic humor in Bellow's work. Some of his characters deflate themselves with self-disparagements, blunders, and eccentricity. The con man (a modern representation of the luft mench in Yiddish literature) enriches American literature by opposing the self-doubting and uncertain hero with "the myth of self-confidence." Martine Chard Hutchinson's paper on humor's function in Bernard Malamud's fiction adds another aspect, no less typical of Jewish humor: "laughter through tears." Nothing, for instance, could be funnier and sadder (especially for an Israeli) than the image of "a Jewish refugee from Israel."

Jay Boyer's paper on the relationship between the traditional shtetl humor and American black humor (black in the sense of gallows humor and not skin color) presents an interesting point of view. The schlemiezel, a naive loser not well adjusted and always hesitating and weak, is the antithesis of the mythical American hero. Life is probably not best represented by Superman or by the schlemiezel, but rather by a mixture of the two. Possibly here again, Jewish humor enlarges the understanding of the world and ourselves by laughing at the "good guy-bad guy" simplistic outlook: there is a schlemiezel in each one of us.

Glenda Abramson's "Mightier than the sword" deals with Jewish cartoonists in South Africa. Rare are research papers on humor dealing with cartoons, and certainly someday a sociologist will study why this is so. Cartoons are an extremely popular form for humorous expression, and Abramson looks at them as a way of transmitting a serious message with a grain of humor. Every form of tyranny has been fought with all kinds of weapons, humor being one of them. In George Orwell's words, "jokes are a tiny revolution." Political cartoons are an expression of political struggle, and Abramson gives some examples of how Jewish cartoonists in South Africa fight with the weapon of caricature against the white oppression there.

Christie Davies addresses himself to the question of self-disparagement in Jewish humor. Much has been written about it, and Davies's analysis is a highly original contribution. He points out that self-mockery is the result of the paradox basic in Jewish history, "being the Chosen People on the one hand and the victims of an anti-Semitic and hostile world." As a good paradox, this one too presents an opening for humor. As he writes, self-disparagement is "the humor not of unbalanced people, but of people seeking and temporarily creating balance in an unbalanced world." An additional aspect of self-disparagement is the focus of Bernard Saper's paper on the Jewish American Princess. As strange as it may seem to Americans, this is a typical Jewish-American invention. For Jews in other countries, the phenomenon is apparently not significant enough to create a stereotype. Saper analyzes JAP jokes based on a cognitive-behavioral approach in which the teller and listener are involved in different ways. His conclusion is that in spite of the aggressive and sexist elements in JAP jokes, their deep meaning is rather positive.

Finally, Ofra Nevo's paper presents an empirical investigation into what makes a joke Jewish. In contrast to all the other authors in this issue, who believe in certain inner characteristics of Jewish humor, Nevo believes that jokes are Jewish because of their external form. Jewish names and expressions make a joke Jewish in the same way French names and expressions would make it French. At the conference, Victor Raskin demonstrated (in a different context) how a joke with Jewish names and expressions was identified by all participants as non-Jewish. However, Nevo's paper is extremely valuable since it is the only one based on empirical data. Very few empirical approaches are used in Jewish humor research, and it is hoped that Nevo's approach will encourage others to pursue the empirical way.

I do hope that for all those interested in Jewish humor, this issue will bring some new ideas and, more importantly, a wish to get involved in the work of the small scientific community working on and enjoying the topic.

Tel Aviv University

References

Ben-Amos, Dan. 1973. The myth of Jewish humor. *Western Folklore* 32(2), 112-131.
Janus, Samuel. 1975. The great comedians: Personality and other factors. *American Journal of Psychoanalysis* 35, 169-174.
Oring, Elliott. 1983. The people of the joke: On the conceptualization of Jewish humor. *Western Folklore* 42, 261-172.

The Jokesmith®

Publisher: Edward C. McManus
               44 Queen's View Road
               Marlboro, MA 01752
Format: Newsletter
Editor: Edward C. McManus
Phone: (508) 481-0979 [FAX: same number]
Founded: 1984
Description: **The Jokesmith** is a comedy newsletter for business and professional speakers. We feature jokes, roast lines, presentation remarks, skits, comedy book reviews, and stories that make a point. Our motto: "Make Them Laugh While You Make Your Point."
Frequency: 4 issues per year
Issues per volume: 4
# of issues published in 1991:   4
# of issues to be published in 1992:   4
# of issues to be published in 1993:   4
Subscription period: Subscriptions run from the date the order is received
Subscription rates:
        1 year/2 years/3 years (U.S. & Canada):   US$40.00   US$70.00   US$99.00
Sample copy: $10.00
Average # of pages per issue: 12
Page size: 8 1/2" x 11"
Production: Laserprinted
Printing: Offset
Binding: Folded and collated loosely
Circulation: 750
Author information:
        Newsletter accepts unsolicited manuscripts
        Acknowledges receipt of manuscripts
        Reports in 30 days
        Author receives 2 complimentary copies of the issue in which the article appears as payment
        Newsletter does not concern itself with copyright of individual articles
        Newsletter is copyrighted
Advertising rates: Advertisements are not accepted
Cross-indexed:
        Joke Service Humor
        Business Humor
        Medicine Humor
        Dentistry Humor
        Nursing Humor
        Regional/Local Humor
        Political Humor
        Education Humor
        Law Humor
        Political Science Humor
        Psychology Humor
        Psychiatry Humor
        Psychology Humor
        Religion Humor
ISSN: 0749-4351

THE
JOKESMITH®

44 Queen's View Road, Marlborough, MA 01752

C Copyright 1991   Phone/Fax (508) 481-0979   Summer, 1991

Abraham Lincoln delighted in reading all the humorists of his day, and he quoted from them shamelessly. I say "shamelessly" by current standards, because he often told the stories as his own, without crediting the author. This apparent plagiarism was quickly noted by the working press.

One presidential news conference, a reporter asked Lincoln if he was the author of all the humorous material he used. "Of course not," laughed the president, "I'm a performer, not a playwright."

That's a story with a point. Here's another:

Two friendly competitors (is that an oxymoron?) were walking through the woods one day when they rounded a corner and came face to face with a great bear. The bear was standing on its hind legs, snarling. All seven feet and one thousand pounds of him was preparing to attack.

One of the walkers gently lowered his pack to the ground. Slowly, not to startle the bear, he opened the pack and started lacing on a sneaker.

"That bear is as fast as he is strong," whispered his friend.

"I know." The first sneaker was on.

"He can hit fifty miles an hour over short distances, you can't outrun him."

"I know that too." The second sneaker was on.

"If you know all that," continued his friend, "why are you bothering with those sneakers?"

"Because," said the other, clapping a hand on his friend's shoulder, "I don't have to outrun him. I just have to outrun you."

Both of these stories originally appeared in The Jokesmith in the late 1980's. They are now classics. Have you heard them before? Our readers had them first.

Journal of Insignificant Research

Publisher: Dr. L. M. Van Valen
             Department of Ecology and Evolution
             University of Chicago
             1101 E. 57th Street
             Chicago, IL 60637-1573

Format: Infrequent periodical

Editor: L. M. Van Valen

Phone: (312) 702-9475

Founded: 1960

Description: **The Journal of Insignificant Research** is mostly whimsical, related to real or exaggerated aspects of the study of natural history and related subjects. Quotations, titles, tidbits, interesting names, and verse are also included.

Frequency: 0-1 issues per year

\# of issues published in 1991:   0

\# of issues to be published in 1992:   1

\# of issues to be published in 1993:   possibly 1

Subscription period: Subscriptions run from the date the order is received

Subscription rates:

1 year:	$5.00 (for next issue—whenever it is)
1 year (Canada):	US$5.00 (for next issue—whenever it is)
1 year (Foreign):	US$5.00 (for next issue—whenever it is)
Sample copy:	$5.00

Average # of pages per issue: 20

Page size: 8 1/2" x 11"

Production: Laserprinted

Printing: Offset

Binding: Stapled on edge

Circulation: 400

Author information:

        Publication accepts unsolicited manuscripts

        Reports in 1 week

        Author receives 1 complimentary copy of the issue in which the article is published as payment

        Publication does not deal with issue of copyrights for individual articles

        Publication is not copyrighted

Advertising rates: Advertisements are not accepted

Cross-indexed:

        Sciences Humor

        Anthropology Humor

        Biology Humor

        Geology Humor

        Poetry Humor

        Zoology Humor

Scrotum humanum Brookes 1763—The First Named Dinosaur

L. B. Halstead, D.Sc., Ph.D.

Several years ago, my wife drew my attention to a detailed account of the discovery of fossil bones which was included in Robert Graves' historical novel "Wife to Mr. Milton." As the action purported to have taken place in the 17th century, I asked Robert Graves if his account was purely imaginary or whether there was documentary evidence for it, which evoked the following response: "in matters like that I don't invent; you'll find it all in Dr. Robert Plot's *Natural History of Oxfordshire*."

Plot's work was published in 1677 and included a figure and detailed description of the distal end of a femur from a quarry in the Parish of Cornwell, which is to the west of Chipping Norton. The engraving from Plate 8, Figure 4 is here reproduced as text—Fig. 1. Plot correctly noted that the specimen had "exactly the figure of the lowermost part of the *thigh-bone* of a *Man*, or at least of some other *Animal*, with the *capita femoris inferiora*, between which are the *anterior* and the larger *posterior sinus*, the seat of the strong *ligament* that rises out of the thigh, and gives safe passage to the *vessels* descending into the leg." He concluded it "must have been a real *bone*, now petrified." With regard to its affinities he recognized that it did not belong to horse, ox, or elephant, and suggested that it may have been the bone of a giant man—this is spite of the circumference of the condyles measuring two feet!

Fig. 1.
Plot.1677.

Fig. 2.
Brookes.1763.

Phillips (1871) pointed out that the specimen came from the Inferior Oolite and naturally enough did not agree with Plot's identification; instead, he thought that the bones "may have been a femur of a large megalosaurus or small ceteosaurus." From Plot's figure it appears that the former alternative is the more likely.

Before Phillips made his identification, the specimen was refigured by Brookes in 1763. His drawing, which is reproduced as text—Fig. 2, is clearly copied from Plot, albeit reversed. In this instance, however, the specimen is given the binomial name *Scrotum humanum*, which undoubtedly referred to the appearance of the condyles. The actual dimensions of the specimen must mean that Brookes could not have intended this name to be taken literally to represent a petrified scrotum; furthermore, he was familiar with the work of Linnaeus, as is evidenced from the title of his book. It only needs to be added that *Scrotum humanum* was for the purposes of zoological nomenclature perfectly valid, as it was post-Linnean, i.e., after 1758. However, as this first valid name given to a dinosaur has never been used in the same context by subsequent workers, then according to the current rules of nomenclature, *Scrotum humanum* should be considered, ironically, a *nomen oblitum*.

Acknowledgements: Sincere thanks are due to Robert Graves and Professor Malcolm Brown for their kind help.

References

Brookes, R. 1763. *The Natural History of Waters, Earths, Stones, Fossils, and Minerals, With their Virtues, Properties, and Medicinal Uses; To which is added, The method in which Linnaeus has treated these subjects.* Vol. V. vi + 364 pp. London.

Phillips, J. 1871. *Geology of Oxford and the Valley of the Thames.* xxiv + 523 pp. Oxford.

Plot, R. 1677. *The Natural History of Oxfordshire, being an essay toward the natural history of England.* x + 358 pp. Oxford.

Reprinted from the **Journal of Insignificant Research**, Vol. 5, #7, by permission of the publisher.

Journal of Irreproducible Results®

Publisher: Blackwell Scientific Publications, Inc.
Three Cambridge Center
Cambridge, MA 02142

Format: Magazine

Editor: Marc Abrahams

Phone: Editorial: (617) 491-4437
Subscriptions: (800) 759-6102 or (617) 225-0401

Send manuscripts to:
Marc Abrahams, Editor
c/o Wisdom Simulators
P.O. Box 853
Cambridge, MA 02238

Founded: 1955

Description: The **Journal of Irreproducible Results**® is a satirical humor magazine written by scientists, doctors, and other people from around the world. **JIR** also sponsors and administers the annual Ig Nobel Prize Ceremony at MIT.

Frequency: 6 issues per year

# of issue published in 1991:   6

# of issues to be published in 1992: 6

# of issues to be published in 1993: 6

1992 volume: Volume #37

Subscription period: Subscription runs from the date the order is received

Subscription rates:

1 year:	$15.00
1 year (Canada):	US$20.00
1 year (Foreign):	US$30.00
Sample copy:	$ 3.00

Average # of pages per issue: 32

Page size: 8 1/2" x 11"

Production: Typeset

Printing: Offset

Binding: Saddle stitched

Circulation: 8,000

Author information:

Magazine accepts unsolicited manuscripts

Reports in 4 months

Author receives 1 complimentary copy of the issue in which the article is published as payment

Magazine owns all rights to the article

Magazine is copyrighted

Advertising rates: Quoted only

Reviews:

"The **Journal of Irreproducible Results** is the funniest thing to happen to Science since Archimedes ran naked through the streets of Syracuse." (*Discover*)

"The **Journal of Irreproducible Results** is a sort of Mad magazine for the Stephen Hawkins crowd." (*Boston Globe*)

"The **Journal of Irreproducible Results** uses a satirical wit as sharply edged as a samurai sword to slice up the useless, pompous and incomprehensible." (*Chicago Tribune*)

Cross-indexed:

General Humor	Political Humor
Sciences Humor	Cartoons/Illustrations/Graphics
Social Sciences Humor	Visual Satire
Humanities Humor	Anthropology Humor
Arts Humor	Astronomy Humor
Business Humor	Biochemistry Humor

Biology Humor
Chemistry Humor
Computer Sciences Humor
Dentistry Humor
Economics Humor
Education Humor
English Humor
Geology Humor
History Humor
Law Humor
Library Sciences Humor
Literature Humor

Mathematics Humor
Medical Humor
Nursing Humor
Philosophy Humor
Physics Humor
Political Sciences Humor
Psychiatry Humor
Psychology Humor
Religion Humor
Sociology Humor
Word Play & Puns
Zoology Humor

ISSN: 0022-2038

A Call for More Scientific Truth in Product Warning Labels

Susan Hewitt and Edward Subitzky
New York City, New York

As scientists and concerned citizens, we applaud the recent trend towards legislation that requires the prominent placing of warnings on products that present hazards to the general public. Yet we must also offer the cautionary thought that such warnings, however well-intentioned, merely scratch the surface of what is really necessary in this important area. This is especially true in light of the findings of 20th century physics.

We are therefore proposing that, as responsible scientists, we join together in an intensive push for new laws that will mandate the conspicuous placement of suitably informative warnings on the packaging of every product in every category offered for sale in the United States of America. Our suggested list of required warnings appears below.

WARNING: This Product Warps Space and Time in Its Vicinity.

WARNING: This Product Attracts Every Other Piece of Matter in the Universe, Including the Products of Other Manufacturers, with a Force Proportional to the Product of the Masses and Inversely Proportional to the Distance Between Them.

CAUTION: The Mass of This Product Contains the Energy Equivalent of 85 Million Tons of TNT per Net Ounce of Weight.

HANDLE WITH EXTREME CARE: This Product Contains Minute Electrically Charged Particles Moving at Velocities in Excess of Five Hundred Million Miles per Hour.

CONSUMER NOTICE: Because of the "Uncertainty Principle," It Is Impossible for the Consumer to Find Out at the Same Time Both Precisely Where This Product Is and How Fast It Is Moving.

ADVISORY: There is an Extremely Small but Nonzero Chance That, Through a Process Known as "Tunneling," This Product May Spontaneously Disappear from Its Present Location and Reappear at Any Random Place in the Universe, Including Your Neighbor's Domicile. The Manufacturer Will Not Be Responsible for Any Damages or Inconvenience That May Result.

READ THIS BEFORE OPENING PACKAGE: According to Certain Suggested Versions of a Grand Unified Theory, the Primary Particles Constituting This Product May Decay to Nothingness Within the Next Four Hundred Million Years.

THIS IS A 100% MATTER PRODUCT: In the Unlikely Event That This Merchandise Should Contact Antimatter in Any Form, a Catastrophic Explosion Will Result.

PUBLIC NOTICE AS REQUIRED BY LAW: Any Use of This Product, in Any Manner Whatsoever, Will Increase the Amount of Disorder in the Universe. Although No Liability Is Implied Herein, the Consumer Is Warned That This Process Will Ultimately Lead to the Heat Death of the Universe.

NOTE: The Most Fundamental Particles in This Product Are Held Together by a "Gluing"

Continued on page 26

Every day, a bird with a silk scarf in its mouth flies over the greatest mountain on earth and brushes it with the scarf. The length of time required for this to reduce the mountain to dust is but one moment in the life of the Buddha.

The emperor wanted to immortalize himself by calculating that time scale in days. Consequently, he constructed a binary abacus having 200 beads and capable of holding a value of $2^{200}-1$ or approximately 10^{60}. Three years into his calculations, the great earthquake of 1299 reinitialized the device. In a rage the emperor ordered all binary abacuses destroyed and exiled Mishugi to China, where he later met Marco Polo.[2]

The origin of the binary abacus is unknown, but clearly it must have sprung from binary counting. The development of the decimal system and decimal abacuses followed logically from finger counting. The vigesimal (base 20) number system used by the Mayans undoubtedly resulted from counting on fingers and toes.[3] Following this reasoning, there has been speculation that the originators of the binary abacus restricted counting to only their thumbs or other paired body parts.[4]

Notes

1. Taka Mitsiya, *Early Eastern Asian Computing Devices*. (Tokyo: Kinahara Publishing Co., Ltd., 1957, in Japanese).
2. Most of Mishugi's work was not utilized during his lifetime. In recent years, Benoit Mandelbrodt has expanded upon other of Mishugi's ideas in developing the field of fractal geometry.
3. There is evidence of an early Central American native people who practiced total nudity. Not surprisingly, they developed a base 21 number system (unpublished report by the 19th century French explorer Count Penilly).
4. Taka Mitsiya, *Op. cit.*

A Call for Truth
Continued from page 21

Continued from page 21

Force About Which Little Is Currently Known and Whose Adhesive Power Can Therefore Not Be Permanently Guaranteed.

ATTENTION: Despite Any Other Listing of Product Contents Found Hereon, the Consumer Is Advised That, in Actuality, This Product Consists Of 99.9999999999% Empty Space.

NEW GRAND UNIFIED THEORY DISCLAIMER: The Manufacturer May Technically Be Entitled to Claim That This Product Is Ten-Dimensional. However, the Consumer Is Reminded That This Confers No Legal Rights Above and Beyond Those Applicable to Three-Dimensional Objects, Since the Seven New Dimensions Are "Rolled Up" into Such a Small "Area" That They Cannot Be Detected.

PLEASE NOTE: Some Quantum Physics Theories Suggest That When the Consumer Is Not Directly Observing This Product, It May Cease to Exist or Will Exist Only in a Vague and Undetermined State.

COMPONENT EQUIVALENCY NOTICE: The Subatomic Particles (Electrons, Protons, etc.) Comprising This Product Are Exactly the Same in Every Measurable Respect as Those Used in the Products of Other Manufacturers, and No Claim to the Contrary May Legitimately Be Expressed or Implied.

HEALTH WARNING: Care Should Be Taken When Lifting This Product, Since Its Mass, and Thus Its Weight, Is Dependent on Its Velocity Relative to the User.

IMPORTANT NOTICE TO PURCHASERS: The Entire Physical Universe, Including This Product, May One Day Collapse Back into an Infinitesimally Small Space. Should Another Universe Subsequently Reemerge, the Existence of This Product in That Universe Cannot Be Guaranteed.

Journal of Nursing Jocularity

Publisher: JNJ Publishing, Inc.
P.O. Box 40416
Mesa, AZ 85274
Format: Journal
Editor: Douglas Fletcher, R.N.
Phone: (602) 835-6165
Founded: 1991
Description: **The Journal of Nursing Jocularity** publishes humorous and satirical works in the fields of Nursing, Medicine, and other related fields. It also includes regular features related to the use of therapeutic humor.
Frequency: 4 issues per year
# of issues published in 1991: 4
# of issues to be published in 1992: 4
# of issues to be published in 1993: 4
1992 volume: Volume #2
Subscription period: Subscriptions run from the date the order is received
Subscription rates:

1 year/2 years:	$12.00	$22.00
1 year/2 years (Canada):	US$16.00	US$26.00
1 year/2 years (Library/Institutions):	$16.00	$26.00
1 year/2 years (Foreign Library/Institutions):	US$20.00	US$30.00

Average # of pages per issue: 44
Page size: 8 1/2" x 11"
Production: Typeset
Printing: Offset
Binding: Saddle stitched
Circulation: 8,000
Author information:
Authors should inquire first before submitting manuscripts
Reports in 6-12 weeks
Authors receive 2 complimentary copies of the issue in which the article is published as payment
Magazine owns 1st serial rights
Magazine is copyrighted
Advertising rates: Advertisements are not accepted
Reviews:
"The humor magazine for nurses...packed with 45 fun pages of great humor and funformation." (*Laughter Works*)
"Providing a hilarious look at our oftentimes crazy experiences, the **Journal of Nursing Jocularity** gives a much needed chuckle at many aspects of the world of nursing. With outrageous cartoons, side-splitting articles, and editorials that will crack you up, it fills a niche in nursing literature." (*The National Nurses in Business Association Newsletter*)
"Filled with quotes and quips, the heart of this 45 page magazine is its many articles written by nurses. Heaven only knows how [they] found this plethora of funny nurses in a time when the nursing shortage is making life anything but funny." (*Laugh It Up*)
Cross-indexed:

Sciences Humor	Biology Humor	Psychology Humor
Research on Humor/Satire	Medical Humor	
Summary of Conferences and/or	Nursing Humor	
Symposiums on Humor	Psychiatry Humor	

ISSN: 1055-3088

How to Read Nursing Employment Ads

by Anita Bush, RN, CCRN

As the worldwide nursing shortage makes recruiters more competitive and our remuneration more equitable, it's easy to become misled by the slick advertising some institutions have adopted. In order to help you avoid feeling misled, here are the real-life definitions of the most common ploys used to attract nurses.

WHAT THE AD SAYS . . . WHAT IT REALLY MEANS . . . .

"Competitive pay"	Pay is as low as we can get away with and still have our body count be reasonable.
"Salary"	Hourly wages based on time clocks or time sheets.
"Challenging environment"	A lot of really sick patients, short-staffed, little support from managers and administrators, a high-density of "difficult" physicians and bitchy nurses.
"Excellent benefits"	Minimum legal requirement, one or two low-cost perks and eventually you will get to take a vacation. . . . maybe a couple of days next year.
"Diversity"	You're required to float to cover units you don't feel competent to work in, and don't say you're not comfortable there. "A nurse is a nurse is a nurse."
"Tuition reimbursement"	We have a written policy, but your schedule will be so bizarre that you'll never be able to complete a course so don't even bother enrolling in one.
"Committed to professional development"	You're expected to serve on many committees and task forces, to participate in your manager's projects but we're so short-staffed right now you'll have to do them on your off-duty time. And no we really can't pay you any extra for this work you do for us, but since we need all this for our accreditation, if you don't do it, we'll have to write that in your performance evaluation.
"Free housing"	We had to close some beds since we couldn't staff them so you can stay right here in-house where we will call you anytime of day or night to come to work.
"Clinical ladders"	12-foot ceilings from which everyone hangs the IV's, i.e. very old building.

"Research opportunities"	We want you to discover how to do 12-hours of work in the 8-hours they pay you. Also they want you to figure out how to care for 50% sicker patients with 33% fewer staff. No statistical knowledge needed.
"Job security"	If you're licensed and breathing you can work 'til you die.
"Inter-facility transfer opportunities"	We have seasonal peaks and troughs so they'll float you 2000 miles away.
"Per diem."	What's that?
"Free parking"	Some places still charge you money to come to work.
"Medical coverage that includes chronic kidney care"	That's part of a new union contract since staff rarely get a chance to go to the bathroom.
"Salary-in-lieu-of-benefits"	Silly goose! Who said you could have both?
"In-house continuing education"	We can't schedule you for 2-3 days off together just because you want to attend a workshop. Even though the class is required for your job, we'll still charge you money to attend.

"And so I thought I'd come cheer you up. Hey! Where do you keep the matches?:

Journal of Polymorphous Perversity®

Publisher: Wry-Bred Press, Inc.
P.O. Box 1454
Madison Square Station
New York, NY 10159-1454
Format: Magazine (Journal)
Editor: Glenn C. Ellenbogen, Ph.D.
Phone: (212) 689-5473
Founded: 1984
Description: The **Journal of Polymorphous Perversity**® is a humorous and satirical journal of psychology (and the closely allied disciplines, including psychiatry, mental health, medicine, social sciences, and education). Typical articles include "The Etiology and Treatment of Childhood," "Psychotherapy of the Dead," "More Clinical Tales: The Man Who Mistook His Wife for a Dishwasher," "New Improved Delusions," and "A Grammatical Overview of Medical Records: The Write Stuff." Boldly going where other journals have feared to tread, **JPP** has treated its readers to a dose of humorous medicine with such zany pieces as an article on "deja vu" that appeared *twice* in the very same issue, hilarious guidelines for diagnosing people by the way they park their cars, and a seminal treatise on the effects of tenure on subsequent productivity of university faculty (the article is completely blank!).

Frequency: 2 issues (Spring and Fall) per year
Issues per volume: 2
# of issues published in 1991: 2
# of issues to be published in 1992: 2
# of issues to be published in 1993: 2
1992 volume: Volume #9
Subscription period: Calendar year (i.e., all subscriptions received in 1992 automatically begin with the Spring 1992 issue)
Subscription rates:

	1 year	2 years
1 year/2 years:	$14.00	$24.00
1 year/2 years (Canada):	US$15.75	US$28.50
1 year/2 years (Foreign):	US$21.75	US$38.00
1 year/2 years (U.S. Library/Institutional):	$20.00	$40.00
1 year/2 years (Foreign Library/Institutional):	US$26.00	US$52.00

Sample copy: $7.00
Average # of pages per issue: 24
Page size: 6 3/4" x 10"
Production: Typeset
Printing: Offset
Binding: Saddle stitched
Circulation: 3,127
Author information:
Magazine accepts unsolicited manuscripts
Reports in 4-6 weeks
Author receives 2 complimentary copies of the issue in which the article is published as payment
Magazine is copyrighted
Author assigns all rights to publisher
Advertising rates:

Full page black & white:	$550
Cover 2 black & white:	$650
Cover 3 black & white:	$600
Cover 4 black & white:	$700

Reviews:

"A social scientist's answer to Mad magazine." (*The Wall Street Journal*)

"Short, snappy, and satiric, the pieces will delight anyone who enjoys language..." (*Library Journal*)

"Unless you're a stuff old fuddy-duddy who takes your professionalism too seriously (as a few of you no doubt are), you'll love this one!" (*The Psychotherapy Newsletter*)

Cross-indexed:

Psychology Humor
Psychiatry Humor
Social Sciences Humor
Sciences Humor
Medicine Humor
Education Humor

ISSN: 0737-1195

Scholarly Image Enhancement
Through a Meaningless Publication

Steven J. Gilbert, Ph.D.
State University of New York at Oneonta

The purpose of this paper is to enhance my perceived scholarly qualifications by padding my Vita and reprint packet with an additional, but entirely bogus, published article (Booth, Mather, & Fuller, 1982). A variety of devices are used to make this paper look like a credible effort, rather than a crass exercise in self-aggrandizement (Freud, 1908; Jackson, Schwab, & Schaller, 1986). For example, the first two sentences of this paragraph contain references. With the exception of the Freud (1908) citation, these references were chosen randomly from the bibliography page of a recent introductory text (Baron, 1989), and have nothing to do with the topic of the paper. I hope, however, that the casual reader will take the string of references to mean that I did an extensive database search, and that this paragraph represents a thoughtful and thorough review of the literature. Actually, there is a theory that explains how this would happen (Petty & Cacioppo, 1985), but it won't be explicated here, because no one who is reading this paper really cares.[1]

Some readers may question whether the *Journal of Polymorphous Perversity* has sufficient prestige to fulfill the author's self-promotional goals. Probably not. It is hoped, however, that the same careless skimming that would enable phony references and a stupid footnote to impress a peruser of my reprints would apply to the name of the journal as well. For example, a reader might assume that the journal is a serious publication dealing with varieties of sexual dysfunction. Some might misread the name as the *Journal of Polyfaceted Perceptivity*, the *Journal of Polysocial Prehension*, or even *Scientific American* (if I luck out). Such assimilation into conventional schemas is a well established phenomenon (Allport & Postman, 1945; Bartlett, 1932; Piaget & Inhelder, 1969), but I won't go into it, because it is too late for a little psychology to transform this enterprise into a real journal article.

And therein lies the danger. A few judges of my credentials actually may recognize that this paper is not a serious piece of psychological work. What, then, will they take it to be? I'm in the most trouble if the content of the paper is accepted at face value; only an amoral creep would attempt to fool his colleagues into thinking he wrote more real papers than he did. Preferably, the paper would be accepted as satire; the author would be understood as wishing to imply that many of the papers that appear in professional journals (and thus, in Curriculum Vitae) are no more significant than a paper about nothing, or a paper about itself (Wittgenstein, 1958).

---

[1] The Freud (1908) reference is included because a Freud reference always looks good, especially to a nonpsychologist on a committee that might be reviewing my file. I make this point in a footnote, rather than in the body of the text, because footnotes suggest that the author has penetrated some phenomenon more deeply than is reasonable to expect an ordinary reader to follow. This makes me look smart, and dedicated to precision and completeness—admirable qualities in any candidate.

The question, then, is whether the author should include the document currently before the reader as an entry into the former's Vita (and should the passive voice be eschewed in further sentences)? Would inclusion of the article devalue the rest of the author's publications, most of which are perfect exemplars of precisely the kind of work the present paper lampoons (assuming the present paper is, indeed, satire)? Can anyone, including the author, know for sure what this paper really is, or is for? And where is R. D. Laing when we really need him?

As it stands, the paper contains five paragraphs and a lengthy footnote. That looks about right for a short, sharp, paradigm-shifting (Kuhn, 1970) manuscript. A few more references will serve to foster the illusion that I'm integrating ideas I've developed here with those of other theorists (Hess, 1975; Phillips & Wills, 1987; Wickes, 1958). Then, I'll insert a quotation from a great psychologist, cautioning the reader to consider "the last of the human freedoms—to choose one's attitude in any given set of circumstances" (Frankl, 1963, p. 104). Finally, with that special mixture of modesty and vision for which I fantasize I am noted, I'll conclude that the new perspectives, and intriguing, nonobvious hypotheses I have developed in this paper, should supply a generation of graduate students with opportunities for parametric extensions and conceptual replications. I trust I will be credited as second author in each.

References

Allport, G.W., & Postman, L.J. (1945). The basic psychology of rumor. *Transactions of the New York Academy of Sciences, Series II, 8*, 61-81.

Baron, R.A. (1989). *Psychology, the essential science*. Boston: Allyn & Bacon.

Bartlett, F.C. (1932). *Remembering*. Cambridge, England: Cambridge University Press.

Booth, D.A., Mather, P., & Fuller, J. (1982). Starch content of ordinary foods associatively conditions human appetite and satiation. *Appetite, 3*, 163-184.

Frankl, V. (1963). *Man's search for meaning*. New York: Washington Square Press.

Freud, S. (1908). Creative writers and daydreaming. In J. Starchey (Ed.), *Standard edition of the complete psychological works of Sigmund Freud, Vol. 9*, pp. 142-152. London: Hogarth.

Hess, E.H. (1975). The role of pupil size in communication. *Scientific American*, Nov., 110-119.

Jackson, S.E., Schwab, R.L., & Schuler, R.S. (1986). Toward an understanding of the burnout phenomenon. *Journal of Applied Psychology, 71*, 630-640.

Kuhn, T.S. (1970). *The structure of scientific revolutions*. Chicago: University of Chicago Press.

Petty, R.E., & Cacioppo, J.T. (1985). The elaboration likelihood model of persuasion. In L. Berkowitz (Ed.), *Advances in experimental social psychology, Vol. 19*. New York: Academic.

Phillips, D.P., & Wills, J.S. (1987). A drop in suicide around major national holidays. *Suicide and Life-Threatening Behavior, 17*, 1-12.

Piaget, J., & Inhelder, B. (1969). *The psychology of the child*. New York: Basic Books.

Schaller, G.B. (1986). Secrets of the wild panda. *National Geographic, 169*, 284-309.

Wickes, I.G. (1958). Treatment of persistent enuresis with the electric buzzer. *Archives of Diseases in Childhood, 33*, 160-164.

Wittgenstein, L. (1958). *Philosophical investigations*. New York: Macmillan.

Just For Laughs

Publisher: Just For Laughs
22 Miller Avenue
#G
Mill Valley, CA 94941

Format: Newspaper
Editors: Jon Fox (Editor & Publisher), Hut Landon (Managing Editor)
Phone: (415) 383-4746
Founded: 1983
Description: **Just For Laughs** is a 9-year-old monthly circulating 50,000 copies to over 300 comedy clubs across the country. The paper covers the national comedy scene with features, reviews, columns, and interviews, as well as national club listings. **Just For Laughs** accepts display and classified ads.
Frequency: 11 issues per year
# of issues published in 1991:   11
# of issues to be published in 1992:   11
# of issues to be published in 1993:   11
1992 volume: Volume #9/10 (July is the anniversary month)
Subscription period: Subscriptions run from the date the order is received
Subscription rates:

        1 year/2 years/3 years: $18.00 $30.00 $40.00

Average # of pages per issue: 24
Page size: 11" x 15"
Production: Laserprinted
Printing: Offset
Binding: Folded and loosely collated
Circulation: 50,000
Author information:

        Newspaper accepts unsolicited manuscripts
        Reports in 1 month
        Newspaper pays between $50 and $150 depending upon length and quality of manuscript
        Newspaper owns 1st serial rights
        Newspaper is copyrighted

Advertising rates:

        Full page black & white: $1,300
        Full page color: $1,800
        (Comedian's rates are available)

Cross-indexed:

        General Humor
        Arts Humor
        Political Humor

Kevin Pollak
He's Making A Good Impression On Screen
By Hut Landon
JFL Managing Editor

Nine years ago, Kevin Pollak established his credentials as a headlining comedian with a strong second place finish in the 1982 San Francisco International Comedy Competition, using a repertoire of celebrity impressions to wow the crowds. Now, after seven years in Los Angeles, he may soon find himself the subject of other impressionists. With his well-received *Avalon* performance available on video, a critically-acclaimed summer TV series, two more movie roles set for fall release, a second HBO special on tap, and last week's signing to act with the likes of Tom Cruise, Demi Moore and Jack Nicholson in the film version of a hit Broadway play, Pollak is making noise with more than just his voice.

First up is "Morton & Hayes," a six-week summer sitcom experiment from CBS. Originally conceived 13 years ago by Rob Reiner as an affectionate tribute to some of the great comedians of the '30s and '40s, the show has traveled a long, long road to fruition. Chick Morton and Eddie Hayes, loosely based on Abbott and Costello, were envisioned as an old vaudeville team that made comedy movies during that Golden era; John Candy and Joe Flaherty, then of SCTV fame, were the first choices for the leads. When they didn't work out, the project sputtered along for several years. "The producers really wanted a team for this," Pollak allows, "because they thought the chemistry would be better. Penn and Teller were very close to a deal for awhile."

Fortunately for Pollak, a suitable team could not be found and he became part of a "strenuous and very painful" casting process that mixed and matched 80 hopefuls (who were expected to rehearse in teams on their own time) before reducing the number to twenty and eventually just six. Pollak read for both the Morton and Hayes parts and was eventually paired with Joe Guzaldo for a pilot that was done two years ago.

The bad news was that Reiner, the show's originator, was unavailable to direct the pilot, so the reins were turned over to, in Pollak's caustic words, "a real idiot. Actually he was an idiot savant, but no one knows what that one thing is he does well."

The resultant product was "a very minute accomplishment," and properly languished in a CBS vault. Then, about a year ago, the network cleaned out its vaults in order to fill summer time slots with the famous "unsold pilot." So here comes "Morton & Hayes," back from the dead. Amazingly, the day of the airing, Daily Variety gave the program a rave review, prompting proud papa Reiner to call new CBS boss Jeff Sagansky, urging him to watch that night. As Pollak tells it, the kicker came when Reiner told Sagansky that "Morton & Hayes" had tested worse than any other show in CBS history and for that reason alone he should watch. Sagansky did, and the next day ordered six shows.

The new incantation now has Pollak as a team's leader, the sarcastic con man Chick Morton (he played Hayes in the pilot), and Bob Amarol as the overweight, put-upon partner. In the first installment, the two play dimwitted private eyes who solve a murder case in spite of themselves. Both Pollak and Amarol have a ball mugging and doubletaking, two boobs in over their heads but comically resourceful nevertheless. Shot in black-and-white (as are they all), the show recreates an era and a comedic genre with great affection and attention to period detail, and both stars look at ease with their characters and each other. Entertainment Weekly has already lavished praise on the sitcom, and noted that Morton is modeled after "the jaded, tough-talking" Bud Abbott but that "Pollak softens the character just enough to make him an interesting boob."

Interestingly, Morton's sarcastic, jaded nature brings to mind a prior Pollak sitcom character, that of a smarmy retirement village manager in the short-lived "Coming of Age." When asked about the similarity, Pollak chuckles and says, "I guess that means I'm good at playing a laughable, fun-loving son-of-a-bitch."

Pollak will barely have time to rest on any laurels that might accrue from "Morton & Hayes" because he begins work in September on an hour-long special for HBO, featuring new stand-up material and a series of live sketches. Then he'll no doubt want to attend the premieres of his two movie openings this fall. *JFL* told you about *Ricochet* last month in Backstage, an action thriller starring Denzel Washington and John Lithgow in which Pollak plays an undercover cop who doesn't make it to the final credits alive.

But it's *Rules of the Game* (title subject to change) that has Pollak seemingly the most excited. The romantic comedy features an ensemble of four—Pollak, Ari Gross, Courtney Cox and Julie Brown. Gross and Cox form the romantic core, while Pollak plays Gross's ball-busting best friend. "He's the last likeable sexist pig," Pollak says, "and, believe me, it was challenging to make him likeable." He is also a scene-stealer in Pollak's view, reminiscent of Jim Belushi in *About Last Night*....

But what he likes best about the role is that, for the first time, he has been given the comedic lead and he can just be funny on camera. He even has an opportunity to show off his impressionist skill by "doing" Ted Koppel in a surreal spoof of "Nightline."

Interestingly, Koppel was the first impression that Pollak had to study to capture the voice. When asked about his toughest voice, he hesitates and then admits that none of them are really hard because "if the impression doesn't come right away, I drop it. I always had this good ear, so a lot of voices just came naturally. If they didn't, I didn't pursue it."

He adds that his respect for good friend Dana Carvey continues to grow as he sees him tackle the impression challenges proffered by "Saturday Night Live." "He's really amazing at them, a real genius," Pollak says with evident feeling.

Pollak will admit that his toughest impression, at least in terms of risk, is of Albert Brooks. The voice itself is no problem—people that are familiar with Brooks realize instantly how well Pollak has him pegged and Johnny Carson has been reduced to near-tears more than once by Pollak "Tonight Show" appearances. But many people, even in comedy clubs, are not familiar with the quirky Brooks, so Pollak must create a funny scenario in which to present the impression. Even then it doesn't always play, but since as a stand-up "you are God on stage," Pollak can always do it for his own amusement.

That somewhat selfish attitude that a single performer can afford to have doesn't usually work for actors, however. Pollak readily acknowledges the shared experience of acting, and how potentially difficult that change can be for stand-ups. So has it been tough for him to become a team player, part of an ensemble rather than the sole focus? He claims not, noting that he

has been involved in show business since age 11 (his first school play) and dreaming of a movie career for almost as long. But he does admit that teamwork is tough when "it's clear that an idea is coming from someone's ego and you know in your gut that it's wrong. Then it can be hard."

But not too much else has been hard for Pollak over the past couple of years. Still, he exudes only cautious satisfaction about his success, well aware that the struggle is not over. "I've been performing since I was 10," he states, "and people have been promising me the world since I was 10, and have always fallen way short."

"I was gullible then, but I'm extremely cautious now. I've seen quick success come and go a little too often; I'm sort of grateful that mine has been a relatively slow climb. Right now, new opportunities are much more exciting than success."

That said, success may be close at hand. Pollak recently auditioned for a movie role that eventually went to Nicholas Cage; what pleased him most was that, even though he was clearly not the right person for the role, he was competing with an established actor like Cage rather than with another comic trying to score a part.

He also admits to enjoying praise bestowed by the likes of Rob Reiner and Christopher Guest (who directed five "Morton & Hayes" episodes). "You work with people of that caliber and they tell you how funny you are; yeah, I'd like to do more of that."

"This is what I dreamed about when I left San Francisco—working with people who I admire and having them like what I do."

Lest he sound too smug (he doesn't) Pollak quickly adds that "I don't want to suggest that offers are pouring in the door. There is a lot of interest in me, but I'm still in the pursuit. What is nice is to be in the position to be very aware of quality and skeptical of just an opportunity to work."

"I guess the bottom line is this: they say when the struggle stops and things come easily, then it's no fun anymore. I think I'd like to be able to say that."

"Morton & Hayes" airs Wednesdays in August on CBS.

Kid Show Quarterly

Publisher: Kid Show Quarterly
               101 Dorchester Drive
               Baltimore, OH 43105
Format: Newsletter
Editor: Mark Wade
Phone: (614) 862-6122
Founded: 1990
Description: **Kid Show Quarterly** is a newsletter dedicated to bringing good, usable comedy
               material to kidshow performers. The material and routines, "Bits-of-Business," and tips
               are aimed at helping kidshow performers do a better job in this specialized field.
Frequency: 4 issues per year
# of issues published in 1991:   4
# of issues to be published in 1992: 4
# of issues to be published in 1993: 4
1992 volume: Volume #3
Subscription period: Subscriptions run from the date the order is received
Subscription rates:

1 year:	$14.00
1 year (Canada):	US$14.00
1 year (Foreign):	US$17.00
Sample copy:	$ 3.50

Average # of pages per issue: 8
Page size: 8 1/2" x 11"
Production: Laserprinted
Printing: Offset
Binding: Folded and loosely collated
Author information:
               Newsletter does not accept unsolicited manuscripts
               Newsletter is copyrighted
Advertising rates: Advertisements are not accepted
Reviews:
               "Mark Wade is doing for children's entertainers what Bob Orben did for adult comedi-
               ans. The material in **KSQ** is current, clean, and funny. The very modest subscription
               price is a small price to pay for the comedy lines you will use. Highly recommended."
               (Samuel Patrick Smith, author and professional kidshow entertainer)
Cross-indexed:
               Joke Service Humor

A "Back-To-School" Opener

Here is a good beginning or "opener" to a school show that involves using comedy props. Whether you are a magician, ventriloquist, clown, or other variety artist, props can do much to enhance the act. This "opener" utilizes some comedy props that can either be purchased from a magic dealer or be made at home. Kids respond well to comedy props and this routine capitalizes on this.

Hi, kids! Well it's back-to-school time (listen to the groans from the children). Oh, I know you're sorry Summer is over but think of the bright side..you'll get to eat all that great cafeteria food again...SOME OF IT LEFT OVER FROM MAY! Hey, I'm kidding!..It's probably left over from JANUARY! Really, though, schools do work hard to give you good food and good learning experiences!

I've even packed my school backpack for my first day of school. Do you want to see what's in it? (Audience answers "YES!") What? I can't hear you!

(Kids scream "YES!") OK, you don't have to shout! I'm standing right here. Sheesh!!

Well, I want to get my day started right so I brushed my teeth..and here is my toothbrush (pull a giant toothbrush out of the bag). It sort of looks like a toothbrush for "Mr. Ed, the Talking Horse". Actually my Mom bought. me a toothbrush she said would fit my mouth! Isn't that nice? Don't laugh..my mouth isn't THAT big!

Next, I'll need a pencil so I can do all my work (pull out a giant pencil about 12-14 inches long and 3-4 inches in diameter). WOW! This looks like it belongs to the "Jolly Green Giant"! I started school last year with a pencil that big and I wrote so much by Christmas it looked like this (pull out a regular pencil). Boy, did we EVER work hard!

I'll also need my glasses so I can do my best (produce a giant pair of glasses)...hey, these are great! I can see everything! (Look down at your tie and shout...) AHHHH!!! I thought my tongue was hanging out, thank goodness it's only my tie! I thought I had a bad case of PAISLEY!!!

Now my teacher will want me to do some writing so I brought some paper along (reach into the bag and produce a roll of toilet paper..act embarassed, and then say...) OPPS! Wrong kind of paper! (Reach back into the bag and pull out a child's writing tablet) This is more like it! Now I'll be able to keep up with my important school work! Well, it looks like I'm ready for school but the big question is : ARE ALL OF YOU READY FOR THE SCHOOL SHOW TODAY?

Continued on Next Page

The Laugh Connection

Publisher: Bob Ross & Associates
                    3643 Corral Cyn Road
                    Bonita, CA 91902
Format: Newsletter
Editor: Bob Ross
Phone: (619) 497-3331
Founded: 1991
Description: **The Laugh Connection** features articles about humorous events and people and "how to" pieces on using humor in personal and professional situations. Special emphasis is given to the role of humor in business and management to enhance communication skills.
Frequency: 4 issues per year
# of issues published in 1991:   4
# of issues to be published in 1992:   4
# of issues to be published in 1993:   4
1992 volume: Volume #2
Subscription period: Subscriptions run from the date the order is received
Subscription rates:

           1 year/2 years: $18.00 $30.00
           1 year/2 years (Canada):   US$18.00 US$30.00 (paid on international money order)
           1 year/2 years (Foreign):   US$18.00 US$30.00 (paid on international money order)
           Sample: Free (include a S.A.S.E. with 52¢ postage)

Average # of pages per issue: 8
Page size: 8 1/2" x 11"
Production: Typeset
Printing: Offset
Binding: Folded and loosely collated
Circulation: 800
Author information:
           Newsletter does not accept unsolicited manuscripts
           All articles are copyrighted
           Newsletter is copyrighted
Advertising rates: Advertisements are not accepted
Reviews:
           "This definitely is one of the best humor letters to come across my desk. And I've received quite a few from a variety of authors." (Jerry Svendsen, Editor, *Sun Life Magazine*)
           "**The Laugh Connection** is for serious humorists...it can help one attain a healthier, happier, longer and more productive life." (*Slow Lane Journal*)
           "**The Laugh Connection** jumps out of my pile and asks to be read. You do your homework and provide useful content you can use right away to put to work the humor advantage." (Terry Paulson, Ph.D., author and professional speaker)
Cross-indexed:
           General Humor
           Business Humor
           Political Humor
           Cartoons/Illustrations/Graphics
           Research on Humor

Case Study
Humor in the Workplace

Some people come to work with the same level of enthusiasm that they'd have for being attacked by a pack of hungry jackals.

Putting humor, fun and play to work in your job is a way of injecting excitement and enthusiasm into the workplace. It is but one major aspect of creating a "nice place to work." But the results are more than altruistic. There's ample evidence that humor at work pays off for the employed in dollars and cents.

Franklin Research and Development took a look at those companies listed in Robert Levering's book *The Best 100 Companies to Work for in America*. They analyzed the seventy companies that were public and found that they were twice as profitable as the average Standard & Poor 500 company and that their stock prices grew at three times the average rate. Clearly, a pleasant workplace is related to corporate success.

What used to be seen by many as Pollyannaism is now being accepted and implemented in many forms, not the least of which is injecting liberal doses of fun into the work environment. It's all part of a caring, sharing atmosphere full of mutual respect—the same thing you'll find by peeking into the make-up of championship sports teams.

Companies are coming up with numerous ways to make the work environment a pleasant one and, through that pleasant environment, communicate that they really care about their employees: *Dress down day*, also known by such sobriquets as "grub day," "jeans day," and "casual Friday," these days are thought to have had

their origin at Hewlett-Packard when Friday was the day products were shipped. When they had a backlog of goods to go out, all workers would come to work dressed casually so they could help with the shipping. The practice spread when HP employees were hired by other Silicone Valley companies. Today, relaxed dress codes are legendary among high-tech firms in that area.

Also common there are the Friday "beer busts." Companies regularly sponsor them so that their employees can come together in a relaxed atmosphere to discuss discoveries and achievements of the week. Through this productive party, management is saying, "We care about you!"

According to its proponents, a beer bust has such ancillary effects as promoting informality among people, which has an equalizing effect. This practice is not confined to high-tech or even manufacturing operations. Even normally stodgy attorneys have gotten in on the act. The Menlo Park (California) firm of Coddington, Hicks & Danforth has adopted the practice. They also have an ice cream break at 3 o'clock in the afternoon.

Besides such things as "dress down day," companies are finding other ways to create positive work places: free day care, two dollar haircuts (at the company barber shop—on company time) and other such amenities all add festivity and a sense of caring to the workplace. One company sponsors an annual "Teddy Day" during which an award is given to the employee who has helped others the most. G.E. put score boards conspicuously around the plant during the World Series as one subtle but effective way of saying "we care."

Some other events used by different companies: silly hat contests, weird shoe competition, and joke telling contests.

National Computer Systems of Minneapolis hired an "Elation Strategist" to "lighten up the joint." The idea: to help people relieve stress and to assist supervisors in becoming better communicators and managers. Other companies have made similar efforts to lighten up their work forces by creating a "Lite Brigade" to come up with ideas for injecting humor, fun and play. Many firms have made their break rooms into "humor rooms" or installed a kiosk to encourage employees to post cartoons and other funny items.

Companies such as Manville Corp., Safeway Stores and Northwestern Bell Telephone have instituted a number of humor programs to help employees unwind.

The message is clear: drill-sergeant management is on the way out. Participative management is alive and well and thriving. This can be seen clearly in examining such companies as General Electric. Their most recent annual report states it quite precisely in a message from John Welsh, Chairman of the Board and CEO: "We want [employees] to go home from work wanting to talk about what they did that day, rather than trying to forget about it. We want factories where the whistle blows and someone suddenly wonders aloud why we need a whistle. We want a company where people find a better way, every day, of doing things, and where by shaping their own work experience they make their lives *better* and [our] Company *best*."

The report adds: "Far-fetched? Fuzzy? Soft? Naive? Not a bit. This is the type of liberated, involved, excited, boundary-less culture that is present in successful start-up enterprises. It is unheard of in an institution our size; but we want it and we are determined we will have it."

A friendly workplace is not a passing trend. It is part and parcel of the "information age," in which we find ourselves. And since the "people approach" (sometimes called "warm-wear") is based on human nature, we can expect to see it around for a long time. Yes, there's ample evidence that the punch line can affect the bottomline.

Reprinted from **The Laugh Connection** by permission of the editor.

Laughing Matters

Publisher: The HUMOR Project, Inc.
110 Spring Street
Saratoga Springs, NY 12866
Format: Magazine
Editor: Dr. Joel Goodman
Phone: (518) 587-8770 [FAX: (518) 587-8771]
Founded: 1981
Description: **Laughing Matters** offers a goldmine of ideas on how to get more smileage out of your life. It is filled with humorous examples of hundreds of practical tips on how to develop and apply your sense of humor personally and on-the-job. Recent articles include "Funny Business: Putting Humor to Work at Work," "Humor for the Health of It," "Fun-Liners Jest for You," "Blooper Scooper: Laughing at Yourself," and personal interviews with Steve Allen, Jay Leno, Victor Borge, Cathy Guisewite, Sid Caesar, Dom DeLuise, Norman Cousins, Allen Funt, Mark Russell, Charles M. Schulz, Buffalo Bob Smith, etc.

Frequency: 4 issues per year
Issues per volume: 4
# of issues published in previous year: 4
# of issues to be published this year: 4
# of issues to be published next year: 4
1992 volume: Volume #8
Subscription period: Calendar year (i.e., all subscriptions received in 1992 are fulfilled with 1992 issues)

Subscription rates:

	U.S. rates*	Outside of U.S.
1 year:	$ 20.00	US$ 23.20
Present year + 1 year of back issues:	$ 36.00	US$ 42.00
Present year + 2 years of back issues:	$ 50.50	US$ 59.10
Present year + 3 years of back issues:	$ 62.50	US$ 75.50
Present year + 4 years of back issues:	$ 75.50	US$ 88.70
Present year + 7 years of back issues:	$108.50	US$129.80
Sample copy:	$ 9.00	US$ 10.00

(*New York State residents should add 7% sales tax)

Average # of pages per issue: 40
Page size: 5 1/2" x 8 1/2"
Production: Laserprinted
Printing: Offset
Binding: Saddle stitched
Circulation: 10,000+
Author information:
Accepts unsolicited manuscripts
Reports in 2-4 months
Author receives 1 free copy of issue in which article appears as payment
Variable copyright terms: Sometimes magazine owns all rights, sometimes 1st serial rights, sometimes author owns rights
Magazine is copyrighted
Advertising rates: Advertisements are not accepted
Reviews:
"**Laughing Matters** is clearly the best periodical on the subject of humor and its uses. If you want more humor in your life, **Laughing Matters** is for you." (Dr. Laurence Peter, creator of The Peter Principle)
"Enthusiastic congratulations on **Laughing Matters**!" (Norman Cousins)
"**Laughing Matters** is an excellent working guide for people seeking to harness the

fantastic powers of mirth. I read every issue cover-to-cover for its countless nuggets on humor in life, humor in work, and humor in health." (Julius Cahn, President of *Health* magazine)

Cross-indexed:

General Humor
Social Sciences Humor
Business Humor
Medicine/Dentistry/Nursing Humor
Political Humor
Cartoons/Illustrations/Graphics
Research on Humor
Summary of Conferences and Symposiums on Humor/Satire
Education Humor
Psychiatry Humor
Psychology Humor
Religion Humor

ISSN: 0731-1788

Mythconception #3:
To Be Humorous, You Have to Be a "Natural" Joke-Teller

Some people think that to be humorous, you had to be born with that quality—or you're out of luck (and humor). I posed this issue to Steve Allen in an interview in Volume 2, #2. His perspective is that we may be born with a certain genetic ceiling and floor when it comes to "humor"—but it's what we do in our lives that influences whether we end up on the ceiling or floor. In other words, there is hope.

Over 300,000 people throughout the United States and abroad have now attended our programs on the positive power of humor. About 80% of these people have indicated that they think they have a good sense of humor. Over 98% of them, however, relate that they can't tell a joke to save their lives.

Although joke-telling is one way to transmit humor, it's not the only way. In fact, there are literally thousands of ways to invite smiles and laughter in addition to joke-telling. So, if joke-telling is not your forte, and if it is inappropriate for you to become the stand-up comic on-the-job, then there are alternatives. Here are some tips to get you going:

(1) *Put humor into the physical environment*—by osmosis, it may filter into the corporate culture. This could be accomplished by having posters with light-hearted sayings: "The brain is a wonderful organ. It starts the moment you get up in the morning and does not stop until you get to the office." (Robert Frost)

(2) *Anticipate ways of injecting humor into potential conflict situations.* This is called "prepared flexibility," which is what leadership is all about anyway. Having available a repertoire of quotes may help you through some sticky situations. One popular phrase I've seen is, "Save time...see it my way!"

(3) *Develop your comic vision.* Look for humor and it will find you. Make believe you are Allen Funt (the creator of the CANDID CAMERA television show) for five minutes each day...especially in the most serious places. For instance, one of my graduate students recently passed along this sign she saw in front of a church announcing the two services for a particular Sunday: "Theme of 9:30 AM Service: Jesus Walks on Water....Theme of 5:00 Service: Searching for Jesus." You are sometimes expected to "walk on water," and yet, you may be searching in the process. Searching for humor is a wonderful way to find yourself.

(4) *Use humor as a tool rather than as a weapon.* Laughing with others builds confidence, brings people together, and pokes fun at our common dilemmas. Laughing at others destroys confidence, destroys teamwork, and singles out individuals or groups as the "butt." In the words of one teacher, "You don't have to blow out my candle to make yours glow brighter." Humor is laughter made from pain, not pain inflicted by laughter. (See the last issue for an article that focuses on this.)

(5) *Laugh at yourself.* Set the tone by modeling your ability to take your job

seriously and yourself lightly. One of the simplest and most powerful ways of doing this is to "tell stories on yourself" whenever possible and appropriate.

My friend, Barbara, tells of a family ritual when she was a child. It went something like this: Every year, at Thanksgiving time, the family would descend on Grandma and Grandpa's. True to form, this particular year, Grandma had spent two days in the kitchen, working on the turkey and everything that went with it. The moment of Thanksgiving dinner arrived—everyone was seated at the dining room table as Grandma emerged proudly from the kitchen with the turkey on a platter. She was about to set the turkey on the table when the turkey slid off the platter and kerplopped on the floor. Grandma hardly missed a beat—she scooped up the turkey, walked back into the kitchen, made a U-turn, and then proudly reemerged announcing, "I'll bring out the other one!"

What could have been an embarrassing, disastrous event has turned into a family legacy of laughter. Each year, at Thanksgiving, the family delights in retelling the time when Grandma felt like a turkey, but was able to use humor to soar above the situation.

Life is Serious...Life Is a Laughing Matter

Life is serious. Life is a laughing matter. Both are true. The wonderful thing is that we have the choice. By choosing humor and laughter, we can survive and thrive.

If you've ever been in a painful or difficult situation in which someone says, "Someday we'll laugh at this!"...you might offer the following suggestion: "Why wait?" Laughing at yourself can have booth immediate and long-term payoffs. Invest in jest now!

Laugh•Makers Variety Arts Magazine

Publisher: Fun Technicians, Inc.
               P.O. Box 160
               Syracuse, NY 13215

Format: Magazine

Editor: Cathy Gibbons

Phone: (315) 492-4523

Founded: 1981

Description: **Laugh•Makers**, "The Variety Arts Magazine for Family & Kidshow Entertainers," is a resource for performers and humor enthusiasts in the US, Canada, and 34 other countries. A network of performers and leaders in their fields provide columns each issue on: clowning, comedy magic, balloonology, puppetry, ventriloquism, storytelling, funny props, comedy techniques, and business/promotion. Feature stories cover broad interests, ranging from interviews with kidshow performers to humor and health, school shows, comedy writing, and more. Each 50- to 60-page issue also includes extensive calendar listings and over 40 advertisers for hard-to-find props, books, and resources. Each summer, the magazine sponsors a week-long conference (Kid Show College).

Frequency: 6 issues per year

# of issues published in 1991:   6

# of issues to be published in 1992:   6

# of issues to be published in 1993:   6

1992 volume: Volume #11

Subscription period: Subscriptions run from the date the order is received

Subscription rates:

1 year/2 years:	$21.00	$40.00
1 year/2 years (Canada):	US$27.00	US$52.00
1 year/2 years (Foreign):	US$27.00	US$52.00
Sample copy: $4.00		

Average # of pages per issue: 52-60

Page size: 8 1/4" x 10 3/4"

Production: Laserprinted

Printing: Offset

Binding: Saddle stitched

Circulation: 3,000-3,200

Author information:

    Prospective authors should inquire first before submitting manuscripts

    Reports in 2-4 weeks

    Author receives 4 complimentary copies of the issue in which the article is published as payment

    Magazine owns 1st serial rights and upon publication rights revert back to author with the stipulation that the article cannot be reprinted in another performer trade publication for one year

    Magazine is copyrighted

Advertising rates:

1/4 page black & white:	$ 50
1/2 page black & white:	$ 90
Full page black & white:	$135
1/2 page Cover 4:	$155

Reviews:

"I have been impressed with the remarkable growth of **Laugh•Makers**. Every issue of this fine magazine just teems with fresh, interesting ideas. The healthy support it has received from advertisers is an indication of its success in the marketplace. I recommend this magazine to all who do family type entertainment. You'll find it refreshing, alive, and encouraging." (Sid Lorraine, *New TOPS Magazine*)

"Lots of practical stuff! If I were working kidshows, I would not be without this magazine." (David Goodsell, *M•U•M* [Society of American Magicians])

"Where in the world have I been? How could I have missed this magazine? I think I'm in love...perusing the pub. in an orgy of fun. I've gotten a new slant into a lot of disciplines with which I was unfamiliar." (Rick Johnson, *Linking King* [International Brotherhood of Magicians])

Cross-indexed:

    General Humor

    Arts Humor

    Summary of Conferences and/or

        Symposiums on Humor

The Big Apple Circus Clown Care Unit:

A Special Kind of Medicine

By Cathy Gibbons

The Queen of Mischief stands in her hospital room doorway. She's eight years old and she's lived in that room a long, long time. Her clown friends from the Big Apple Circus Clown Care Unit visit every week. She can count on them. Newly crowned by "Dr. E B D B D" (Laine Barton), in a ceremony worthy of any Shakespearian fool and attended by her Mom, nurses, clowns, and anyone else in the hallway, the Queen smiles and asks, "What is mischief?"

The crown, like many of the Clown Care Unit props, is fashioned from simple things. Laine finds a box of tin foil under puppets, juggling scarves, squeaky toys, and clown stuff overflowing the little wagon she pulls behind her. She fashions the crown before our very eyes, encrusting it with sticker dot jewels.

Not so simple are the psychological depth, responsible planning, on-going training, teamwork and personal dedication that have defined the Clown Care Unit since its inception at Babies Hospital, a division of The Presbyterian Hospital, Columbia Presbyterian Medical Center.

Like its "parent," the prestigious one-ring Big Apple Circus founded a decade before, the Clown Care Unit began as one individual's vision and grew to encompass a working community of artists, friends and practical thinkers. Inspired to perform in hospitals after losing his older brother to cancer, Big Apple Circus clown Michael Christensen said his first hospital show was "the most fulfilling 20 minutes I'd done in my career."

Christensen's goal was clear from the start. He wanted to create a program of service not only to the children and their families, but also to performers and hospital staff. He initiated a collaborative effort that continues today. Circus directors and fundraisers, clown performers and hospital staff (from top physicians to behaviorists, counselors, nurses, housekeeping personnel and development/public relations specialists) worked together to forge a pilot program sensitive to each other's needs. All involved feel a sense of intellectual or emotional "ownership" of the program, a factor that also helps insure longer term survival. And they are united in the shared purpose of helping children cope with illness. Rather than an entertainment "slapped on" the hospital, the Clown Care Unit is an integral part of hospital life.

With Jeff Gordon ("Disorderly Gordoon"), a fellow Big Apple Circus professional clown, Christensen, now "Dr. Stubs," began the first Clown Care "rounds" at Babies Hospital in 1986. Performance parameters established then continue in place now, including:

1)Working as clown characters who parody the medical routine, usually as "Doctors," with the intention of helping children feel less traumatized by scary aspects of the hospital environment and painful medical procedures;

2) Designing clown faces more in the European or Auguste tradition with real skin showing, keeping a more human rather than cartoonish quality, which they consider less potentially frightening to children in the hospital situation;

3) Always working in teams of two clowns (not as solo performers and preferably including both a man and a woman clown) who make their rounds in the same hospital on the same floors on a consistent basis creating the opportunity to build relationships;

4)Hiring professional performers skilled in clowning, magic, puppets, juggling, music, etc., who also have the adaptability and sensitivity required in a hospital environment where the child, not the performance, comes first;

5) Paying performers for their work with the Clown Care Unit from a pool of private and corporate donations (last year when I was there, the clowns were given $110.00 each day they worked, with their schedule being 10:00 a.m. to 3:00 p.m. including an hour for lunch, and a maximum of 3 days a week allocated each clown to help prevent "burn out").

Babies Hospital continues to be the training center for the Clown Care Unit, but the program has expanded and now sends clown teams to St. Luke's/Roosevelt Hospital Center, The Montefiore Medical Center, the Jack D. Weiler Hospital of the Albert Einstein College of Medicine, and other New York City medical institutions.

With expansion, of course, has come the need to formalize procedures for clowns invited to become members of the Clown Care Unit. A full-time Program Administrator was recruited. An audition and training process, scheduled seminars and counseling sessions on issues related to working with sick children, and monthly group rehearsal meetings have been established. Fundraising and grant writing continue their demanding course.

Despite the challenges of practicality and structure required to make dreams functioning reality, the spirit of the work remains the same. The clowns, with their allies' support and encouragement, extend a precious gift—the healing gift of wonder, of knowing that within the pain we are still intact, sturdy, alive. We know because our moments with the clowns, pristine like the bubbles they blow around our heads, prove we still can laugh.

Mischief still can reign.

Reprinted with permission from **Laugh•Makers Variety Arts Magazine**.

The Laughter Prescription

Publisher: Karen Silver
              17337 Septo Street
              Northridge, CA 91325
Format: Newsletter
Editor: Karen Silver
Phone: (818) 886-1951
Founded: 1989
Description: A 6-page newsletter dedicated to the art of humor and healing.
Frequency: 12 issues per year
# of issues published in 1991:   12
# of issues to be published in 1992: 12
# of issues to be published in 1993: 12
1992 volume: Volume #4
Subscription period: Subscription runs from date the order is received
Subscription rates:

1 year:	$18.00
1 year (Canada):	US$18.00
1 year (Foreign):	US$18.00

Average # of pages per issue: 6
Page size: 8 1/2" x 11"
Production: Laserprinted
Printing: Xeroxed
Binding: Folded and loosely collated
Circulation: 250
Author information:
          Newsletter accepts unsolicited manuscripts
          Reports in 1 week
          Author receives 3 complimentary copies of the issue in which the article is published as
              payment
          Newsletter does not deal with the issue of copyrighting individual articles
          Newsletter is not copyrighted
Advertising: Advertisements are not accepted
Reviews:
          "**The Laughter Prescription.** Jest what the doctor ordered. Each page is chock full of
              information and entertaining clean jokes to tickle your funnybone. Great for patients
              and nurses alike." (*Journal of Nursing Jocularity*)
          "Lighten up. Having trouble forcing a smile? Noticing more frown lines than laugh
              lines? **The Laughter Prescription**, a newsletter dedicated to the healing art of humor,
              could be just the ticket. It's a monthly publication that costs $18 a year, offering jokes,
              heart-warming articles on how to deal with subjects such as death and dying and a list
              of professional humorous speakers for your club or church event." (*The Daily News*)
          "Karen Silver, comedy writer and newsletter publisher, puts together one of the best
              humor publications I've come across in a long time. **The Laughter Prescription**
              newsletter is a monthly newsletter dedicated to bringing humor to healthcare. In the
              belief that laughter has positive benefits, each newsletter will contain brand new
              contemporary, clean jokes to entertain both patients and care givers. It is also an ideal
              gift for hospital chaplain visits." (*The Laugh Report*)
Cross-indexed:
          General Humor
          Research on Humor
          Medical Humor
          Nursing Humor
          Joke Service Humor
ISSN: 1046-5588

THE LAUGHTER PRESCRIPTION

THE LAUGHTER PRESCRIPTION NEWSLETTER

prepared by
KAREN SILVER

subscription rate
**12 MONTHLY ISSUES - $18
SAMPLE ISSUE - $1**

ISSN 1046 5588

*address all inquiries, correspondence
and address changes to*
**17337 SEPTO STREET
NORTHRIDGE, CA 91325**

phone
**(818) 886-8737
(818) 886-1951**

the board of advisors
**MS. LOU ANNE BOSWELL
MS. JUDY BROWN
DR. IRVING M. BUSH
MR. ART GLINER
DR. BARBARA HANNA
MR. ED HERCER
MS. LINDA H. MACKEY
DR. J. MITCHELL PERRY
SPANKY
MRS. MARY JO CROWLEYSTEINER
DR. TOM STEINER
DR. VIRGINIA TOOPER
MR. DAVID A. VAN GORDER
MS. RAHLA KAHN**

cartoonist
JOE SUMRALL

typesetter
**BONNIE LAMBERT
DESKTOP PUBLISHING**

graphic design
**DAVID LYNCH
GRAPHIC DESIGN**

NOOZ ROUNDUP

✳ Actress Hedy Lamarr was recently arrested for shop lifting. I didn't know she was in the cast of Different Strokes.

✳ A giant cockroach found in a Florida school captured the World's Biggest Roach title... and they say cafeteria food has no nutritional value.

✳ *Esquire Magazine*'s September issue will feature two separate covers. One shows a smiling, and the other a frowning David Letterman. I thought he was alone when they announced Leno got the Tonight Show job.

✳ Happy anniversary... 56 years ago this month the government launched the first multi-level marketing plan, Social Security.

✳ LA City schools are reducing their budget shortfall by increasing class size. If this plan really works, the district will end up with a student/teacher ratio of 600,000 to 1.

✳ LA Police Department reform cost put at $31.8 million, boy am I glad they're not orthodox!

✳ A group of former high-ranking intelligence officials quickly raised funds to help pay the legal expenses for Iran-Contra defendants. They have been so sneaky, I wouldn't be surprised if the CIA really *was* made up of Counterfeitors In Action.

✳ Dan Quayle went before the American Bar Association and complained to thousands of lawyers that the nation was being bogged down with too much costly litigation. That's right Dan, if you can't join 'em, beat 'em up.

✳ The phone company is going to charge for 911 emergency service, but freeway callboxes still won't cost anything. This means victims of drive by shootings can still report that their car has been filled with leaded gas against their will.

✳ LA City Department heads have received two raises in two weeks, but there isn't enough money to keep neurosurgeons in town. It's a shame too, because the city council members really *should* have their heads examined.

HUMOR IS HEALING

2

ON A ROLL WITH
GENE MITCHENER

Gene Mitchener's motto is, "Do not let what you can't do stand in the way of what you *can* do." He should know. For years he dreamed of doing comedy, until at the age of 27 his musician friends plunked Gene's wheelchair on stage for his first set. Gene realized once he let go of the stand up part, he could do the comedy. No one has been able to stop the founder of Rolling Productions since.

Gene Mitchener, professional sit-down comedian, wastes no time when it comes to breaking down barriers as he appears in his wheelchair on stages throughout the country. "I was born this way," says Gene. "It was a difficult birth, my head was caught in the spokes…" Gene has a rare form of muscular dystrophy. However, it has not prevented him from becoming a very well-established entertainer. He has hosted his own television show, performed in comedy clubs nationwide, and appeared on numerous television talk shows, and has been featured in countless newspaper and magazine articles.

Gene created the annual television special "Standup Comics Take a Stand," a fund raiser that has donated money to United Cerebral Palsy. He has also authored a cartoon book that features Gene in his many humorous situations. All this with one goal in mind, that the disabled are people too. Talking with Gene, I am struck with his great intelligence, energy and facile wit. It is clear he is passionate about his work and definitely an inspiration to all who come in contact with him. Somehow in addition to his busy schedule Gene also finds time to use humor therapy while doing volunteer work in a drug and alcohol rehabilitation half way house.

GENE
MITCHENER

Gene explained, "It has been said tragedy plus time equals comedy. You can look back later and laugh about it. I believe if you can actually bring laughter into the moment it is healing. "He cited this example. During a Disability Awareness Day program at a Midwestern college, Gene was introduced and his wheelchair literally rolled downstage, and fell into the orchestra pit. Here were two thousand people collectively holding their breath watching a potential tragedy. Even though he broke his collarbone and his glasses, Gene went right back on stage and in his best Don Pardo voice announced, "Live from New York, it's Saturday Night!" Humor had broken a tension that could be cut with a knife.

Gene quoted from Psalms, "A merry heart doeth good like a medicine." He added, in the original Greek the merry translates as hilarious. So, Gene heals with comedy wherever he goes, and challenges the able bodied not to let mental handicaps keep them from achieving their dreams.

Contact Gene through Peterson & Fisher public relations (213) 461-9975.

Gene

"Do not let what you can't do stand in the way of what you can do."

HUMOR IS HEALING

Laughter Works® The Newsletter

Founder: Jim Pelley
Publication: **Laughter Works The Newsletter**
Publisher: The Newsletter Company
            222 Selby Ranch Road, #4
            Sacramento, CA 95864
Format: Newsletter
Editor: Jim Pelley
Phone: (916) 484-7988
Organization founded: 1985
Publication founded: 1988
Description of organization: **Laughter Works** gives people the tools and skills for applying humor in their life to reduce stress and to solve problems with creativity. **Laughter Works** sponsors a Humor in the Hills 2 1/2-day retreat program every fall.
Description of publication: **Laughter Works The Newsletter** features humor news and current comedy including hilarious cartoons; a guest authors section where one can see how humor relates to Health Care, Education, Business, etc., from some of the leading people in their fields; a complete calendar of Humor Events; a 10 tips section, providing ideas for using humor and laughter personally and professionally; quotables—knowledge, insight and laughter from the Famous, Funny and Unknown; and Mirth Management Ideas that are working in businesses, schools and hospitals.
Frequency: 4 issues per year
# of issues published in 1991:   4
# of issues to be published in 1992:   4
# of issues to be published in 1993:   4
1992 volume: Volume #4
Subscription period: Subscriptions run from the date the order is received
Subscription rates:

1 year/2 years:	$18.00	$31.00
1 year/2 years (Canada):	US$25.00	US$38.00
1 year/2 years (Foreign):	US$25.00	US$38.00
Sample copy: $6.00		

Average # of pages per issue: 8
Page size: 8 1/2" x 11"
Production: Typeset
Printing: Offset
Binding: Folded and loosely collated
Circulation: 10,000
Author information:
        Newsletter accepts unsolicited manuscripts
        Reports in 4 months
        Authors receive 100 complimentary copies of the issue in which the article is published as payment
        Author owns rights to article
        Newsletter is copyrighted
Advertising rates: Advertisements are not accepted
Reviews:
        "Excellent Resource! **Laughter Works The Newsletter** offers practical and effective techniques...inspirational advice to increase serum fun levels!" (Patty Wooten, R.N., B.S.N., C.C.R.N.)
        "The best humor newsletter on the market, no question about it!" (Edward & Rita Pelley [Jim's parents])
        "**Laughter Works The Newsletter** is fun-derful. I can't wait for it to be made into a musical." (Allen Klein)
Cross-indexed:

General Humor	Summary of Conferences and/or
Business Humor	Symposiums on Humor
Research on Humor	Nursing Humor

Guest Author

Headline humor

How to translate the headlines into humor

By Kurt Kilpatrick, J.D., CSP, CPAE

The literary giant T.S. Eliot said, "Humor is another way of saying something serious." When broken down into its component parts we begin to see the pattern: ALL humor springs forth from serious subject matter which, on its face, is not particularly funny. But it is in knowing what is serious that we recognize what is or can be humorous. The contemporary comedy writer's task is to take the serious and twist the standard meaning and search for ways to misdirect the meaning toward the unlikely, the bizarre and the non-standard meaning.

The raw material for writing humor from the headlines comes, of course, from newspapers, magazines, popular books, TV shows, radio talk shows, and other sources of news. A great deal of information is required and a broad knowledge of world and local events is necessary. After the raw material is accumulated the writer begins to categorize the information and begins looking for relationships between the serious and the absurd or comedic point of view.

Sometimes the headlines themselves are humorous right from the start. They jump out at you. The headlines, for example, "Lawyers must try case in Union Suit," "Former man dies in California," or "Woman is shot and the bullet is in her yet," are all funny in themselves. When the standard meaning is applied the headlines almost appear normal. When, however, we distort the meaning in our minds they take on a non-standard meaning. Can't you imag-

Kurt Kilpatrick, J.D., CSP, CPAE

ine the lawyer trying a case in his Union Suit? The man who died in California was a former man. What was he before that? A woman was shot and the bullet is in her "yet." In what part of the anatomy do we find a woman's "yet"? Sometimes the comedy writer's work is already done by the people who write the headlines. Often times the simple powers of observation and awareness will create funny material right before our eyes.

Generally, however, the writer has to do a little work to come up with funny "humor from the headlines." I do it in the following way. First I pick a subject, then do a spreadsheet based on the journalistic formula of "who, what, where, when and how," after which I begin looking for relationships between the serious and the humorous. The second step involves looking for the standard versus the non-standard meaning.

The third step is then a process of tying together the relatable items, looking for the comedic twist, then finally eliminating all but the funniest lines. Like most successful endeavors, it's simple but it's not easy.

After I've accumulated my raw data, my brain goes through a process like the following: Who's involved?, What's involved? , What's going on?, How will it effect me (us)?, Is there a common ground everyone can relate to?, When is it happening?, Where is it occurring?, What are the relationships? Then I begin to look for connecting points to tie it all together.

If my subject was, for instance, "Politics," we could have a field day. In order to help balance the budget, Congress has installed a 1-900-number and is asking for your suggestions.

By connecting the standard meaning with the non-standard meaning, using comedic misdirection and distortion you can take almost any serious subject, when appropriate, and turn it into a humorous line.

The humor writer, the professional humorist, gives us that relief by As As one great philosopher said, "It is in knowing what is serious that we can find what is humorous." Keep laughing!

Kurt Kilpatrick is a professional humorist, author and radio personality.
For more information call (205) 945-8607 or write:
606 Forest Dr.
Birmingham, Alabama 35209

If you would like to be a guest author please contact us at: LAUGHTER WORKS, 222 Selby Ranch Road #4, Sacramento, CA 95864-5832, (916) 484-7988

Leadership

Publisher: The Economics Press
               12 Daniel Road
               Fairfield, NJ 07004
Format: Magazine
Editor: Arthur F. Lenehan
Phone: (201) 227-1224
Founded: 1985 [formerly entitled *Soundings*]
Description: **Leadership** is the sister publication to *Bits & Pieces*, published to satisfy *Bits & Pieces* readers who want more of the same. Also aimed at executive and management personnel, **Leadership** has a fast-growing following among female management personnel. Features brief (100-200 words) articles about dealing with people, sandwiched between humorous anecdotes, aphorisms, proverbs, etc.
Frequency: 12 issues per year
Issues per volume: 12
# of issues published in 1991:   12
# of issues to be published in 1992:   12
# of issues to be published in 1993:   12
1992 volume: Volume #8
Subscription period: Subscriptions run from the date the order is received
Subscription rates:
               1 year: $17.55
               Sample copy: Free
Page size: 4" x 6 1/2"
Production: Typeset
Printing: Offset
Binding: Saddle stitched
Circulation: 42,000
Author information:
               Magazine does not accept unsolicited manuscripts
Advertising rates: Advertisements are not accepted
Cross-indexed:
               General Humor
               Business Humor

THE U.S. PRESIDENTIAL CANDIDATES are out in full force in New Hampshire. We're told one of them had been speaking for 20 minutes to a small audience in a meeting house.

An elderly woman in front turned to the row behind her and said, "I can't quite hear him. What's he talkin' about?"

The group in back of her conferred for a few moments. Then one of them finally leaned forward and said, "He don't say."

WE NEED more people who can bring to their jobs the same enthusiasm for getting ahead as they display in traffic.

The common cold is positive as well as negative. Sometimes the eyes have it, and sometimes the nose.

A MAN CAME into the doctor's office with both ears badly burned.

"I was ironing some shirts and I had the telephone sitting on the ironing board," he explained. "When the phone range, I picked up the iron by mistake and put it to my ear. And to make it worse, the call turned out to be a wrong number."

"But how did you burn the other ear?" asked the doctor.

"The dumbbell called back again," said the man.

—James Dent
Charleston, W.Va. Gazette

The difference between horse races and political races is that in a horse race the whole horse wins.

In spite of the cost of living, it's still popular.

A DEPARTMENT STORE buyer passed away and went to his eternal resting place.

When he arrived in the other world, he was greeted by a salesman who had unsuccessfully tried to get an appointment with him many times while on earth.

"Hello, Jack," said the salesman, greeting him. "I'm here for the appointment."

"What appointment?" snarled the buyer.

"Don't you remember?" replied the salesman. "Every time I used to try and see you in your office, you'd tell me you'd rather see me here."

Sign in a hardware store: Shovels. Salt. *Sympathy.*

A WOMAN EXECUTIVE to whom time is precious has devised a defense against unexpected guests. When her doorbell rings, she puts on her hat and coat and opens the door.

It it's someone she doesn't want to see, she says, "Oh, isn't this too bad! I'm just on my way out!"

If it's someone she wants to see, she says, "What great timing! I just got in!"

Before you decide about your aim in life, check your ammunition.

THERE ARE now so many substitutes on the market, it's sometimes hard to remember what the original was.

The Loonies

Founder: Barry Gantt
Address: **The Loonies**
             P.O. Box 20443
             Oakland, CA 94620
Phone: (510) 451-6248
Founded: 1978
Description: **The Loonies** is a "salon" in the traditional sense—we gather about every six weeks to exchange contacts, show work, get feedback, socialize, whatever. We are a very informal, yet well-connected group, with no formal rules, publications, or bureaucracy. And people have always liked it that way. Guests have ranged from Gahan Wilson and Paul Krassner (author of the recently published *Best of the Realist*) to Gilbert Shelton. The only publication of **The Loonies** is a flyer announcing periodic salons. A recent flyer welcomed humorists, cartoonists, performers, ad biz and media mavens, art directors, animators, publishers, and anyone with a sense of humor and/or creativity.

Annual membership dues: None
# of members: 350 on the organization's mailing list (To get on mailing list, send a self-addressed, stamped envelope)
Cross-indexed:
             General Humor
             Cartoons/Illustrations/Graphics

MAD®

Publisher: E. C. Publications, Inc.
               485 Madison Avenue
               New York, NY 10022
Format: Magazine
Editors: Nick Meglin, John Ficarra
Phone: (212) 752-7685
Founded: 1952
Description: **MAD®** is "humor in a jugular vein."
Frequency: 8 issues per year
# of issues published in 1991:   8
# of issues to be published in 1992: 8
# of issues to be published in 1993: 8
Subscription period: Subscriptions begin about 10-12 weeks after the order is received
Subscription rates:

1 year/3 years/5 years:	$13.75	$33.75	$53.75
1 year/3 years/5 years (Foreign):	US$18.75	US$46.75	US$74.75
Sample copy: $1.75			

Average # of pages per issue: 48
Page size: 8 3/8" x 10 1/2"
Production: Typeset
Printing: Offset
Binding: Saddle stitched
Circulation: 1,000,000+
Author information:
               Magazine accepts unsolicited manuscripts
               Reports in 1 month
               Pays $350 per printed page minimum
               Magazine buys all rights
               Magazine is copyrighted
Advertising rates: Advertisements are not accepted
Cross-indexed:
               General Humor
               Social Sciences Humor
               Arts Humor
               Political Humor
               Cartoons/Illustrations/Graphics
               Visual Satire
               Education Humor
               Film Media Humor
               History Humor
               Literature Humore
               Medical Humor
               Poetry Humor
               Word Play & Puns
ISSN: 0024-9319

The MAD WRITER'S Fantasy

The MAD WRITER'S Reality

As you can see from the nifty little drama depicted above, things in life often don't "pan out" as one might like. Sometimes things turn out rather poorly. All too frequently, they turn out even worse! The rest of the time... KABLOOIE! Take this intro— we wanted something short, compact, concise and to the point. What we got was a long, boring, tedious, meandering gabfest! Nonetheless, it did do the job and introduced...

CONSUMER FANTASY
vs.
PRODUCT REALITY

ARTIST: BOB JONES   WRITER: MIKE SNIDER

The MR. MICROPHONE Fantasy

The MR. MICROPHONE Reality

The AIR JORDAN Fantasy

The AIR JORDAN Reality

Maledicta Monitor

Publisher: Maledicta Press
P.O. Box 14123
Santa Rosa, CA 95402-6123
Format: Newsletter
Editor: Reinhold Aman
Phone: (707) 523-4761
Founded: 1990
Description: Quotations of (humorous) insults and "bad" words by and about famous people; colorful, uncensored language; new joke topics; comments on taboo language and censorship; new words and books.
Frequency: 4 issues per year
# of issues published in 1991: 4
# of issues to be published in 1992: 4
# of issues to be published in 1993: 4
Subscription period: By sets of 4 issues (1-4, 5-8, 9-12, etc.)
Subscription rates:

1 year:	$ 8.00
1 year (Canada):	US$ 8.50
1 year (Foreign):	US$10.50 (includes Air Mail postage)
Sample copy:	$ 2.00

Average # of pages per issue: 4
Page size: 8 1/2" x 11"
Production: Typeset
Printing: Offset
Binding: Folded
Circulation: 2,000
Author information:
Prospective authors should inquire first
Reports in 1 week
Author receives 2 complimentary copies of the issue in which the article is published as payment
Newsletter owns all rights to articles
Newsletter is copyrighted
Advertising rates: Advertisements are not accepted
Reviews:
"Documenting bad words, the annual **Maledicta** has a fun, malicious, equally bent scholarly cousin." (Bill Katz, *Library Journal*)
Cross-indexed:

General Humor	Educational Humor	Religion Humor
Sciences Humor	English Humor	Sociology Humor
Social Sciences Humor	Film Media Humor	Word Play & Puns
Arts Humor	Geology Humor	Zoology Humor
Business Humor	History Humor	Joke Service Humor
Regional/Local Humor	Law Humor	
Political Humor	Literature Humor	
Cartoons/Illustrations/Graphics	Limericks	
Scholarly Reviews of Humor as a Subject of Study	Mathematics Humor	
Research on Humor	Medical Humor	
Anthropology Humor	Poetry Humor	
Computer Sciences Humor	Political Science Humor	
	Psychiatry Humor	

ISSN:1041-8504

Opera Magazine, but in prudish America, Prick was offensive. Alas, now we can only dream of such headlines as "Prick Wilts in *Aida*."

Toy-Boy & Older Woman

After two years of marriage, clothes designer Mary McFadden, 52, divorced her fourth husband, Kohle Yohannan, 23, calling him a **"spaced-out delinquent," "complete flake," "homosexual,"** and a **"cheap toy-boy."** Yohannan about her: she is **"an aging couturière"** and a **"much older, selfish, willful, alcoholic woman"** who demanded "to be slapped around during sexual relations." (*SFC*, 19 June 91: D3)

Crude Strine

A reader complained in a letter to the editor of the *Herald-Sun* (Melbourne, Australia) about Prime Minister Bob Hawke, who uses at official functions, press conferences, etc., such terms as **"bloody," "bugger,"** and **"bullshit."** (17 Oct 90: 14. Robert B.)

TV Twits

After an improved performance by his network, CBS president Howard Stringer beamed: "I've gone from **blithering idiot** to **cheerful oaf.**" (*Newsweek*, 5 Aug 91: 15) • CBS chairman Laurence Tisch, a strong supporter of Israel, was angered by CBS correspondent Mike Wallace's 1988 critical report on AIPAC, a pro-Israel lobby, and called him a **"self-hating Jew."** (*Newsweek*: 8)

COLORFUL MISCELLANY

Miscellaneous material from the Maledicta Archive or sent by our readers. *Colorful Miscellany* items, from written and oral sources, include insults, slurs, curses, threats, blasphemies, and similes. *See* inside front cover of **Maledicta 10** for more topics. We prefer short, clever, witty, creative, concrete examples. Please identify your source (person or publication) and *see also* introduction to "Elite Maledicta" for more information on how to submit material.

Airplane vs. Condom

Northrop, the giant airplane makers of the B-2 Stealth Bomber, is suing tiny Stealth Condoms, Inc., a Texas company, for allegedly confusing or deceiving the people with its name and packaging. The condom's slogan: **"They'll Never See You Coming."** (*National Lampoon*, April 91: 67; *Washington Post*, 24 Oct 90) – Actually, no confusion is possible: People use Stealth condoms for screwing, whereas Northrop misuses Stealth airplanes for screwing the people.

Taboo *Jew*

Hyper-sensitive *goyim* seem to be afraid of offending Jews with the neutral word *Jew*, thus use *quasi*-euphemisms: an Associated Press caption under a photo showing two white-bearded Jews gingerly described them as "two Hasidic **Jewish men**" (not: "Hasidic Jews"; *SF Examiner*, 25 Aug 91: A4). Jon Carroll, an otherwise no-nonsense, anti-p.c.-bullshit columnist, described Woody Allen's movie character as a "neurotic, brainy, insecure, funny New York **Jewish person**" (not: "New York Jew"; *SFC*, 22 Aug

91: E8). Remember, Sensitive Ones, in the Bible (John 19.19), Jesus is called "King of the **Jews**," not "King of the **Jewish persons**." • *Jewess* is even more taboo among the Sensitive Ones, in part because of its goshawful "sexist" suffix *-ess*. But Cuban lawyer and secretary of the Hebrew Community of Cuba, Adela Dworin, says of herself: "I remember I was a **Jewess**...." (*SFC*, "Sunday Punch," 1 Sept 91: 5)

Gimme a Good Fockink, Shitto-Breath!

Could you guess by their names what the following products are? They are marketed by foreign companies: **Ass Glue** (blood tonic from donkey parts, China); **Black Nikka** (whiskey, Japan); **Blue Peter** (canned fish, Norway); **Fockink** (liqueur, The Netherlands); **Green Piles** (lawn fertilizer, Japan); **Hornyphon** (video recorder, Austria); **Last Climax** (paper tissues, Japan); **Mucos** (soft drink, Japan); **Pansy** (men's underwear, China); **Pipi** (orangeade, Yugoslavia); **Polio** (detergent, Czechoslovakia); **Pshitt** (soft drink, France); **Shitto** (hot spiced pepper sauce, Ghana); **Superglans** (car wax, The Netherlands); **Trim Pecker** (trousers, Japan). (From my files and several contributors, with many thanks.)

Eat My Crusties!

Foreign companies aren't the only ones who come up with dorky brand names. Consider **KRUSTEAZ**. No, that's not a brand of underpants worn by hygienically challenged lumberjacks but a pancake mix. The company explains the name on their packages: in 1932, the ladies of a Seattle bridge club developed a secret recipe for pie crust and came up with the name, from "Crust-Ease."

O.B.F.

Glenn Dudley, a San Francisco artist, uses the abbreviation *O.B.F.* after his name. I asked him whether the initials refer to some obscure religious order. Nope. They stand for **"Old Bald Fruit."** His self-portrait shows that he's indeed balder than Buddha's balls.

-meister

The German suffix *-meister* ("master") is a new fad in U.S. English. Popularized by a character on the "Saturday Night Live" TV show who adds (*the*) *-meister* mainly to people's names or professions (**the Brucemeister; filmmeister**), this suffix is appearing in advertising and elsewhere: "Stupid lawsuits filed by **jerkmeister** lawyers...." (*SFC* columnist Jon Carroll, 16 Aug 91: F16). This fad will be fun until it's killed by overuse. One could call Pee-wee Herman **"the whackmeister,"** Arnold Schwarzenegger **"musclemeister,"** Johnny Carson **"divorcemeister,"** Jesus **"Savemeister,"** and Casanova **"humpmeister."** I'm, of course, **"the MALmeister."**

Lyrics Needed

Two readers have asked for complete texts of bawdy songs or poems, not in my files. If you have the complete texts, please send them, so that I can pass them on: (1) "Rangy Lil," containing: *Til over the hill from Drag Ass Creek / Came a sawed-off shit named Half-Assed Pete.* (Gene O'K.) • (2) "The Ballad of Piss Pot Pete," con-

Mark Twain Circular

Publisher: Mark Twain Circle
c/o James S. Leonard
English Department
The Citadel
Charleston, SC 29409

Format: Newsletter
Editor: James S. Leonard
Phone: (803) 792-5138
Founded: 1987
Description: The **Mark Twain Circular** is the newsletter of the Mark Twain Circle of America. The newsletter features news of meetings; short articles and notes on the life and works of Mark Twain and persons relevant to Twain studies; annotated bibliography of current books and articles on Twain.
Frequency: 4 issues per year
# of issues published in 1991:   4
# of issues to be published in 1992:   4
# of issues to be published in 1993:   4
1992 volume: Volume #5
Subscription period: Calendar year (i.e., all subscriptions received in 1992 automatically begin with the first issue of 1992)
Subscription rates:

1 year/2 years/3 years:	$7.00	$14.00	$21.00
1 year/2 years/3 years (Canada):	US$8.00	US$16.00	US$24.00
1 year/2 years/3 years (Foreign):	US$8.00	US$16.00	US$24.00
Sample copy: Free			

Average # of pages per issue: 12
Page size: 8 1/2" x 11"
Production: Laserprinted
Printing: Quick copy
Binding: Stapled
Circulation: 1,050
Author information:
    Newsletter accepts unsolicited manuscripts
    Reports in 2 weeks
    Author receives 3 complimentary copies of the issue in which the article is published as payment
    Newsletter does not deal with the issue of copyright of individual articles
    Newsletter is not copyrighted
Advertising rates:

1/2 page black & white:	$12.50
Full page black & white:	$25.00

Cross-indexed:
    Literature Humor
ISSN: 1042-5357

Another Stab at the Origin of No. 44 as a Name

William M. Gibson has offered several knowledgeable and appealing theories about the meaning of "No. 44" as the name for Young Satan. Though Mark Twain used it first in the Schoolhouse Hill version of the "Mysterious Stranger," it is now best known as the title for the last of the related manuscripts. After following up his ideas, Gibson concluded, "None of these explanations, however, seems totally adequate."[1] So far as I know, nobody has improved on Gibson, yet Twainians feel there's probably an identifiable, logical source for such an unusual touch, and even more probably for that particular number rather than some other. I hope they will be interested, therefore, to learn about Part Three, Act One, Scene Five of *Dziady* (or *Forefather's Eve*, 1822-32), a drama-pageant by Adam Mickiewicz. In it a Polish priest, held in a Czarist prison, has an ecstatic vision of a hero who will marshal nationalist fervor and rescue the generation of idealistic intellectuals wasting away in Siberia. That hero will be named "forty-four."[2] Once having perceived him, the priest's vision grows in passion and scope, sanctioned by a choir of angels. That hero, though earthborn, appears more and more god-like, with even "a threefold countenance/And threefold brow." But before the priest swoons, he repeats that the savior of Polish identity will be a "man" and "his name, that shall resound/For ages unto ages, shall be forty-four!"

Dziady has long held among Poles the status of virtually a national scripture. But so what for Twainians? Well, according to A.B. Paine's biography, Clara Clemens "wished to study the piano under Leschetizky, and this would take" the family to Vienna in the fall of 1897. Her memoir *My Husband, Gabrilowitsch* (1938) opens by recalling her "Polish professor" there and especially a dinner in the family apartment during the spring of 1898 at which her father and the pianist discussed politics animately. Though Poland as a country had disappeared under partitions by 1795, Theodore (Teodor) Leszetycki (the original spelling changed later to match the pronunciation among the circles in which he moved) came from parents who considered themselves Polish, and his mother was an especially ardent patriot.[3] Both parents, well-educated, had high-culture interests; surely (that most glib word of all in studies of influence) they knew the major writings of Mickiewicz (1798-1855), revered by nationalists, deservedly, as both a poet-bard and a political martyr.

Admittedly, I have no proof that son Theodore knew, much less admired, *Dziady* in particular. But the record does show he took that lively interest in politics typical for the nineteenth-century intelligentsia and that, more relevant here, he identified himself as a Pole throughout a career in St. Petersburg and then Vienna. The record also shows greater social interplay with the Clemens family than Paine or even Clara suggested. Ethel Newcomb, another young American, started out in Clara's cohort of Leschetizky students, and she kept a diary on which she later built a memoir. She recalls that "during the two years" Clemens spent in Austria "he and Leschetizky often came together. They became great friends and seemed to understand each other perfectly."[4]

An obvious move would try next to triangulate Ossip Gabrilowitsch, a star pupil of the pianist and increasingly Clara's suitor. But, intriguingly, Clemens complained, in a letter of 20 February 1898, about daughter Jean: "She could be learning Russian, which has a large literature and is a beautiful language besides, but it is her caprice to learn Polish."[5] Somewhat elliptically, Ethel Newcomb indicates that Jean had a warm friendship with Leschetizky. Of course the content, depth, and sequence of relationships have grown hazy by now, but John Tuckey's study of Mysterious Stranger manuscripts shows that No. 44 as a name appeared no earlier than November 1898, more than a year after the family brought Clara to study under the Polish master.[6]

What do I think I have proved? Nothing. Even if we learn for sure that somebody introduced Mark Twain to *Forefather's Eve* or to Mickiewicz's broader interest in numerology, we may not advance far. A Polish edition that glosses the name of forty-four supports a Hebrew source as the most plausible but concludes—like Gibson for the Twainians—that of the many ideas offered so far, none sweeps the field.[7] The editor of the latest English translation adds a somewhat firmer footnote: "Possibly the numerical value of the letters in the Hebrew alphabet which spell out Mickiewicz's first name, Adam. A prophetic numerology typical of the Cabala." Actually, Twain did poke around in Jewish lore during his stay in Austria, and he could have picked up forty-four as a tag for a prelapsarian quasi-god. Maybe Twain and Mickiewicz scholars can get UNESCO funding for a conference in Vienna to solve their mutual puzzle.

Notes

1. William M. Gibson, ed., *Mark Twain's Mysterious Stranger Manuscripts* (Berkeley: U of California P, 1969), 472-73. *In Mark Twain's Mysterious Stranger: A Study of the Manuscript Texts* (Colum-bia: U of Missouri P, 1978, 205-6), Sholom J. Kahn speculates on "some possible meanings," including patterns from Hebrew numerology based upon twenty-two.

2. See pp. 125-27 of *Polish Romantic Drama: Three Plays in English Translation*, ed. Harold B. Segal (Ithaca: Cornell UP, 1977).

3. See Nicholas Slonimsky, *Baker's Biographical Dictionary of Musicians*, 6th ed. (New York: Schirmer, 1978), and, for first-hand detail, Angele Potoka, *Theodore Leschetizky* (New York: Century, 1903), 3-8.

4. Ethel Newcomb, *Leschetizky as I Knew Him* (1921; rpt. New York: Da Capo P, 1967), 186-88, 210, 300. Also see *Mark Twain's Notebook*, ed. Albert Bigelow Paine (New York: Harper, 1935), 352-53.

5. Letter to Laurence Hutton; quoted in *Mark Twain's Correspondence with Henry Huddleston Rogers, 1893-1909*, ed. Lewis Leary (Berkeley: U of California P, 1969), 292-93.

6. John S. Tuckey, *Mark Twain and Little Satan* (West Lafayette:Purdue UP, 1963), 41.

7. See p. 508 of Adam Mickiewicz, *Utwory Dramatyczne*, ed. Julian Kryzyanowski et al. (Warszawa: Spoldzielnia Wydawnica/Czytelnik, 1955). As a sign of the early prominence of this detail, see Erazm Krzyszkowski, *Czterdiesci i cztery: Przyczynek do studyow nad "Dziadami" Michiewicz* (Czerniowce, 1888). Or, *Forty and Four: A Contribution to Studies of Mickiewicz's "Forefather's Eve."*

Louis J. Budd
Duke University

Reprinted from the **Mark Twain Circular** by permission of the editor.

Mark Twain Journal

Publisher: Mark Twain Journal
           c/o Department of English
           The College of Charleston
           Charleston, SC 29424

Format: Magazine
Editor: Thomas A. Tenney
Phone: (803) 723-0487
Founded: 1936
Description: The **Mark Twain Journal** publishes well-documented factual articles based on sources in Mark Twain's own time, including letters, photographs, and cartoons of Mark Twain.
Frequency: 2 issues per year
# of issues published in 1991:   3 (Fall 1988, Spring 1989, Fall 1989)
# of issues to be published in 1992:   4 (1990 and 1991 volumes)
# of issues to be published in 1993:   4 (1992 and 1993 volumes)
1992 volume: Volume #30
Subscription period: Calendar year (i.e., all subscriptions received in 1992 automatically begin with the Spring 1992 issue). However, note we are behind in publishing; the two 1989 issues appeared in 1991.
Subscription rates:

1 year/2 years/3 years:	$17.00	$30.00	$45.00
1 year/2 years/3 years (Canada):	US$19.00	US$32.00	US$47.00
1 year/2 years/3 years (Foreign):	US$19.00	US$32.00	US$47.00
Sample copy: $5.00			

Average # of pages per issue: 40-50
Page size: 7 3/4" x 10 1/2"
Production: Laserprinted and word processed
Printing: Offset
Binding: Saddle stitched
Circulation: 900
Author information:
        Magazine accepts unsolicited manuscripts
        Reports in 2-3 weeks
        Author receives 10 complimentary copies of the issue in which the article is published as payment
        Magazine owns all rights to the article (unless the copyright is reserved by the author)
        Magazine is copyrighted
Advertising rates: Advertisements are not accepted
Cross-indexed:
        Literature Humor
ISSN: 0025-3499

ALLISON R. ENSOR

"Mightier than the Sword": An Undetected Obscenity in the First Edition of *Tom Sawyer*

ALMOST EVERY Mark Twain enthusiast has heard of the "obscene illustration" in the first edition of *Adventures of Huckleberry Finn*, the illustration in chapter 32 captioned "Who do you reckon it is?" to which some never-discovered mischief-maker added a notable detail, so that Uncle Silas Phelps appears to have been caught by Huck in a flagrant act of

Tom Sawyer, was not entirely serious in his work, as is evidenced by his placing his own name on one of the stones in the graveyard where Dr. Robinson is murdered: "SACRED TO THE MEMORY OF T. W. WILLIAMS."[1] I would suggest that Williams also smuggled an undetected joke—indeed, an obscenity—into another illustration. In "EXAMINATION EVENING"

exposure. But nothing seems to have been said concerning an illustration in *The Adventures of Tom Sawyer* in which the word rather than the object makes a subtle appearance.

True Williams, the illustrator of the first edition of

(chapter 21) Williams pictures the crowded schoolroom where the exercises ending the school year are taking place. Twain's narration makes no mention of any slogans or mottoes on the wall, but Williams decided to supply a few. Most are typical and exactly what one might expect: "TIME FLIES," "KNOWLEDGE IS POWER," "INDUSTRY MUST THRIVE."

MARK TWAIN JOURNAL, 27:1 (SPRING, 1989)

The remaining motto is so familiar that it might scarcely attract our attention but for the placing of the words. It reads: "THE PEN IS / MIGHTIER / THAN THE / SWORD." As Williams has drawn them, the spacing between the second and third words of the first line is hardly perceptible.

I suggest that Williams acted deliberately, perhaps chuckling to himself over having gotten a forbidden word into a book which children would be reading, at the same time secure in knowing that most readers would be so familiar with the saying that they would disregard Williams' placing of the words. I further suggest that Mark Twain saw what Williams had done, was amused by it, and years later used the revised statement himself. In the fall of 1898 Twain began a burlesque poem entitled "AGE–A *Rubáiyát*"; two quatrains in what was once intended to be a part of the longer poem lament the impotence which may accompany old age and contrast it with former vitality. The first line reads: Behold–the Penis mightier than the Sword."[2] The similarity can hardly be coincidental. Twain ap-

pears to have recognized what Williams had written, even if his more innocent readers did not.

University of Tennessee
Knoxville

NOTES

[1]Beverly David, *Mark Twain and His Illustrators, 1869-1875* (Troy, NY: Whitston, 1986), p. 230. David refers to Williams' "whimsical though perverse sense of humor" but makes no mention of the illustration I discuss here.

[2]Quoted in *Mark Twain's Rubáiyát*, intro. by Alan Gribben (Austin, TX and Santa Barbara, CA: Jenkins Publishing Co. and Karpeles Manuscript Library, 1983), p. 21. The line also appears in Twain's *The Mammoth Cod*, ed. Gershon Legman (Milwaukee: Maledicta, 1976), p. 11.

The Marx Brotherhood

Founder: Paul G. Wesolowski
Publication: **The Freedonia Gazette**
Publisher: **The Freedonia Gazette**   In Europe: **The Freedonia Gazette**
28-B Darien   137 Easterly Road
New Hope, PA 18938-1224   Leeds LS8 2RY England
Format: Magazine
Editor: Paul G. Wesolowski (Senior Editor), Raymond D. White (U.K. Editor)
Phone: (215) 862-9734
Founded: 1978
Description: **The Marx Brotherhood** was started in 1978 as an organization within the National Film Society. The NFS organized several "study units" by bringing together members with a common interest. We realized from the start that our group had a lot of things to share with the rest of the world, so the **Marx Brotherhood** quickly opened up membership to anyone who was interested, even if they were not NFS members. Our first project was to begin publishing **The Freedonia Gazette**. (In the 1933 film DUCK SOUP, Groucho is dictator of Freedonia.) In addition to photographs, drawings, and comics, articles include well-researched biographical pieces about particular aspects of the Marxes' lives and/or careers, interviews with people who knew the Marxes, reviews of books which mention the Marxes, reviews of stage shows which impersonate the Marxes, and interviews with the stars of these shows. From time to time we correct errors which other writers have made, just to set the record straight, and we publish a regular column of current news about the Marxes and their films and their impact on popular culture. The information for many of our articles comes from the archives of our publisher, Paul G. Wesolowski. The archives include over 30,000 magazine and newspaper clippings dating to 1905. We host an open house every year so that members/readers can meet others with the same interest, trade memorabilia, watch videotapes and films, and examine our publisher's collection of several hundred Marx-related movie posters. **The Freedonia Gazette** has historically included more news, biography, and reviews relating to the Marxes and their humor than original humor, but the scholarly research articles are fun and never pompous or preachy. We'll print good humor when it's submitted, but won't print mediocre humor just to fill space. We never analyze why anything is funny.
Frequency: 2 issues per year
# of issues published in 1991: 2
# of issues to be published in 1992: 2
# of issues to be published in 1993: 2
Subscription period: Generally calendar year (i.e., subscriptions received in a given year begin with the first issue of that year) but we may move the subscription ahead or back depending on when the last issue was published and when the next issue is expected.
Annual membership dues: $10.00 (includes newsletter)
# of members: 400
Subscription rates:

1 year/2 years/3 years:	$10.00	$20.00	$30.00
1 year/2 years/3 years (Canada):	US$10.00	US$20.00	US$30.00
1 year/2 years/3 years (Foreign):	US$12.00	US$24.00	US$36.00
Sample copy: $5.00			

Average # of pages per issue: 20
Page size: 8 1/2" x 11"
Production: Typed
Printing: Offset
Binding: Saddle stitched
Circulation: 400

Author information:

        Magazine accepts unsolicited manuscripts

        Reports in 1 month

        Author receives 1 complimentary copy of the issue in which the article is published as payment (or more than 1 copy depending on the length of the manuscripts)

        Magazine owns all rights to the article

        Magazine is copyrighted

Advertising rates:

1/2-page black & white:	$30
Full-page black & white:	$60

Reviews:

        "You probably think Wesolowski is a crackpot [whose] mental transmission is slipping from drive to reverse." (Steve Hedgepeth, *Bucks County Courier Times*)

        "A literate if somewhat idiosyncratic fanzine." (Leonard Maltin, *The Whole Film Sourcebook*)

Cross-indexed:

        General Humor

        Arts Humor

        Film Media

ISSN: 0748-5247

Confessions of a Marx Brothers Addict

P.S. Fragola

I have come here today to tell my story, in order to alert others to the dangers of film addiction. If you're sitting there thinking that these things only happen to ghetto kids, or unwed mothers, you're wrong. You're dead wrong. And if you don't believe me, you could be just that: dead. I'm here to prove that film addiction does happen, and it happens to all types of people; it doesn't discriminate. Everyone is susceptible. The only way we can prevent this terrible disease—it is a disease—is through education.

I came from a closely knit family, middle class origins. I have two brothers and one sister. Our parents worked hard to make sure we got everything we needed or wanted. I was far from being a neglected child. My parents did, however, neglect to teach me how to say "no" to film addiction. They never expected that their baby was going to grow up to be a Marx Brothers Addict.

I was fourteen when I saw my first Marx Brothers film. An older friend of mine had rented *Duck Soup* and invited me over. His parents didn't care. They let him watch at home. They always said they'd rather he watch at home than in some grungy theater. Nobody back then understood the dangers involved. It was a good time. Something we did for fun. At first, I didn't really like it. It seemed so silly. People running every which way. Infantile plots. But all my friends watched. I wanted to fit in, I wanted to be cool, so I kept watching until I was hooked.

I tried to hide it from my family. It was easy at first. They didn't notice. My viewing habits began to change. My parents just figured it was a stage I was going through. Every chance I got, I watched a Marx Brothers film. My family didn't notice, I didn't even notice. I was hooked. I couldn't go a day without my fix. I began staying up late on school nights to tape them off t.v. (without commercials). I went on like this throughout high school. My grades started to slip. Teachers began to complain about my double talk in class when I hadn't done my homework. Then one day the principal caught me selling a tape to another student. My parents were notified and I was expelled from school.

Life at home became a living hell after that. My mother wouldn't let me watch t.v. alone anymore. I couldn't even watch the news alone. My father kept pressing me for my source. They let me back in school after awhile, but I started to skip. Since I couldn't watch the films at home, I had to go to matinees at the local theater. I finally stopped going to school all together. I was spending all my money at the movies, so I had to find some way to make money. Selling was the natural thing to do. It wasn't long before my parents found out that I had quit school and could no longer get into the college of my choice. They gave me an ultimatum. Quit or move out.

I took the VCR and rented a small, dirty flat down on Vid-row. Now that I was alone, I sunk deeper into my comic quagmire. I had gotten up to six films a day. Sometimes, I would get so desperate that I would watch the movies with just Harpo and Groucho, or even just Groucho. I remember meeting a girl during this period. She kept telling me to quit. "That stuff'll kill you! Switch to something safer, like Laurel and Hardy, I did."

I took her advice. I tried to switch to something safer. I tried Laurel and Hardy. I tried Abbott and Costello. I even tried the 3 Stooges. Nothing gave me as much pleasure. I went back to Groucho, Harpo, Chico, and yes even Zeppo. I went back and it was worse than ever! I got so bad, I would have sold my own mother just to see *Animal Crackers*. I still didn't think I had a problem. Whenever I got a hold of a newspaper, I no longer read the headlines or even the comics. I'd flip to the theater section to see if there was anyone—anywhere!—showing *Cocoanuts*. But I didn't have a problem.

My old friends didn't call me anymore. If I passed them on the street, they looked the other way. I didn't care. I had enough friends: Groucho, Harpo, Chico, Zeppo and Margaret. They understood. Well at least the boys did. As weeks went by, I got worse and worse. I began to use cheap grade tapes for the stuff I sold. I would sell to anybody. I needed the money. I had sunk so low, that I even began to sell to children.

I woke up one day and realized that all over the flat were unsmoked cigars and all my clothes were baggy. Even though I had begun to speak with an Italian accent, I thought I could still handle it. Then when the phone rang, instead of saying "Hello," I honked a horn!! I needed help and I needed it bad.

I began to look for help. At that time, not many people knew about Marx Brothers addiction, let alone how to treat it. I spent two weeks going cold turkey. Those were the worst weeks of my young life. I thought I was going crazy. The doctors thought I should have been committed. I kept screaming "Hail, Hail Freedonia!" and singing "Hooray for Captain Spaulding" at the top of my lungs. Several times, I was overcome by the urge to chase a blond nurse down the hall and steal the doctor's stethoscope. I didn't think I was going to make it out of there alive. I almost didn't.

I'm telling you now, because no one told me then. Don't be stupid. Don't be fooled into thinking that all that zaniness is glamorous or cool, because it's not. It's dangerous, it could kill you. Don't be lured by the thought of a quick double entendre, a quick laugh. It's not worth it. If someone asks you to come over and watch a Marx Brothers film, don't be stupid, just say "No."

Minne Ha! Ha!

Publisher: Minne Ha! Ha! Inc.
               Box 6626 Minnehaha Station
               Minneapolis, MN 55406
Format: Newspaper (Tabloid)
Editors: Lance Anger, Bruce Carlson
Phone: (612) 491-1818
Founded: 1979
Description: America's first local humor tabloid—avant-garde and political cartoons, satire, short
               humor pieces, and comics.
Frequency: 10 issues per year
# of issues published in 1991:   6
# of issues to be published in 1992:   10
# of issues to be published in 1993:   10
1992 volume: Volume #5
Subscription period: Subscriptions run from the date the order is received
Subscription rates:

1 year/2 years/3 years:	$16.00	$31.00	$45.00
1 year/2 years/3 years (Canada):	US$20.00	US$40.00	US$60.00
1 year/2 years/3 years (Foreign):	US$22.00	US$44.00	US$66.00

               Sample copy: $3.75
Average # of pages per issue: 20
Page size: 11" x 13 1/2"
Production: Laserprinted
Printing: Offset
Binding: Folded and loosely collated
Circulation: 30,000
Author information:
               Newspaper accepts unsolicited manuscripts
               Reports in 4 months
               Newspaper pays $5-$35 per article
               Author owns copyright to article
               Newspaper is copyrighted
Advertising rates:

1/2 page black & white:	$ 315
1/2 page color:	$ 755
Full page black & white:	$ 605
Full page color:	$1,420
Cover 2 black & white:	$ 805
Cover 2 color:	$1,600

Cross-indexed:
               General Humor
               Social Sciences Humor
               Arts Humor
               Political Humor
               Cartoons/Illustrations/Graphics
               Visual Satire

BULLWINKLE:
The Minnesota Connection

By Bruce Carlson
Copyright 1991 by Minne HA! HA!

After spending years in television's gutter of reruns and orphaned time slots, Bullwinkle has been plugged into the 1990s and (ta da!): he's hot. The release of six videocassettes from the original Rocky and Bullwinkle TV series (through Disney's Buena Vista Studios) has launched an outbreak of "Moosemania." The critics are gushing, Disney's marketing campaign is massive (moosive?), and video sales have exceeded expectations (over two million copies already). Time and Newsweek have run features on the moose and squirrel, and a retrospective entitled "Of Moose and Men" recently put Bullwinkle and pals in the ironic position of fund raising for public television.

Minnesota played prominently in the development of the Rocky and Bullwinkle show, both on and off screen. Most obvious is the fact that our heroes maintained residence in Frostbite Falls, MN, shunning the fast-paced Hollywood lifestyles of the rich and famoose. A trip via Mr. Peabody's Way-back machine, taking us back to the late 1950s when Rocky and Bullwinkle came on the air, would remind us that the show was made possible by the sponsorship of Twin Cities based General Mills, Inc. It would also remind us that TV, and the world itself, were a bit more innocent back then— when TV was young, the Cold War was heated, and a box top was worth a box top.

The first Bullwinkle shows were introduced live by show creator Jay Ward, with the help of a Bullwinkle hand puppet. Given Ward's penchant for unbounded satire, it's little wonder that the live portion of the program didn't last long. One incident, prompted by ratings pressure from NBC, proved to be the final straw for network executives: Ward and his puppet told viewers that the continuation of the Bullwinkle show was endangered by recent overall drops in NBC ratings. The puppet jokingly instructed children to remove and hide the TV channel knob to assure that NBC would get better ratings, thus saving the show. Phone calls from 20,000 angry parents of children who actually did this flooded the phone lines of NBC affiliates around the country. Two weeks later, after Ward reassured the children that it was okay to put the knobs back on the sets, the live introductions were stopped by NBC. (IF SOMEONE IN YOUR FAMILY DID THIS, WRITE TO MINNE HA! HA! IMMEDIATELY!)

Ward and his staff often concocted elaborate publicity stunts to promote the TV show. One of these involved Minnesota, where Ward purchased a remote island (in Lake of the Woods) and began a campaign for its statehood. The drive to induct "Moosylvania" as the 51st state included a cross-country trek ending at the White House, with the intent of lobbying (and humoring) President Kennedy. The stunt turned sour as Ward and his crew were ordered away from the White House gate at gunpoint by a surly guard—bad timing had them arrive the same day the President announced the detection of Soviet missiles in Cuba. (Maybe they would have had better luck if they named it "Moosachoosetts," in honor of the President's home.)

General Mills sponsored broadcasts of the Rocky and Bullwinkle show beginning in 1959. The television sponsorship included animated commercials of Bullwinkle, the Cheerios Kid and Sue. Bullwinkle also promoted Cheerios (and other products including Trix and Cocoa Puffs) in print ads, comic books, on cereal boxes and in other promotions through 1968. Some examples of these promotions are reproduced here (courtesy of the General Mills archivists).

Best of all for kids were the premiums General Mills offered for saving box tops and a little change. These prizes included the "How To Have Fun Outdoors Without Getting Clobbered" coloring kit (the cover drawing of Bullwinkle was reproduced from this book); Bullwinkle's electronic quiz Fun Game; a Bullwinkle breakfast set (made of indestructible Melmac); Rocky and Bullwinkle rub-off tee shirt transfers (including Boris and Natasha), and a Bullwinkle magnetic bulletin board.

The kids who scraped their hard earned box tops together thirty years ago presumably make up the bulk of the "kids" that are buying the videocassettes like crazy today. The videos have been a hit—all six titles landed simultaneously in Billboard's top ten listing this year. This success should be attributed not only to the lasting appeal of the shows' contents, but also to the care taken in programming and restoring the shows to their original condition.

The Monthly Independent Tribune Times Journal Post Gazette News Chronicle Bulletin

Publisher: T. S. Child
             1630 Allston Way
             Berkeley, CA 94703
Format: Magazine
Editor: T. S. Child
Founded: 1983
Description: Try to remember: When at the age of eight, you were exploring the basement of a condemned house and you came across a box containing old mimeographed papers that you couldn't understand; and how, when traveling in the tropics three years ago, you became ill and went to a doctor who babbled to you in a foreign tongue and gave you pills you didn't trust and threw away so you ended up vomiting for five days straight. Now, you look back at those golden moments and wonder—what were those mimeographs, what was that illness? It is just that exact emotion we're trying to capture with every issue of **The Monthly...Bulletin.**
Frequency: Varies
# of issues published in 1991:   1 or 2
# of issues to be published in 1992:   1-6
# of issues to be published in 1993:   1-6
Subscription period: Subscriptions run from the date the order is received or subscribers can have any issues of their choice
Subscription rates:
             Per issue: .50 or 2 first class stamps
             Sample copy: .50
Average # of pages per issue: 8
Page size: 5 1/2" x 7 1/2"
Production: Varies (may be typeset, laserprinted, word processed and/or typed)
Printing: Offset or xeroxed (varies from issue to issue)
Binding: Saddle stitched
Circulation: 500
Author information:
             Magazine accepts unsolicited manuscripts
             Reports in 4 weeks
             Author receives 3 complimentary copies of the issue in which the article is published and a free 2-issue subscription as payment
             Magazine does not deal with the issue of copyrights for individual articles
             Magazine is not copyrighted
Advertising rates: Advertisements are not accepted
Cross-indexed:

General Humor	Astronomy Humor	Medical Humor
Sciences Humor	Education Humor	Philosophy Humor
Social Sciences Humor	English Humor	Physics Humor
Humanities Humor	Film Media Humor	Religion Humor
Arts Humor	Foreign Language Humor	Sociology Humor
Cartoons/ Illustrations/Graphics	History Humor	Word Play & Puns
Visual Satire	Literature Humor	
Anthropology Humor	Mathematics Humor	

Professional Hide-and-Go-Seek League Standings

NOOK DIVISION

East	W	L	T		West	W	L	T	
Chattanooga Choo-Choos	30	2	1	.924	Fairbanks Frostbite	24	6	3	.773
Philadelphia Brotherly Lovers	19	14	0	.576	Kansas City Crazy Little Women	20	12	1	.621
Indianapolis 500s	15	16	2	.485	Oakland Theres	18	15	0	.545
Macon Bacon	9	21	3	.318	El Paso Wetbacks	12	20	1	.378
Buffalo Springfields	3	30	0	.091	Santa Fe Trails	7	21	5	.288

CRANNY DIVISION

East	W	L	T		West	W	L	T	
Detroit Blight	28	5	0	.848	Salt Lake City Bigamists	23	3	7	.803
Boston Baked Beans	22	9	2	.697	Hilo Hulas	22	8	3	.712
Tallahassee Lassies	14	18	1	.439	Phoenix Heat	17	15	1	.530
Little Rock Segregationalists	5	25	3	.197	San Francisco Nights	13	14	6	.485
Harrisburg Meltdowns	2	27	4	.121	Los Angeles Smog	5	27	1	.167

The Salt Lake City Bigamists, with their recent double-header victory over the Hilo Hulas (34-26, 20-11), have strengthened their lead in the Cranny Division West. The Bigamists' head coach Elder Young called their double success "a victory of morality over those topless heathen polynesians," but the Hulas are protesting both results, claiming in their official complaint to the league commissioner that the Bigamists' famous woman-man-woman offensive tag formation violated not only league rules but also Hawaii marriage laws. The Los Angeles Smog's last-place standings in the Cranny Division West can be largely attributed to the team's insistence on driving during their games and their marked inability to successfully hide their cars. The Detroit Blight have used their expertise in Victim Isolation and Police Avoidance Tactics to establish a lead over Boston and Tallahassee in the Cranny Division East. Six of the Blight's victories have been on forfeits by the Little Rock Segregation-alists who refuse to share the field with any team that has black members. The Harrisburg Meltdowns' new glow-in-the-dark uniforms spelled disaster for them this season since they discovered too late that all their hiders could be effortlessly located, especially during night games.

Chattanooga's seemingly unstoppable "caboose-whip" scoring technique has terrorized the entire Nook Division this season, but some analysts believe their unnerving "Choo-choo!" has intimidated their opponents more than anything else. The all-male Philadelphia Brotherly Lovers have fallen short of their high expectations this year as many of their best players have been afflicted by an unnamed venereal disease. The usually speedy Indianapolis 500s have been hampered by their crash helmets and fire-resistant body suits and have had a mediocre season, although they have not incurred a single injury this season. In the Nook Division West, the Fairbanks Frostbite is making a bid for its first division championship, though the Rules Committee is still discussing whether snowmobiles are permissible on the playing field. The Crazy Little Women from Kansas City, whose lascivious on-field antics are rivalled only by the notorious Macon Bacon squad, have slipped from first place after winning their first twelve games in a row; it seems as if their unique strategy has backfired because over half the team is now pregnant. Few people will ever forget their four-hour-long 0-0 tie against Macon Beacon earlier in the season. The El Paso Wetbacks, suffering from language problems, have been unable to capitalize on their highly-touted camouflaging methods since no one on the team can understand the rules booklet or referees. The Sante Fe Trails, who insist on traveling to all their away games in covered wagons, have arrived too late numer-ous times and have lost nine games on forfeit.

Prediction: look for the superbly-choreographed but underrated Hilo Hulas to overtake the Bigamists and defeat Detroit in the Cranny Division finals. The Frostbite will hang on to win the Nook Division West but will be stomped by Chattanooga in the finals as they were earlier in the season. The Choo-Choos will beat the Hulas in the Nook & Cranny World Series by five games to two.

©The Monthly...Bulletin

National Lampoon®

Publisher: National Lampoon
155 Avenue of the Americas
New York, NY 10013
Format: Magazine
Editors: Sam Johnson, Chris Marcil
Phone: (212) 645-5040
Founded: 1970
Description: **National Lampoon®** is the humor magazine for adults.
Frequency: 6 issues per year
# of issues published in 1991: 6
# of issues to be published in 1992: 6
# of issues to be published in 1993: 6
Subscription period: Subscriptions run from the date the order is received
Subscription rates:

1 year/2 years/3 years:	$11.95	$18.95	$24.95
1 year/2 years/3 years (Canada):	US$21.95	US$28.95	US$34.95
1 year/2 years/3 years (Foreign):	US$21.95	US$28.95	US$34.95

Sample copy: $3.95
Average # of pages per issue: 96
Page size: 8" x 10 7/8"
Production: Typeset
Printing: Offset
Binding: Perfect bound
Circulation: 250,000
Author information:

Magazine accepts unsolicited manuscripts
Reports in 2 months
Payment depends upon length of manuscript
Magazine owns 1st serial rights
Magazine is copyrighted

Advertising rates:

1/2 page black & white:	$3,170
1/2 page color:	$4,115
Full page black & white:	$5,275
Full page color:	$6,870

Reviews:

"Best magazine published in America today." (*Village Voice*)

Cross-indexed:

General Humor
Cartoons/Illustrations/Graphics

ISSN: 0027-9587

The Code of Hammurabi
Translated by Doug Kenney

I Hammurabi the Just, true son of King Zestab-pez-necco and conqueror of the evil tyrant Ashur-du-smelbad, by this stela set in the marketplace do set down my Code.

Let it be known throughout all Mesopotamia, both to Assyria and Babylonia, that these laws will make the flesh of the people glad, and are not to be leaned on.

* * *

- If two oxcarts meet at a crossroad, the oxcart on the right has the right-of-way.
- If an oxcart meets a war chariot at a crossroad, the vehicle equipped with bows, arrows, spears, slings, and scythe-blade hubs has the right-of-way.
- If traveling in congested cities, charioteers shall set melons on the points of their scythes.

* * *

- If a man split the ear of his wife, the ear of his favorite dog shall be split.
- If a man split the ear of his slave girl, his first and second wife shall split the sewing.
- If a man deflower another's slave girl, he shall pay one-half mina of silver and the cost of new sheets.
- If a woman in a quarrel damages the testicles of a man, her testicles shall be damaged.
- If a man damages the testicles of a eunuch, he shall inform the eunuch.
- If a man flog his wife, pluck our her hair, or smite and damage her nose, she shall have been flogged, had her hair plucked out, been smote, and had her nose damaged.

* * *

- If a temple prostitute refused the silver coin of an undiseased freeman, she shall be made to lie with his ox in the square, and miniature bas-reliefs of the event may be sole to adult males above the age of fourteen.
- If a slave strikes his master's son, the slave's hand shall be cut off.
- If a son kills his father's slave, his allowance shall be cut off.
- If a son says to his father, "You are not my father," he shall be sent upstairs without supper and smothered.

* * *

- If a freeman kills a tax collector of the King, he shall be sent on in his place, swordless, to Palestine.
- If a house of mud brick collapses, killing the owner, the mason shall be

pressed under every tablet relating to building codes.

- If a surgeon, using a bronze instrument, blinds, kills, or cripples a slave, his fee must be drastically reduced.
- If a royal physician prescribes to a King a strict regimen of diet and exercise, he shall be set on stakes.
- If a teacher kills a student for whispering, a note must be obtained from the parents.
- If, in the course of building a great ziggurat tall enough to reach Heaven, the workers suddenly lay down their tools claiming they no longer understand each other, the usual Jews shall be rounded up for questioning.

* * *

- If a man copulates with an ape, the child must be exposed or apply for Egyptian citizenship.
- If a man's orchard bears fruit, but at harvest time the fruit is found on the neighbor's side of the wall, and the neighbor accounts for this with a tale of great wind in the night, the windfall fruit belongs to the neighbor and the neighbor's testicles belong over the first man's fireplace.
- If a merchant measures with false weights in the market, his weight shall be guessed by his customers, and he shall before them consume ox droppings in this amount.
- If a man in the King's game reserve slays a spotted lion under ten spearpoints in length, he has slain a hyena.
- If a man unlawfully enters a ziggurat and defaces the walls with vile cuneiforms, he shall inscribe on a stone tablet, "I will not deface ziggurats" one thousand times with his nose and be put to death.
- If a man be overheard telling tales concerning the goddess Ishtar, his tongue shall be torn out and put to death.
- If I find out who keeps singing popular songs under my window, he shall be thrown in the Holy River.
- If a man's brother-in-law lives under his roof, and does no work and stirs not, after four years he may be considered furniture and sold.
- If a man damage the eye of another man's horse, the first man shall be responsible for future moving violations.

* * *

- If a wet nurse substitutes a changeling for a freeman's son, and the real son returns years later by accident as part of a traveling acrobatic troop and is immediately recognized by the father by means of a distinctive ring or birthmark, the rights to any resulting poem, song, or bas-relief shall belong to the King.
- If a scribe makes an error in the transcription of a royal edict, he shall be [text unintelligible].

National Organization Taunting Safety and Fairness Everywhere (N.O.T. S.A.F.E.)

Founder: Dale Lowdermilk
Publication: **Quagmire**
Publisher: **N.O.T. S.A.F.E.**
             Box 5743-DHM North
             Montecito, CA 93150
Format: Newsletter
Editor: Dale Lowdermilk
Phone: (805) 969-6217
Founded: 1980
Description: **N.O.T. S.A.F.E.** activities and events include periodic press releases, "Letters to the Editor," and radio interviews, all of which lampoon stupid regulations, laws, and paternalistic attitudes. We encourage members to send and redistribute news clippings of strange events and safety hazards which can be editorialized upon. We use reverse subliminal messages to convey subliminal messages, e.g." "LIVEL-LAFOTOOREHTSITNEMNREVOG" (GOVERNMENT IS THE ROOT OF ALL EVIL). **Quagmire** is the official newsletter of **N.O.T. S.A.F.E.** and highlights the absurdities that come about when the government attempts to apply rules and regulations to all spheres of the individual's life. For total safety, we encourage everyone to stay in bed...and get plenty of exercise! We also have four serious goals: limit the number of laws introduced, limit the terms of office, allow taxpayers to spend $1.00 of their tax return in the Department of their choice, and allow voters to choose from none of the above on ballots!
Frequency: 1 issue per year
# of issues published in 1991:   1
# of issues to be published in 1992:   1
# of issues to be published in 1993:   1
Subscription period: Subscriptions run from the date the order is received
# of members: 896
Subscription rates (includes membership and newsletter):
             1 year: $25.00
             Life: $99.00
Average # of pages per issue: 4
Page size: 8 1/2" x 11"
Production: Word processed
Printing: Xeroxed
Binding: Stapled on surface of publication
Circulation: 1,200
Author information:
             Newsletter accepts unsolicited manuscripts
             Reports in 4 months
             Newsletter may pay up to $1.50 per article and may or may not provide authors with
                1 complimentary copy of the issue in which the article is published
             Author owns rights to the article
             Newsletter is copyrighted
Advertising rates: Advertisements are not accepted
Reviews:
             "...The World's Most Sarcastic Organization." (*National Examiner*)
Cross-indexed: Politics Humor   Law Humor   Medical Humor   Political Science Humor

Press Release

STI—Strategic Trash Initiative

In an effort to help lawmakers approach difficult problems from an imaginative "angle," the National Organization Taunting Safety And Fairness Everywhere (NOT-SAFE) would like to offer a proposal for an issue which touches the life of everyone on earth...NATIONAL DEFENSE.

Instead of focusing mental and fiscal resources on research and development of exotic (non-testable) X-ray lasers, unreliable deployment systems, and electronic gear that sometimes goes "blink-in-the-night" (offspring of that famous NORAD computer which is totally fail saf...fail saf...fail safe), the Department of Defense should look for simple, less expensive solutions which are "litter-ally" in our own back yards. Yes folks, America has state-of-the-art, "off-the-shelf" (and out-of-the-box) technology to build TODAY...not 10 years from now, a *STRATEGIC TRASH INITIATIVE (S.T.I.)*.

By using obsolete ICBM's, Minuteman, and self-destructing Atlas rockets to launch millions of tons of junk, the United States could construct an impenetrable defensive barrier of garbage so effective that no incoming missile could pass through without becoming a disintegrated contribution to the orbiting shield. If a 50 pound pelican can bring down a 500 m.p.h. B-1 bomber, imagine what would happen to a Soviet rocket traveling 17,000 m.p.h. when it collides with an STI soup can, beer bottle, or half-eaten chicken bone. Any military strategist knows that the best DEFENSE is a good OFFENSE, and even a non-military moron knows how "offensive" garbage can be, especially after being heated and frozen every 90 minutes for 10 or 20 years.

Precisely launched litter, such as billions of bottle caps or smashed aluminum cans, could be positioned over the polar "caps" to help reflect deadly ultra-violet radiation which has begun leaking through the ozone-depleted atmosphere. As these items fall back to earth over a period of years, astronomers would be able to observe man-made Aurora Borealis with spectacular new hues and colors.

Trendy "REGIONAL REFUSE" themes could be adopted where trash surpluses existed. For example, empty suntan lotion bottles, discarded surfboards, and black market computer chips would orbit over Southern California while orange peels, pecan shells, and confiscated drug paraphernalia would be positioned over Florida and the southeast portions of the United States. The midwest would utilize surplus rock-hard corn and abandoned oil drilling equipment while the northeast would be protected by a thick, rich layer of "stellar sludge" contributed by the human feces capital of the world, New York City.

For those who are vegetarian-optimists, we could launch tons of grains of winter wheat which, after we earthlings have figured out how to live with each other, could be retrieved after a hundred years or so, and eaten...or maybe planted.

Even more important than the immediate "protection" an STI would provide are it's future applications for space anthropologists who will judge whether or not we did the right thing by "trashing" our national defense program. If it's worth doing right, it's worth OVER doing!!!

Cautiously,

Dale Lowdermilk
Executive Director, NOT-SAFE

P.S. You can show your support for this proposal by sending uncooked spaghetti to your elected representatives with your ideas on where they can put it.

News of the Weird

Publisher: Chuck Shepherd
                 P.O. Box 57141
                 Washington, DC 20037
Format: Newsletter
Editor: Chuck Shepherd
Founded: 1990
Description: Compilation of contemporary true, bizarre news from the syndicated column, "News of
                 the Weird." Subscribers to this newsletter also receive the editor's personal newsletter
                 of weird news, *View from the Ledge*.
Frequency: 7 issues per year
# of issues published in 1991:   7
# of issues to be published in 1992:   7
# of issues to be published in 1993:   7
Subscription period: Subscriptions run from the date orders are received
Subscription rates:

1 year:	$10.00
1 year (Canada):	US$11.00
1 year (Foreign):	US$16.00
Sample copy:	$ 1.00

Average # of pages per issue: 4
Page size: 8 1/2" x 11"
Production: Typeset
Printing: Offset
Binding: Folded
Circulation: 1,100
Author information:
                 Newsletter does not accept unsolicited manuscripts
                 Accepts newspaper or magazine clippings but makes no payment for these submissions
                 Newsletter is copyrighted
Advertising: Advertisements are not accepted

[column of November 9, 1990]

Lead Story

● Featured at the June Elvis Presley Impersonators Convention were a 7-year-old Elvis, a female Elvis, a Hindu Elvis, and 40 others. Panel workshops were held on the serious issues of whether impersonators focus too heavily on the Vegas era (rather than the Leather era and the Gold Lamé era) and whether there should be a code of ethics for Elvis impersonators.

Odds and Ends (Mostly Odds)

● Six years ago, Walter DeBow won a judgment for $3.4 million in damages against the city of East St. Louis, Ill., but he has been unable to collect, as the city is bankrupt. In September, DeBow was given title to the city's main municipal building and its 220-acre industrial park as compensation. (He had sued the city for a crippling beating he took while in city jail.)

● Over 100 "tobacco rebellions" were reported in Moscow in August because of the unavailability of cigarettes. Several work stoppages were reported in other cities, including some by farmers refusing to bring in harvests. Twenty-two of the 24 cigarette factories in Russia were closed for the summer for repairs. (A pack of Marlboros was costing 30 rubles on the black market—$48 at the official exchange rate—and a small jar of butts was going for one ruble.)

● Michael Faircloth, unsuccessful candidate for the Senate in Australia, promised as part of his campaign in March that he would introduce legislation giving a $7.50 grant to everyone who voted for him.

● The India Association of Sex Educators, Counselors and Therapists has set February 1991 for the first International Conference on Orgasm, in New Delhi, and has issued a call for papers.

● Chicago's WGN-TV earlier this year reopened its reservations list for the long-running *The Bozo Show*, whose ticket list had been frozen 10 years ago at 200,000 names. The station set up a special phone line for five years' worth of shows, and 27 million attempts from Illinois alone were made to call it. The 140,000 reservations were gone in five-and-a-half hours.

● In Natick, Mass., John Patrick McKenna was born at precisely 56 seconds after 12:34 in the morning of 7/8/90.

● In August, Charles A. Hinkle, 38, was shot while in his car in Riverview, Fla., by a woman to whom he had given a lift home from a bar. The bullet passed through the windshield, through his lip, but was stopped by his dentures. Hinkle later told police, "[No more] Mr. Nice Guy."

● Brent Paladino, 3, just out of diapers and into nursery school in September, plays golf six days a week in Hartford, Conn., hitting about 300 balls a day. His father calls Brent "obsessed": "In the winter, I'll sit in the car with the heater on, and he'll be on the putting green."

● A large-scale study of American television-watching supported by the National Institute of Mental Health, released in May, found that it takes more skill and concentration to eat a meal than to watch TV and that the longer people watch, the more drowsy, bored, sad, lonely, irritable, and hostile they become.

● At least 4,500 Muslims have made pilgrimages to Leicester, England, in recent months to see Zahid Kassam's discovery of an eggplant whose seeds spelled the name of Allah, and in March an Asian in Nottingham found another one.

● It took 5,000 hours in the editing room, but director Armando Acosta recently finished his two-hour film of *Romeo and Juliet*, featuring one actor (John Hurt) and 150 cats, which he will premiere at the Venice Film Festival. Juliet is played by a white Turkish Angora, and she and Romeo fight and eat canaries in Brooklyn and Venice.

● George Hassapis, 6, took 10 minutes and 19 moves to beat U.S. chess master Orest Popovych in London in August.

● In June, Sayed Abdel-Aal, 40, left a suicide note in Cairo, explaining that he had hanged himself in despair at the Egyptian soccer team's first-round elimination in the World Cup.

● The National Association of Brick Distributors presented its prestigious "Brick Achievement Award" in June to MTV because of the many music videos that contain brick motifs. (NABD cited M.C. Hammer's "U Can't Touch This," which features 62 seconds of brick walls, and Elton John's "Club at the End of the Street," which "uses meticulous detail in texturizing the brick" in the video.)

[column of November 16, 1990]

Lead Story

● Steven Walter Henderson, 21, of St. Charles County, Mo., was involved in an auto accident in July, when his car slammed into the back of a police car. He said he lost control of his car as he was applying Vaseline to the tail of his pet bulldog, which had just had tail-trim surgery.

Too Much Time on Their Hands

● Fran Trutt, 33, pleaded no contest in April to charges that she attempted to kill the president of a supply firm that uses anesthetized dogs to help train surgeons on new procedures. She expressed hope that her own pet dog would be allowed to visit her in prison.

● Joseph and Dottie Hardy of Farmington, Pa., spent about $187,000 at a London auction recently to acquire an estate and titles in Warwickshire. Said Joseph, "Lord and lady are sort of a big thing here. It's a mini, mini, mini thing of the whole country, you know, Queen Elizabeth?"

● Responding to the New York law banning dwarf-tossing contests, promoter Baird Jones complained that "we're being lumped with bar sports. This is not someone promoting Jell-O wrestling. It's performance art designed to satirize the values of mainstream America."

● In May, 200 people participated in the Third Annual Hill Country Machine Gun Shoot near Helotes, Texas, firing rounds from more than 100 automatic weapons and shredding washing machines, refrigerators, and other targets. Said one, "Can you think of a better way to spend a holiday weekend? Soldiers died so we'd have the right to shoot all we want."

● A London TV executive (who preferred anonymity) purchased the rights to a personalized license plate at a government auction in July, paying about $54,000. The plate he wanted was "FAX IT."

● Birmingham, Ala., talk show host Tim Lennox was suspended in July after announcing on the air that, for a segment on crime, he wanted to hear only from white callers.

Questionable Judgments

● Robert C. Jackson, 21, was arrested in Silver Spring, Md., in July for carrying a handgun, and, during a body search, police found in Jackson's rectum a brown paper bag with 78 plastic packets of rock cocaine and a razor blade. A police sergeant told reporters, "That's a pretty large amount [to be inside a rectum]."

● Blumita Singer of Brazil was invited, as one of 52 finalists, to perform at the International Violin Competition in Indianapolis in September as the result of an audition tape she submitted. However, when she started to perform, she played so poorly that it became apparent that she could not have been the person on the tape, and some of the judges walked out while others began giggling. She did not offer an explanation of what she intended to accomplish.

● Workers at a Ford plant in Cuautitlan, Mexico, staged a "nude-in" in July to protest layoffs.

● When police arrested Thomas "Tommy Karate" Pitera in June as a suspected Mafia hitman in New York City, they found a well-stocked library in his home that included such books as *The Hitman's Handbook*; *Kill or Be Killed*; and *Torture, Interrogation, and Execution*.

● Denver police announced in June they could not arrest the man who occasionally stood in the doorway of his apartment wearing only a diaper and calling to neighbors, "Hi, I'm wearing a diaper," because he was on his own property at the time.

● Animal trainer Arian Seidon, 60, who had kidnapped two elephants five years before in order to protect them from abuse by their owners, was arrested in April. Seidon supposedly had to procure 600 pounds of food per day during that time and dispose of 500 pounds of droppings.

● The Arlington County, Va., school board announced last spring that it was cutting back some sex education classes, including the popular game "Pin the Organ on the Body."

● Darlene Brown's house in Lusby, Md., was destroyed by fire in May after a neighbor tried to help her get rid of a non-poisonous black snake. The neighbor ignited the snake outside a bedroom window, 10 feet from the pilot light of the furnace. Thirty-five firefighters were called, and damage was reported at $50,000, but the snake was killed.

[column of November 23, 1990]

Lead Story

● At the Minnesota State Fair in August, passengers on the midway ride "Enterprise" (a flat board that starts parallel to the ground and then spins for four minutes until it is perpendicular to the ground)

Nonsense

Publisher: Nonsense
Hofstra University
203 Student Center
Hempstead, NY 11550
Format: Magazine
Editor: Al Rotches
Phone: (516) 463-6965
Founded: 1983
Description: **Nonsense** is the college humor magazine of Hofstra University.
Frequency: 6 issues per year
# of issues published in 1991: 6
# of issues to be published in 1992: 6
# of issues to be published in 1993: 6
1992 volume: Volume #9
Subscription period: 3 issues per semester
Subscription rates:

1 year/2 years/3 years:	$5.00	$10.00	$15.00
1 year/2 years/3 years (Canada):	US$5.00	US$10.00	US$15.00
1 year/2 years/3 years (Foreign):	US$5.00	US$10.00	US$15.00

Sample copy: $1.00
Average # of pages per issue: 36
Page size: 7 1/4" x 10 3/8"
Production: Laserprinted
Printing: Offset
Binding: Saddle stitched
Circulation: 4,000
Author information:

Prospective authors should inquire first before submitting manuscripts
Reports immediately
Author receives 10 complimentary copies of the issue in which the article appears as payment
Magazine owns all rights to articles
Magazine is copyrighted

Advertising rates:

Full page black & white:	$175
Cover 2 black & white:	$175
Cover 3 black & white:	$175
Cover 4 black & white:	$175

Cross-indexed:

General Humor
Sciences Humor
Social Sciences Humor
Humanities Humor
Arts Humor
Business Humor
Regional/Local Humor
Political Humor
Cartoons/Illustrations/Graphics
Visual Satire
Education Humor
English Humor

Film Media Humor
History Humor
Limericks
Philosophy Humor
Poetry Humor
Political Science Humor
Word Play & Puns

I had a great job, a beautiful wife, and two loving children.
But that's all gone now because I'm...

HOOKED ON PHONICS

Phonics ruined this man's life, and it can ruin your's too. Phonic tapes use subliminal messages to control your new and addictive habit...

"Phonics is goooood."

"Verbs help you smell better."

"Chicks dig guys who know their adverbs."

Stop Phonics now before it rewrites the rest of your life.

Reprinted from **Nonsense** by permission of the editor.

The Nose

Publisher: Acme Publishing Company, Inc.
           1095 Market Street
           Suite 812
           San Francisco, CA 94103
Format: Magazine
Editor: Jack Boulware
Founded: 1989
Description: **The Nose** is a satirical investigative magazine covering all aspects of the Wild West.
Frequency: 6 issues per year
# of issues published in 1991:   5
# of issues to be published in 1992: 6
# of issues to be published in 1993: 6
Subscription period: Subscriptions run from the date the order is received
Subscription rates:
           1 year: $12.00
           1 year (Canada):   US$15.00
           Sample copy: $ 3.00
Average # of pages per issue: 64
Page size: 8 3/8" x 10 7/8"
Production: Typeset
Printing: Offset
Binding: Saddle stitched
Circulation: 50,000
Author information:
           Magazine accepts unsolicited manuscripts
           Reports in 1 month
           Author receives either payment or complimentary copies of the issue in which the article
              appears (depending on current finances of the magazine)
           Magazine acquires 1st serial rights and reprint rights
           Magazine is copyrighted
Advertising rates (for insertion orders, contact the Industria Media Group at [415] 775-9718):
           1/2 page black & white: $ 635
           1/2 page color: $1,000
           Full page black & white: $1,150
           Full page color: $1,900
           Cover 2 color: $3,100
           Cover 3 color: $3,000
           Cover 4 color: $3,200
Reviews:
           "Stands out amongst the skads of hyper-hip magazines." (*San Francisco Chronicle*)
           "Very much like *Spy* magazine but without the swelled head." (*Gannett News Service*)
Cross-indexed:
           General Humor
           Regional/Local Humor
           Cartoons/Illustrations/Graphics
           Visual Humor

One to One:™ The Journal of Creative Broadcasting

Publisher: CreeYadio Services
                P.O. Box 9787
                Fresno, CA 93794
Format: Newsletter
Editor: Jay Trachman
Phone: (209) 226-0558
Founded: 1976
Description: **One to One** carries weekly info, talent, prep., and humor, providing broadcasters with information on improving their technique, plus day-to-day calendars of history and events, artist bios, promotions, production tips—and 5 pages of weekly topical humor, jokes, one liners, and record intros. (Material from **One to One** is also available for computers on-line via Broadcast Professionals Forum of CompuServe.)
Frequency: 50 times per year
# of issues published in 1991:   50
# of issues to be published in 1992:   50
# of issues to be published in 1993:   50
1992 volume: Volume #XVII
Subscription period: Subscriptions run from the date the order is received
Subscription rates:

1 year/3 years:	$150.00	$300.00
1 year (Canada):	US$175.00	US$350.00
1 year (Foreign):	US$185.00	US$370.00
Sample: N/C		
On-line format: Inquire		

Average # of pages per issue: 16
Page size: 7" x 8 1/2"
Production: Laserprinted
Printing: Offset
Binding: Saddle stitched
Circulation: 2,500-3,000
Author information:

      Newsletter generally accepts unsolicited manuscripts only from subscribers—inquire first
      Newsletter owns all rights to articles
      Newsletter is copyrighted

Advertising rates:

1/2 page black & white:	$150
Full page black & white:	$275

Cross-indexed:

General Humor	Political Humor
Sciences Humor	
Social Sciences Humor	
Humanities Humor	
Arts Humor	
Business Humor	
Medicine Humor	
Dentistry Humor	
Nursing Humor	
Regional/Local Humor	

Here's one to add to your collection of self-canceling phrases, like "military intelligence" and "postal service": How 'bout—"Reagan memoirs"...

Biosphere II, the experiment to see how humans do in an artifical environment, will be sealed up on September 26th; eight people will be sealed inside a glass and steel dome for two years; the environment is completely self-sustaining, and it's the only place on earth where people can be completely safe, from junk mail...

You know what's really scary about the dropping scores on the S.A.T.'s? Research shows if the current trends continue, but the time he runs for president in '96, Dan Quayle could be considered an intellectual leader...

Little-known sidelight to history: William Tell, the Swiss archery hero, was also a great bowler; he and his family played for one of the local merchants...but eventually, many merchants who didn't bother to sponsor them also claimed the name...and because of poor records, today it's impossible to know for whom the Tells bowled...

An Evansville minister's advertising in the paper, trying to get Madonna to attend Sunday services while she's in town filming her new movie; he points out Jesus was always more comfortable among open sinners than with religious hypocrites...and he might even be able to get her a picture spread in his new magazine, Repent-House...

I hope things start calming down in what's left of the Soviet Union for a few weeks, to give us all a chance to catch up on the changes...So do the people in the map-making industry...They're still waiting to take their summer vacations...

The courts have agreed to Arista's plan to reimburse people who bought Milli Vanilli records; anyone who purchased "Girl You Know It's True" gets a refund from $1 to $3...Oh—and they have to change the name to "Girl, You Know It's *Not* True"...

A 49-year-old prospector became an instant millionaire last week, after finding the largest black opal ever discoverd in Western Australia...It'll be named "Opal Winfrey"...

Medicine has made great strides in the twentieth century, you know...In olden days, doctors used to bleed a sick patient; today, they just soak you...

Pop quiz; how does Roseanne Barr take a bath? Answer: first she fills the tub...Then, she adds water...

I like the card the boss sent me when I was out sick last week; it said, "Get well— by 8 a.m. Monday!"

Ostriches Anonymous Association

Founder: Robert O. Besco
Publication: **Ostrich Watchers Newsletter**
Publisher: Professional Performance Improvement
                10887 Crooked Creek Drive
                Dallas, TX 75229
Format: Newsletter
Editor: Robert O. Besco
Phone: (214) 361-1908
Organization founded: 1990
Publication founded: 1990
Description: The **Ostriches Anonymous Association** (OAA) is totally autonomous, anonymous, and
                innocuous. It is in no way endorsed or supported by any sane, competent, or respectable
                individuals, organizations, or societies. The sole purpose of the OAA is to promote
                aviation safety and risk awareness by sponsoring the Oliver Ostrich "Head in the Sand"
                Anonymous Annual Award, awarded to any anonymous individual or organization who
                contributes most by conscious action, decision, or purposeful neglect to either the denial,
                the discounting, or the ignoring of significant aviation risks or opportunities. OAA also
                sponsors an annual dinner.
Frequency: 3 issues per year
# of issues published in 1991:   3
# of issues to be published in 1992:   3
# of issues to be published in 1993:   3
Subscription period: Calendar year (i.e., all subscriptions received in 1992 automatically begin with
                the first issue of 1992)
Annual membership rates (newsletter is included in the price of membership):
                Regular member: $ 5.00
                Corporate member: $50.00
                Lifetime member: $50.00
# of members: 43
Average # of pages per issue: 2
Page size: 8" x 10"
Production: Laserprinted
Printing: Xeroxed
Binding: Stapled in corner or on edge
Author information:
                Newsletter accepts unsolicited manuscripts
                Reports in 6 weeks
                Authors receive no compensation, either in cash or free copies
                Newsletter owns all rights to articles
                Newsletter is not copyrighted
Cross-indexed:
                General Humor
                Social Sciences Humor
                Business Humor
                History Humor
                Philosophy Humor
                Psychology Humor

Previous Nominees

Year	Position	Risk Denying Statement
1990	Attorney	"My clients' high blood alcohol did not degrade his flight deck performance. He is an alcoholic and has a high degree of tolerance."
	Aircraft Manufacturer	"The take-off warning system is a back-up system and the loss of that by itself in no way affects the safety of the airplane."
	Personality Theory Psychologist	"Most Airline Cockpit Resource Management problems never would have materialized if airlines had not hired military fighter pilots or other pilots with stereotyped "macho" personality traits.
	Accident Investigator	"It sounds like the cause of this accident is going to be a repeat. I have known for a long time that this thing was going to reoccur. I'll bet that when we get into this, my pet theory of causation will be confirmed."
1989	Government Official	"The structural failure was a *rogue accident*. Inspection and maintenance procedures do not need to be changed." (Anonymous statement describing a 1988 structural failure and decompression incident, Aviation Week, Jan 2, 1989).
	Sr. Military Officer	"Don't you realize how much negative response your safety recommendation will generate?"
1988	Aviation Publisher	"Since this no-cost safety procedure can not guarantee that we will never have another accident, we should not publish it"
	Government Official	"The whole industry is now so sensitized to the no-flap takeoff error that it will be many years before we are at risk from a no flap mistake being repeated." (Address made to a professional organization 23 months after the first accident and one month before the second accident).
1987	Airline Executive	"We needed the wage concessions of $350 million to keep the Airline in business." (statement made prior to realizing a $350 million personal gain from a stock merger, privatization and debt restructure transaction with that same airline.)
1986	Wingman	"Blue Leader, it is my personal feeling, based on my current analysis of the situation, that you might want to reconsider your current plan of action. I recommend that you seriously consider an alternative tactic which would involve the detachment of the bogey from your six o'clock position by responding promptly to the following suggestion: "BLUE LEAD, BREAK HARD LEFT, NOW!" (Warning call by wingman made *after* completing leadership sensitivity and assertiveness training).
1985	Flight Crew & All of The Guys Ahead	"It must be all right to approach and land, all the guys ahead of us made it."
	Airline Chief Pilot	"A copilot is never supposed to question the Captain."
1984	Airline Flight Instructor	"They will teach you about the Digital Guidance System during your Initial Line Operating Experience."
1984	Aviation Medical Examiner	"I can prescribe Valium for this airline pilot without putting it into his medical records. He will act responsibly and not use it within 24 hours of flying."

10/02

2

1983	Airline Executive	"We don't need to raise our pilots wages. We can find plenty of licensed pilots to hire at less than $1500/month."
1982	Airline Hot-Line Tech'l Advisor	"If your only abnormal indication is a high vibration indication on No. 3 engine, you might as well leave it run and continue on to your destination." (Advice given two hours before the complete inflight disintegration of a multi million dollar engine)
	VP of Flt. Training	"Sure Boss, we can reduce training costs and still pass the FAA inspections."
1981	Avionics Expert	"Our Digital Flight Management Systems and Glass Cockpits of the future will greatly reduce the workload on the flight crews."
	Air Force Commander	"Do you want and need the legal minimun number of generators for takeoff? If you do, we will have to scrub the mission."
1980	Airline Executive	"Our pilots are the cream of the crop. They won't make those type of errors."
1979	Government Official	"Safety margins will remain the same after deregulation."
1978	Manufacturer & Government Officials	"These pylon cracks are not immediately dangerous. There is no reason to be alarmed about structural integrity."
1977	Airline President	"The pilots involved in the accident chose to ignore everything that they were trained to do."
1976	Airline President	"There is practically no turnover in the airline pilots work force. Therefore, we don't need to be concerned about the quality of a pilots' work life."
1975	Jet Engine Designer	"The vibration indicators are so unreliable that we should remove them from the engines."
	Pilot	"If it is legal, it must be safe. They wouldn't send us out to fly it if it weren't safe. Besides, it hasn't caused any accidents."
1974	Airline Executive	"We cannot send out job offers to pilots more than two weeks before reporting dates. We cannot afford to commit to a pilot staffing plan months in advance."
1973	Aircraft Designer	"Overdesign is desirable but is practical only for structural engineers in buildings and bridges."
1972	Approach Controller	"Pilots would never be that far off of an assigned low altitude, my equipment must be malfunctioning again."
1971	Airline Capt.	"Flying these airplane is as easy as driving a tricycle."
1970	Airline Co Pilot	"Its great to fly with fully qualified and experienced Captains. You don't have to be constantly on the alert for their mistakes."
1969	Probationary Co Pilot	"If I tell the Captain he is doing something wrong, he will write me up, and I will be discharged without right of appeal."
	Aircraft Manufacturer	"We can make this cargo door lock foolproof. But we cannot make it damn fool proof."
1968	Check Airman	"If you test that warning system every flight, you will wear it out." 10/02

The Peter Schickele Rag

Publisher: The Peter Schickele Rag
               P.O. Box 1188
               Woodstock, NY 12498

Format: Newsletter

Editor: Peter Schickele

Founded: 1979

Description: **The Peter Schickele Rag** publishes information about the activities of Peter Schickele and P. D. Q. Bach, along with music (usually rounds), crossword puzzles, miscellaneous articles, inexcusable puns, and assorted hype.

Frequency: 2 issues per year

# of issues published in 1991:   1

# of issues to be published in 1992:   3 (the 1 extra issue making up for 1991)

# of issues to be published in 1993:   2

Subscription period: Subscriptions run from the date the order is received

Subscription rates:

          5 issues: $7.00
          Sample copy: $1.00

Average # of pages per issue: 8

Page size: 8 1/2" x 11"

Production: Typeset

Printing: Offset

Circulation: 750-1,000

Author information:

          Newsletter does not accept unsolicited manuscripts
          Newsletter is copyrighted

Advertising rates: Advertisements are not accepted

Cross-indexed:

          Arts Humor
          Music Humor

The Plague

Publisher: The Plague at NYU
21 Washington Place
Box 189
New York, NY 10003

Format: Magazine

Editors: Seth Minsk (Managing Editor), Lawrence V. Lewitinn (Executive Editor), Amy Marie Zucca (Art & Layout Editor)

Founded: 1977

Description: **The Plague** is New York's downtown college humor magazine. We've been making New York University and the rest of the city sick since 1977. An equal opportunity offender. **The Plague**—sensitive topics, insensitive treatment.

Frequency: 4 issues per year

# of issues published in 1991:   4

# of issues to be published in 1992:   4

# of issues to be published in 1993:   4

1992 volume: Volume #15 (volume numbers run by academic year; Volume #15 is 1991-92)

Subscription period: Academic year (September to May)

Subscription rates:

1 year:	$12.00
1 year (Canada):	US$15.00
Sample copy:	$ 3.00

Average # of pages per issue: 24

Page size: 8 1/2" x 11"

Production: Laserprinted

Printing: Offset

Binding: Saddle stitched

Circulation: 8,000

Author information:

Prospective authors should inquire first before submitting manuscripts

Reports in 2-4 weeks

Author receives complimentary copies of the issue in which the article is published as payment

Magazine owns all rights to articles

Magazine is copyrighted

Advertising rates:

1/2-page black & white:	$ 350
Full-page black & white:	$ 600
Cover 2 black & white:	$1,000
Cover 3 black & white:	$1,000
Cover 4 black & white:	$1,600

Reviews:

"My legal department would not be too pleased with your parody. But I was, so I won't show it to them." (Hugh M. Heffner, in a letter to **The Plague**'s editors, regarding May 1991's "Plagueboy" issue of **The Plague**, a *Playboy* parody)

Cross-indexed:

General Humor	Education Humor
Social Sciences Humor	History Humor
Arts Humor	Law Humor
Regional/Local Humor	Literature Humor
Political Humor	Political Science Humor
Cartoons/Illustrations/Graphics	Religion Humor
Visual Satire	Word Play & Puns

CAUCASIAN HETEROSEXUAL MALE STUDIES (69)

1600 Pennsylvania Avenue
Chairman : **Professor A. Nal Retentive**
Director of Undergraduate Studies: **Professor I.M. White**

The Department of Caucasian Heterosexual Male Studies has a threefold objective: first, to examine the history of the CHM, as they have done everything important in this world; second, to probe the depths of American culture as a CHM society; and finally, to discover the roots of their domineering and sexually frustrated psyche.

The Department offers numerous courses designed to explore the concentrations above, and has a wide range of resources to achieve its purpose since, in fact, Caucasian Heterosexual Males really do control everything. In addition, the department offers an exciting internship program through its many connections in high level government and corporate bodies. Indeed, it was one of CHM's interns who gave the go ahead to Gen. Norman Schwarzkopf to invade Kuwait. Now that's power.

Professors: Jones, Morgan, Smith, Stevens, Vanderbilt, Winchester; **Assistant Professors:** High, Michaud, Silberman, Zimmerman; **Special Fellowship in Minority Studies:** Professor Michael Levine; **NAAWP Endowment for Studies in Creative Persuasion:** David Duke; **Visiting Professor in Economic Oppression Tactics:** William F. Buckley Jr.

Major

A major in CHM Studies requires eight four-point classes, including:

(1) *History : Oppression or Protection?* A69.0001, (2) *Whitespeak for Beginners Level I* A69.0004, and (3) at least one course in the Rural Studies Division. Membership in the Republican Party recommended for any student to be taken seriously.

Minor

As we feel that this Department is of such a major concern to the world in general, offering a minor would be offensive to actual Caucasian Heterosexual Males. However, we are working on a "Minority Studies from a Majority View" program that will be offered as a more acceptable minor in the near future. Those interested please contact Prof. Levine.

Independent Study

The Department will accept applications from Juniors and Seniors who wish to be placed with a Caucasian Heterosexual Male in order to observe and participate in daily events such as golf, cruising for babes, and invading small countries. Prerequisite: *Buttkissing for Upward Mobility* V69.0105

Honors

The Department will award Honors to all Caucasian Heterosexual Males who graduate, demonstrate a mastery of lynching ettiquette, and pay an additional $25,000.

Courses

Introductory Courses

History : Oppression or Protection? A69.0001 *LEP Area 6. 4 points.* Examines the recent flap about Multiculturalism and compares similar movements against CHM power such as Civil Rights, Womens' Rights, and rights in general.

Heterosexuality I A69.0002 *LEP Area 8. 4 points.* Explores a concept alien to the Greenwich Village area; studies the proper ratios of the female form, as embodied by Barbie,

and shows why men shouldn't fuck other men because only AIDS-carrying, felching, dick-sucking faggot liberals do that.

Heterosexuality II A69.0003 *LEP Area 8. 4 points.* Advanced studies; provides instruction on the integral mechanics of mating: the missionary position. How to condemn sex while secretly enjoying it. Focus on the art of preventing premature ejaculation.

Note: The Department is accepting applications from women who want to earn extra credit by offering themselves as demonstration aids. Free contraceptives.

Whitespeak for Beginners I A69.0004 *LEP Area 1. 4 points.* A course designed primarily to teach the elements of Whitespeak grammar and language structure through an oral tradition. Special attention is paid on how to confuse *them* on standardized examinations and in the workplace. Introduction to and usage of Whitespeak words such as "Republican" (the real American party), "Conservatives" (the good people of our country), and "WASP" (true red-blooded Americans).

Whitespeak for Beginners II A69.0005 *Prerequisite: A69.0004 LEP Area 1. 4 points.* A more advanced course that delves into such complex concepts as Affirmative Action, Liberalism, Sodomy, and Homosexual Love, with emphasis on why none of these are legitimate or moral.

Advanced Courses

The Conflict of Ethics and Power V69.0100 *LEP Area 3. 4 points.* Instruction on how to make people think you care when you are really a money-grubbing thug. Patriotic manipulation to avoid the truth and/ or domestic problems. Special lecture by George Bush.

Creative Racial Slurring V69.0101 *4 points.* In conjunction with the Linguistics Department, we now offer a course which will teach students the true root of such

8

THE PLAGUE • NOVEMBER 1991

---

oppressive terms as "Women," "Black," and "Oriental" as well as the proper uses for such words as "Cunt," "Alabama Porch Monkey," and "Slanty-Eyed Job-Stealing V.C. Chink." Focus on the "it's all in the intent" or "it's a white thing; you wouldn't understand" arguments for those sticky situations.

Real Estate and Preserving the Suburbs V69.0102 *4 points.* Explores the concept and methodology of keeping your neighborhood "pure." How to reinterpret the Constitution to oppose bussing and support the separate but equal doctrine even though *they* are not actually equal. Teaches surveillance methods to keep track of neighbors and how to discourage real estate agents from showing homes in one's area to undesirables.

Loopholes in Quota Legislation V69.0103 *4 points.* Examines recent examples of quota dodging. Skills are developed in the art of articulating such views as maintaining that minorities just don't have the brain capacity to sweep floors so they don't get hired. Demonstrates a fallback position where society is blamed for not turning out any qualified minorities, thus preventing the employer from hiring any.

Cocktail Hour as a Social Priority V69.0104 *4 points.* Intended for those new to the CHM social scene to develop the proper habits of social drinking. Involves avoiding such faux pas as exposing one's cock to the boss' wife and telling her to "ride it like the wild woman you are," vomitting in one's hostess' drawer of sex toys, and attempting to alternately buttfuck and felch one's best friend's poodle.

Buttkissing for Upward Mobility V69.0105 *4 points.* How and whom to choose to suck up to. Explores the different methods, from constantly hanging around superiors and agreeing with everything they say to using kneepads and mouthwash. Special section for

women on how to avoid the glass ceiling without compromising their dignity...too much.

Rhythm V69.1234 *4 points.* This is the course that asks the eternal question, "Can white people clap on the backbeat?" Why Negroes, due to their jungle-adapting traits, have better rhythm, and why it doesn't matter.

Women as Sex Objects V69.6969 *4 points.* Studies of societal institutions and how they are designed to keep women at bay. How to build a glass ceiling in your corporation. Pornography as a tool to abuse and basically fuck women over. Studies the proper terminology of "babe," "chick," and "lust puppy."

Dumb Fraternity Tricks V69.1325 *4 points.* Describes and explores traditional frat activities such as panty raids, excessive imbibing of alcohol, drug running, circle jerks, and elephant trains. Will cover modeling as introductory material. (Note: class open to prospective Fiji and Psi U. pledges only.)

Rural Studies

This division focuses on the... less cultured members of the Caucasian Heterosexual Male family. Special focus on language and lifestyle for prospective "hicks".

Terminology and Dialect V69.1001 *4 points.* How to talk even funnier than Long Island JAPs. Explains the proper references to women as "bitches" and everybody else as "buddy".

Beer and Booze V69.1002 *4 points.* The joys of brewing. Examines the great debate over "tastes great, less filling." The class will also profile Adolf "Hitler" Coors as an important figure in the life of any hunter, and will attempt to find out just what the fuck "dry beer" is.

Hunting and Drinking V69.1003 *4 points.* Explains how, contrary to popular belief, a few dead cows and Boy Scouts each year still don't

prove that hunting and drinking don't really mix. Also, how to distinguish your buddies from your targets under extreme intoxication.

Truck Ettiquete V69.1004 *4 points.* Chevy versus Ford; where to hang your shotgun racks; creative places for beer cans; how to hang a dead animal on your hood without blocking your view; the ethics of claiming road kill as a hunting trophy.

The Hidden Sexuality of Farm Animals V69.1005 *4 points.* For those really desperate moments.

Professional Wrestling Appreciation V69.1006 *4 points.* Why the Good Guys are always white and the Bad Guys always talk funny. Will present a seminar on "The Dynamics of Having a Female Manager: From Sex to Rescuing Her From Your Enemies."

Techniques of Wife Beating V69.1007 *4 points.* We know you all do it; here's how to do it without leaving brusies.

History of the John Birch Society V69.1008 *4 points.* Explores this freedom-loving, patriotic organization and its glorious defense of our country against the loathsome Communist Oppressors. Will prove how the metric system is really a Communist plot to confuse us.

Music Appreciation V69.1009 *4 points.* Explains why country music is the only legitimate art form left 'round here, and why every other type of music is Satanic.

History and Development of Lynching : From Cross Burning to Castration V69.1010 *4 points.* Techniques of purification and creative persuasion. How to make an impact in flowing white robes on top of a horse. History of the KKK and why their targets deserved it.

Advanced Lynching Techniques V69.1011 *4 points.* What more can you do? You'll find out in this class. Emphasis placed on genitalia.

9

NYU: NAZIS, YOKELS, & UNIONS

Procrastinators' Club of America

Founder: Les Waas
Publication: **Last Month's Newsletter**
Publisher: Procrastinators'' Club of America, Inc.
             1111 Broad-Locust Building
             Philadelphia, PA 19102
Format: Newsletter
Editor: Joesph H. Weiss
Phone: (215) 546-3861
Description: The purpose of the **Procrastinators' Club of America** is to promote positive procras-
             tination and to bring together honest procrastinators. Nothing is scheduled on a regular
             basis. National Procrastination Week is the first full week in March. National Be Late
             For Something Day is September 5th. **Last Month's Newsletter** is a humorous, tongue-
             in-cheek 4-page publication, with many articles continued on Page 5.
Frequency: Published irregularly
Membership dues and subscriptions (includes subscription to newsletter): $21.00 to join
# of members: 9,000
Average # of pages per issue: 4
Page size: 8 1/2" x 11"
Production: Combination of typeset, typed, and press-on
Printing: Offset
Circulation: 9,000
Author information:
             Newsletter does not accepted unsolicited manuscripts
             Newsletter is copyrighted
Cross-indexed:
             General Humor
             Cartoons/Illustrations/Graphics

Winner Announced

Winner of Club's 1958 essay contest on "How Procrastination Has Helped Make My Life Better," has just been announced. She is Mrs. Walter Treftz of suburban Philadelphia. Her wining letter read "I'll write tomorrow."

Our Protest Against the War

We are extremely happy to report that our 1967 Protest against the War of 1812 has been appraised as a super success. A peace treaty has now been signed.

> REMINDER: PAY YOUR DUES LATE AND AVOID THE BIG 5% PENALTY.

National Procrastination Week is listed in Chase's Calendar of Events as the first week in March. Sincere Procrastinators are urged to celebrate this great holiday the second week in March.

> Once a Procrastinator makes up his mind to take a firm stand on something, nothing in the world can stop him from possibly getting around to it—some day.

AWARDS

Note: Every year we pay homage to one specific person or thing who warrants the famed "Procrastinator of the Year Award." When you get around to it, why not submit a nominee you consider worthy? Past honorees include:

A Topless Dancer *(for putting things off, of course)*...

Jack Benny *(for never getting around to "turning 40")*...

Murray Rappaport *(for breaking the world's record for an overdue library book)*...

Dean Martin & Jerry Lewis *(as the comedy team of the year)*...

Methodist Hospital *(for not placing their cornerstone, dated 1968, until 1972)*...

Illinois Central *(for the latest of trains—left in 1903 and hasn't arrived yet!)*...

Elmer T. Klassen *(former Postmaster General for obvious reasons)*.

It's interesting to note that Postmaster Klassen, to inform us that he was unable to attend the banquet in his honor, sent us a telegram. Perhaps, like the rest of us, he just couldn't trust the mails.

1972-73 Membership Drive Underway

If you have a friend (or enemy) who is thinking about joining (or not joining) PCA, he (or she) might (or might not) consider joining (or not joining) in 1972 or 1973, one of our most active (and therefore most successful) years. Have this potential member (or nonmember) contact our 1972-73 Membership Committee Chairperson after this chairperson is named.

"Hank" Hanish, long time neophyte procrastinator, when chosen from so many thousands to serve as editors of earlier issues of **Last Month's Newsletter**, expressed sincere joviality, as well as disbelief, at his having been chosen from so many thousands to serve as editors of earlier issues of **Last Month's Newsletter**.

"They're honors that come twice in a lifetime, if at all," Hanish, who hails from Willingboro, N.J., as does his lovely wife Helen, exclaimed.

He admitted, however, that he'd have preferred being named editor of this issue, although he realized, of course, that it is far too early for such a selection to have been made at this time already.

Hanish would have relished the opportunity to write of the Club's trip to the Whitechapel Bell Foundry in London in 1970 to demand that they honor the warranty on the Liberty Bell (which is cracked). He would have loved to write about our 1974 Zoo Year's Eve Party...our Day-Old Cake Sale for Muscular Dystrophy...our visit to Spain in 1972 to raise money for 3 ships to discover America...our fantastic summer ski party and winter picnic...our celebration of May Fool's Day...our junket to Rome in 1974 to use the tickets we got to see Christians battle lions in the Circus Maximus...our Procrastinators' Race in which the last horse won...the resignation of Bob Dome because of too much activity—although he hadn't even applied for membership yet...our Christmas gift buying seminar in January...our trip to the N.Y. World's Fair a year after it closed...our discovery of Africa...and stuff like that there.

But what the heck. To be realistic about it, Hank don't write all that good anyway.

PUNCH Digest for Canadian Doctors

Publisher: Punch Digest for Canadian Doctors
               14845 Yonge Street
               Suite 300
               Aurora, Ontario L4G 6H8
               Canada
Format: Magazine
Editor: Simon Hally
Phone: (416) 841-5607 [FAX: (416) 841-5688]
Founded: 1990
Description: **PUNCH Digest for Canadian Doctors** is a humour and lifestyle magazine for practis-
               ing physicians in Canada.
Frequency: 6 issues per year
# of issues published in 1991:   6
# of issues to be published in 1992: 6
# of issues to be published in 1993: 6
Subscription period: Subscriptions run from the date the order is received
Subscription rates:

1 year/2 years:	not available	$40.00 (Canadian dollars) for 12 issues
1 year/2 years (Canada):	not available	$25.00 (Canadian dollars) for 12 issues
1 year/2 years (Foreign):	not available	$60.00 (Canadian dollars) for 12 issues
Sample copy: $4.00 (Canadian dollars)		

Average # of pages per issue: 48
Page size: 8 1/2" x 10 7/8"
Production: Laserprinted
Printing: Offset
Binding: Saddle stitched
Circulation: 37,000
Author information:

    Magazine accepts unsolicited manuscripts
    Reports in 2-4 weeks
    Magazine pays 30¢ per word
    Magazine owns 1st serial rights
    Magazine is copyrighted

Advertising rates (Canadian dollars, 1-time rates):

1/2 page black & white:	$1,595
1/2 page color:	$2,945
Full page black & white:	$2,350
Full page color:	$3,700
Covers black & white:	not available
Cover 2 color:	$4,810
Cover 3 color:	$4,810
Cover 4 color:	$5,550

Cross-indexed:

General Humor	Nursing Humor
Sciences Humor	Psychiatry Humor
Regional/Local Humor	
Political Humor	
Cartoons/Illustrations/Graphics	
Summary of Conferences and/or	
Symposiums on Humor	
Medical Humor	

ISSN:1182-5405

FIRST PERSON

JUST FOLLOWING ORDERS

BY DR. SYLVIA KERESZTES
KITCHENER, ONT.

Many a moon ago, I arrived late one night at our mission post in Central America. The next morning, Sister and I were all set at 6 a.m. to start the out-patient clinic when a call came for Sister to go to the Aldea for a delivery. She asked me if I'd be all right on my own. She knew that since I'd served in India, Africa and Haiti, tropical medicine shouldn't be a problem, but Spanish might be.

I assured her that for six weeks prior to my departure, my husband, who speaks many languages fluently, had drilled me in Spanish for two hours a day, and that he thought I should be all right.

My first patient was a soldier with bloody diarrhoea. I thought his problem was most likely to be hookworm. I asked him to produce a stool sample. He couldn't, so I gave him a jar and told him to return when he'd had a B.M.

Two minutes later he came back; he wondered how his B.M. would fit into such a small bottle. I explained to him that all he had to do was take a little branch from a tree and deposit a small amount of his stool in the jar and return with it as soon as possible,

Sister came back from the Aldea and we worked our way through many patients.

Suddenly we heard a commotion outside. We looked through the window and there was my soldier patient with six other soldiers who were carrying a tree. On the very tip of the tree was the patient's stool sample, and on top of that was the jar I'd given him

I had a sneaking suspicion that my Spanish needed some improvement!

MISINFORMED CONSENT

BY DR. BRIAN BOYD
TORONTO

As a junior surgical resident in Liverpool, I was once asked by my chief to a "minor" surgical list in the operating room adjoining his. One of the patients was a 15-year-old mentally retarded male booked in for circumcision at his mother's request.

The operation went smoothly enough, but in the post-operative period he developed a massive haematoma, giving his penis the appearance of a large grapefruit grasped in the hand of a small child. I like to think it was the patient's propensity for masturbation rather than any deficiency in

surgical technique that resulted in this unfortunate complication.

The problem (like the penis) was handled aggressively from the outset, with the gamut of therapy ranging from surgical drainage (difficult) to medicinal leeches (interesting). After a week's prostration and pain, the unlucky young man miraculously recovered and was limping out of the ward when I first met his mother and sister.

It appeared that the sister, who was two years younger than the patient, was also mentally retarded. In the course of my conversation with the mother, it became clear that the two of them had struck up an incestuous relationship.

"I know the boy suffered, Doc," the mother said, "but was the operation a success? Are you sure he won't have no babies?"

"Mrs. S., your son had a circumcision, not a vasectomy!"

"Dammit, *that*'s the word I was looking for!"

THE 58th VARIETY

BY DR. JEAN LAVALLÉE
QUEBEC CITY

One night about ten years ago, while I was on duty in the Emergency Department of a Quebec City hospital, I was awakened by the nurse at 5 a.m.

She wouldn't tell me on the phone the reason for the patient's visit, and I soon realized why: here he was, about 35 years old, six feet tall, 250 pounds, bleeding heavily from the anal region. The cause? He had put a junior-size Heinz fruit bottle in his anus, and it had slipped into his rectum, where it was now stuck.

The surgeon that I woke up didn't believe my story at first, and he had a good reason not to: it was April 1.

In the operating

"Look, a hospital owning a funeral home is not a conflict of interest. It's vertical integration."

Pun Intended

Publisher: Gary Hallock
                 1124-A Clayton Lane
                 Austin, TX 78723
Format: Newsletter
Editor: Gary Hallock
Phone: (512) 453-4431
Founded: 1991
Description: **Pun Intended** features puns, puzzles, cartoons, limericks, letters, contests, poetry, and
                 news (with the emphasis on puns).
Frequency: 4 issues per year
# of issues published in 1991:   3
# of issues to be published in 1992:   4
# of issues to be published in 1993:   4
1992 volume: Volume #2
Subscription period: Subscriptions run from the date the order is received
Subscription rates:

1 year:	$ 8.00
1 year (Canada):	US$ 8.00
1 year (Foreign):	US$10.00
Sample copy:	$ 1.00

Average # of pages per issue: 4
Page size: 8 1/2" x 11"
Production: Laserprinted
Printing: Xeroxed
Binding: Folded
Circulation: 100
Author information:

          Newsletter accepts unsolicited manuscripts
          Reports in 1 week
          Author may receive some complimentary copies of the issue in which the article appears
             as payment
          Newsletter does not deal with the issue of copyright of individual articles
          Newsletter is copyrighted
Reviews:

          "...Very good, very witty....pun crammed...it's getting better and better." (*The Pundit*)
          "A collection of puns to rival O. Henry...Some are truly brilliant." (*Factsheet Five*)
Cross-indexed:

          General Humor
          Sciences Humor
          Social Sciences Humor
          Humanities Humor
          Arts Humor
          Business Humor
          Political Humor
          Cartoons/Illustrations/Graphics
          Visual Satire
          Limericks
          Poetry Humor
          Word Play & Puns

LET US STEW THE EDITOR

Some of our new startups are real upstarts. Some sent dirty ditties that I can't **ink lewd** here but may **lecher** read later. While I am not exactly a **prude gent y'all, Allstate** my policy **adjust** once more for the **wrecker. "EYE ONE TWO KEY PIT ASS KLEENEX PSYCH CANNES"**

When I **ladies** rules out, I was **soaping** it wouldn't **detergents** from sending cards and **lathers.** I was **soap** proud that most readers did come clean as I **washed** they would.

Steve Sisson of Arlington Tx. warns me that he thinks that **subscriptions** should only be written by Navy Pharmacists. (I believe their **subordinates** have the right to write those too)

Sunil Kapahi wanted me to **tally** you that he counted 80 puns in the previous issue. He enjoyed eight of them so much that he's decided to subscribe. His conclusion: **"A PUN IN TEN DID IT!"** Mr. Kapahi lives in Dunwoody Ga. and has **done what he** can to transcend the cultural gap between **America 'n' India in** his new newsletter known as **"PHUN".** I called him a **"Kapahi Kat," Hindi** responded by dubbing me **"Guru."** It sounds like he's off to a strong start and there's nothing **weak Hindu** about it. (e.g. Do you know the difference between Yehudi Menuhin and Mahatma Gandhi? Menuhin was a **viol inist,** and Gandhi was a **Non-violenist.**) If you need more of this foolishness, write to him at 4632 Dellrose Dr., Dunwoody, GA 30338.

Chronic contributor, **Chuck Burgess** of El Campo Tx. has sent me his recomended reading list. Some of his favorite books titles include; *Be Specific,* by U. Noe Hu, *Traveling the USA,* by Sally Forth, *Cartoons,* by Anna Mashun and *Subliminal Advertising,* by Mibuk.

Another repeat offender, **Lee Jackson**, relates the tale of a lazy dictionary editor who was accused of being a laxicographer. He must have suffered from writer's block, because he spent a lot of time in the bathroom. The publisher eventually fired him and he became an ex-laxicographer.

Yukon imagine how it **Anchorages** me to **Bearing strait** from **Ken Landfield** that we now have a reader in **Alaska**? He's a **Homersapien**. No, that's not an **Aleutian** to **Homer's sects** ya'll, that's **Seward** those residents of the southern inlet **Cooked** up to make pun of themselves. I **Canada side** if I should pull that tired old pun that both **Kenai & Juneau,** so next time icy him, **Isle ask Ken.** In fact, I did **Ketchiken,** and I **totem** I wanted his impression of **Valdez** puns. He **offjord** no response, made no **sound** and his **ice** got **glacier.** How could I **eskimo**?

Now that he's had his **off fish oil** introduction, you might enjoy **herring** Ken's story **red**. Even though it spawned that babbling stream of **brooken** english in the paragraph above, after I **egg salmoned** it, I **thawed** it to be a **kipper,** so I'll be in **sardine** it here if I **can**.

"I work at a radio station with a woman named Susan. Now, if we could get her to read the headlines at 12:00, we could call it the **'SUE NOON NEWS.'"**
(Isn't that the Maine man's main man?)

The woman who usually delivers mail to **George McClughan** has been ill. When she resumed her duties the following week, George inquired as to the nature of her illness. Obviously uncomfortable with the question, she responded, "Uh, female problems". Not wanting to embarrass her further but equally reluctant to let the opportunity pass, George resp**unded**, "Oh, I see, it was a **mail lady malady, m'lady"** *[letter alone, George]*

The Quayle Quarterly™

Publisher: The Quayle Quarterly
              P.O. Box 8593
              Brewster Station
              Bridgeport, CT 06605
Format: Magazine
Editors: Deborah Werksman, Jeffrey Yoder
Phone: (203) 333-9399
Founded: 1990
Description: Political satire—a watchful eye on the Vice Presidency. Humor, analysis, readers' feedback, press reviews, letters, cartoons.
Frequency: 4 issues per year
\# of issues published in 1991:   4
\# of issues to be published in 1992: 4
\# of issues to be published in 1993: 4
1992 volume: Volume #3
Subscription period: Subscriptions run from the date the order is received
Subscription rates:

1 year:	$14.95
1 year (Canada):	US$17.95
1 year (Foreign):	US$21.95
Sample copy:	$ 3.95

Average # of pages per issue: 20
Page size: 8 1/2" x 11"
Production: Laserprinted
Printing: Offset
Binding: Saddle stitched
Circulation: 15,000
Author information:

        Magazine accepts unsolicited manuscripts
        Reports in 3 months
        Payment is negotiable
        Magazine owns 1st serial rights
        Magazine is copyrighted

Advertising rates:

1/2 page black & white:	$275
Full page black & white:	$500
Cover 3 black & white:	$500
Cover 4 black & white:	$500

Reviews:

        "...witty, irreverent and informative." (*Inside Media*)
        "...a splendid addition to the public enlightenment." (Arthur Schlesinger, Jr.)
        "...just shows how much interest there is in the Vice President." (David Beckwith, Press Secretary to Dan Quayle)

Cross-indexed:

        Political Humor
ISSN: 0149-5452

The Once and Future Quayle

by Tim Grana

I am old enough to remember a time when Barry Goldwater was widely regarded as a crazed fanatic capable of unspeakably lunatic acts (sending U.S. Marines into Vietnam, say, or bombing Cambodia). And I fled America after the '72 election on the grounds that no nation which returns Nixon to power can be safe. I did not understand, as Edgar learns in King Lear, that

> *The worst is not*
> *So long as we can say 'this is the worst.'*

If I thought then that we Americans had a monopoly on mediocrity, I now know from my long exile that Outstanding Imbeciles can be found in every corner of the globe. But only in America are they afforded such power and prestige.

The rest of the world marvels at us, crediting us with superhuman self-confidence in placing our National Embarrassments so firmly centre on the Global Stage. Countless foreigners have asked me why we can put a human on the moon, but not in the White House.

I have met Frenchmen astounded by the farcical "'L'etat, c'est moi'" pronouncements of Dick Nixon and Germans dumbstruck by the suicidal Prussian loyalty of G. Gordon Liddy. Incredulous African dissidents fleeing the notorious Emperor Bokhassa have demanded of me how Gerald Ford could ever have become a Head of State. On the topless beaches of the Algarve, I have struggled to translate for bewildered Portuguese the true meaning of brother Billy Carter's "FREE BEER FOR NAKED WOMEN" offer.

To this day, few Europeans believe Reagan actually served two terms and challenge me to tell how it came to pass. I have witnessed the most stolid BBC correspondent unable to stop giggling while reporting Ollie North's testimony. I have even faced a dozen Shi'ites aching with laughter at the phenomenal religious fanaticism of Oral Roberts held hostage in the Tulsa Prayer Tower by God Himself. Through all these tribulatons, I have loyally endeavoured to defend our nation's Good Name.

And then came Danforth.

This, surely, is the *pons asinorum* of American patriotism. From the moment he was selected, Europeans have been aggressively insisting I explain the inexplicable.

And heaven knows I've tried. "Bush," I tell them, "took a strong pro-life stance and thus had to balance his ticket with Quayle, who embodies all the arguments favoring abortion." Few are convinced by this, so I usually go on to quote H.L. Mencken: "Nobody ever went broke underestimating the American taste."

But the problem is power, not aesthetics. Quayle calls into question the efficacy of our democratic restraints. Caligula was an absolute dictator when he foisted his steed upon the Roman Senate, but even he felt constrained to appoint the whole horse.

The British keep asking me if we'll finally admit 1776 was a terrible mistake, beg forgiveness and return to the colonial fold. My American pride rejects this solution outright, but the proposal does il-

---

Foreigners ask me why we can put a human on the moon but not in the White House.

---

luminate the problem. And that, it seems, is that our unquenchable thirst for razzmatazz and showmanship, although 'good box office', does not entail 'fit to govern.' There is no reason why someone clever enough to understand the complexities of our economy and foreign relations should also be photogenic, yet such is our disastrous expectation. But if we were to adopt the British model, whereby a crowned head presides over official Pomp and Circumstance without actually exercising a drop of power, then we could safely continue to indulge our national predilection for elevating the unlikely.

In other words, it's time to install an All-American Monarchy. Quayle should be King.

This may seem to go against the American temper, but in fact we have always harbored a secret longing for Royalty. Washington himself proposed "Your Mightiness" as the form of address for the president. Note how those who today stand by their Dan are reduced to wailing, "As VP, he should be respected" — as if the job were a regal inheritance. This kind of deference spared George III and Ludwig of Bavaria the grisly fate of many an elected leader, and reappears in the unbounded American enthusiasm for the antics of Charles and Di.

As King Danforth the Ever-Ready, Quayle could reign, but not fool. His lavish coronation at L.A.'s Crystal Cathedral will bring hope and comfort to Senator Hruska's fabled hoards of 'ignorant and ill-read' Americans. Heritage USA can be the Royal Palace from which the enthroned King Quayle will shine forth as a 'beacon of hope' to our numerous Conservatives who miss the Middle Ages. Mr. Izzo may find himself dubbed with a 7-iron and told to "Arise, Sir Paul, Duke of Connecticut." At colorful tourneys, such Knights of the Round Think Tank can compete for the favors of Lady Kirkpatrick by jousting against liberal strawmen — while the actual government quietly sets about correcting the trade deficit from the Reagan years.

The future investiture of Tucker as Prince of Disneyland will be full of photo opportunities and Right Royal soundbites. *Time* will speculate on Princess Corinne's choice of worthy commoner (Matthew Broderick or Michael J. Fox?) for her Consort. CNN will bring us hourly updates as the Foremost Family makes its Royal Progress across the fairways of the Midwest. While efficient (if dull) officials guide our nation towards peace abroad and prosperity at home, sufferers of genital herpes can ceremonially petition Queen Marilyn for her Royal Touch of healing.

Vivat! Vivat Rex Americae!   QQ

Tim Grana is an American living in Europe.

Saddam, continued from page 11

tacks Saudi Arabia and support in the U.S. begins to erode?

Quayle avoided this question and instead pointed out that support of the Arab community was a prerequisite to Bush's deployment of U.S. troops. "We do need to have the Arab unity," Quayle emphasized. Koppel decided not to press the original question since Quayle now actually raised perhaps a more serious one - what if the resolve of the Arab nations weakens?

Koppel: "You're telling me if we don't have the Arab unity we might have to rethink whether we stay in there?"

Quayle: "I'm not saying that we rethink about staying in there. I'm saying it is essential to the policy to have Arab unity. We have it, we have it now, and it was one of the requirements that the President wanted to make sure that he had before we went in there."

This Q&A set had the remarkable quality of being infinitely repeatable — Koppel's question would sound like a logical follow-up to Quayle's answer, and Quayle's response would sound like an answer each time. If Arab unity was a prerequisite, what do we do if it fades? Not answered.

Endless loops make bad television, so Koppel moved on. If a military solution is what it takes, how can we avoid a protracted conflict with a "minimum loss of life"?

Not to worry says Quayle, "from an historical basis, Middle East conflicts do not last a long time." Koppel struggled to hide his disbelief. What about the last 40 years

"From an historical basis, Middle East conflicts do not last a long time."

of Arab-Israeli conflict, the war in Lebanon since 1982? Koppel cited more examples without even mentioning the bloody 8-year Iran-Iraq war, and stopping short of the arguable truth that conflict in the Middle East has gone on uninterrupted for over 3,000 years.

Quayle suddenly remembered the "key to peace" phrase that had obviously been in his script. The key to peace and stability, he blurted, is for Saddam Hussein to withdraw from Kuwait and release the hostages. The VP clearly felt he had returned to safe ground.

But Hussein would probably be overthrown if that happened, Koppel noted. "I don't know what would happen to Saddam Hussein," Quayle admitted. An honest enough answer, but if the key to peace relies on an action that Hussein would never take, then it's a key to a door that's nailed shut.

In his closing remark, Quayle finally came clean in his own muddled way: "This is the Middle East, and anybody that can predict with any precision what is going to happen in the Middle East, I just happen to disagree with them. You cannot make a prediction one way or another. The only thing you can do is the right thing, and the President is doing the right thing, he's pursuing every door to peace, and we hope that's the answer, but we don't know."

End of interview, with the big question still hanging: What are these mysterious "doors to peace" that Bush is pursuing?

The Realist

Publisher: Paul Krassner
                  P.O. Box 1230
                  Venice, CA 90294
Format: Newsletter
Editor: Paul Krassner
Phone: (213) 392-5848
Founded: 1958 (operations suspended in 1974); (begun again in) 1985
Description: **The Realist** is a newsletter of social-political satire.
Frequency: 4 issues per year
Subscription rates:
                  12 issues: $23.00
Page size: 8 1/2" x 11"
Production: Laserprinted
Printing: Offset
Binding: Folded
Circulation: 3,000
Author information:
                  Newsletter accepts unsolicited manuscripts
                  Newsletter acknowledges unsolicited manuscripts
                  Reports in 3 weeks
                  Newsletter pays 10 cents per word
                  Author owns rights to article
                  Newsletter is not copyrighted
Advertising rates: Advertisements are not accepted
Reviews:
                  "The best satirical periodical published in America." (*Library Journal*)
                  "Acid comedy in the tradition of Lenny Bruce and Mort Sahl." (*Playboy*)
                  "Krassner not only attacks establishment values; he attacks decency in general." (Harry
                  Reasoner)
Cross-indexed:
                  Social Sciences Humor
                  Arts Humor
                  Political Humor

Roasted

Nancy Cain

Of all the things that Harlan Ellison has yelled out (and he has a black belt in Mouth), of all the times he has lunged across the desk at a terrified producer, threatening to rip out his liver, he never expected to be sued by an unknown writer for a compliment.

At the Hollywood Press Club on a Saturday night, Ellison is being roasted for the benefit of his own defense fund. Film critic Digby Diehl hosts a group on the stage which, he says, "personifies Ed Meese's personal nightmare."

The roasters: comedian-actor Robin Williams; Ray Bradbury, the grandfather clock of science-fiction; screen-writer David Gerrold; Phil de Guere, producer of *Twilight Zone*; Stan Lee, the dirty old uncle of comic books; Robert *Psycho* Block; sci-fi writer Robert Silverberg; *The Realist*'s Paul Krassner; and, of course, the lawyer, Henry Holmes, Jr.

The auditorium is packed to the rafters at $25 a head. Bradbury notes that "no bigger crowd has gathered since Harry Cohn's funeral—give 'em what they want and they all show up." And what do we get? An insult, meta-insult orgy for one of the angriest short guys in town. Why? So that Harlan can pay his legal fees.

"It's an eerie feeling," says Gerrold, "to think that the proceeds from tonight's benefit are going directly to pay the maintenance on Henry Holmes' Rolls Royce." He exaggerates. "Really, Paramount Pictures paid for the Rolls. We're buying the cellular phone."

It is reported that Harlan is the most famous native of Painsville, Ohio. It is revealed that "his parents were normal, but the milkman was a syphilitic dwarf."

Dwarf? "Harlan Ellison is so short that he goes up on his girlfriend," says Silverberg. On the dais, Williams and Krassner simultaneously cross that joke off their imaginary lists.

Short? "Actually, this isn't a roast," says Krassner, "it's more like a microwave."

There are more short jokes than you can shake a toothpick at. "Short? I carry a life-sized portrait of Harlan in my wallet." Or, "Nasty, brutish and short. It's a multiple choice. A: Hobbes' description of the conditions of life; B: Harlan Ellison; C: Sex with Harlan Ellison?"

Speaking of sex with...: "If it's true that you are what you eat, Harlan would be a vagina."

Gerrold is still on the lawyer. "Henry Holmes is really a very religious man. Every day before he goes into court he says the lawyer's prayer: Oh, Lord, let there be evil-doers and thieves; let there be strife among our children; let there be hardship and travail; lest they servant perish."

Gerrold must be reminded that this is a roast for Ellison. "I know, but it's hard to concentrate on Harlan when there are so many other tempting targets."

A telegram is read from Isaac Asimov, with a P.S.: "Kick him in the balls—signed, Frank Sinatra."

But seriously, folks, it's a first Amendment thing. Michael Fleischer, a comic-book-novel writer is suing Ellison for a statement he made in a review in *Comics Journal* back in 1980. He thinks that Harlan defamed him in print. Ironically, Harlan in his way really meant to compliment Fleischer, calling him "crazy" like H.P. Lovecraft and other renowned writers. But Fleischer is seeing a psychiatrist and an attorney, so he takes the epithet literally. This makes Ellison very mad.

"Angry? Harlan has had a chip on his shoulder so long his armpits are infested with termites."

Holmes remarks that instead of suing, Fleischer should have just stood up in the same forum and said that Harlan is full of shit. But now, it's pending—the defendants are Ellison and Gary Groth of Fanagraphics, publisher of *Comics Journal*. The plaintiff is suing for a million dollars plus punitive damages, interest and attorney fees.

"The fact that Ellison is a self-made man," says Gerrold, "relieves God of a great responsibility." He admits to being Harlan's friend for six years. "Of course, I've known him for eighteen years...."

De Guere has the dubious distinction of having given Harlan his longest period of employment. "It took him nine months before he figured out how to shoot himself in the foot at *Twilight Zone* and get canned. But of all the people I have worked with, Harlan is by far the shortest."

Childhood friend Silverberg takes exception. "He's not so short any more. He's wider than he used to be, he's thicker, and he's taller. By damn, he's moving in all directions." They are so close that Silverberg is "the only one who would stab Harlan in the front."

"Harlan doesn't have a short fuse," says de Guere, "he *is* a short fuse."

Lee disagrees. "Harlan is a very difficult person to arouse. Ask any of his former wives." Ellison has a special place in his heart. "He's right up there with the tax collector and the periodontist."

Block, "who has provided a permanent career for Tony Perkins," is amazed at how many people have nothing to do on a Saturday night. He recalls first meeting Harlan in 1952. "He was 18, and I was unlucky."

Back in those days, Block reminisces, "Harlan was interested in re-writing other people's work. He took me into a nearby drug store and showed me how he had erased all the M's off all the Murine bottles." But I wanna tell ya...

Harlan is not all bad. Block notes that he never stops working—"except for those four glorious weekends when he got married."

And he's got politics too. Krassner points out that "Harlan is on the right side of a lot of important fights. He's fought against racism and sexism. That's why this whole panel is white males." Harlan an egomaniac? Krassner says that's true, "partially because at the moment of sexual climax, Harlan calls out his own name."

Williams shouts: "Was it good for *me*?"

Krassner continues: "Harlan has a typewriter with only two letters—M and E. And on it, he has written 42 books as well as 300 of Steve Allen's songs plus a few of Lyndon LaRouche's speeches."

Krassner says that "Harlan has always refused to get involved with the drug world—as a user. However, he *is* a dealer. In fact, he was the connection for Kathy Evelyn Smith."

There is a long "Oooooooh" from the audience, now in Roast Heaven. They know that Williams and Robert DeNiro had been with Smith and John Belushi the night of Belushi's death.

"Oh, that's a good one," says Williams, holding himself in his chair.

"Listen, " Krassner says, "if she didn't plea-bargain, you wouldn't be here tonight."

Mock steam pours out of Williams' ears.

Roasting.

Silverberg tells about the time Harlan passed his new watch around. It was one of those watches with huge numbers. What with Harlan not being the punctual type and his buddies knowing it and all, one of the guys set the thing two hours ahead just to see if he'd notice. He didn't notice, and he was on time for all of his appointments the whole next week. Well, that worked so well they decided to push his desk calendar a year ahead, and Harlan actually met three deadlines.

Now it is time for the star of the evening, "the Messiah of comedy," as Rona Barrett has called him.

"Robin Williams has been called the king of improv," says Diehl, "and he has proven it tonight by interrupting everybody, stepping on their lines, doing schtick. He's been about as annoying as he can be."

"I loved that review, though," says Williams, referring to Diehl's pan of *Club Paradise*.

"I was hoping you hadn't seen it, Robin. It's said of you in Hollywood that you don't read your scripts. Anyway, ladies and gentlemen, I'd like to bring you Robin Williams, fresh from *Club Paradise*, his biggest failure yet."

Say, whose roast is this anyway?

"Thank you, Gary Franklin [the film reviewer Diehl replaced]. What can you say about a man who's a TV critic? A man who looks at a good film and letters it like a report card. Is that art? I think not. And I'd like to thank Harlan's lawyer for proving, God, is there a reason for law? I think not. And I'd like to thank Mr. Krassner for all the Kathy Smith references. That's some funny stuff." Fake hostility.

"I really don't know Harlan for shit," confesses Williams. He calls him "a tall Paul Williams, a white Paul Simon."

Words fly like a swarm of gnats on speed. Williams is visiting Ellison's house. "It's like Notre Dame done by Sears. There's Harlan, naked, playing in his toys with a beautiful shiksa goddess jumping up and down saying, "I like him. He's smart."

Now Williams is Georgie Jessel, now he's a little boy in the bathroom—"I'm reading Bradbury, dad." Now it's *Star Trek*, wait, a penis joke. "If you're hung like a field mouse, don't stand in the wind." And now a toast, gee, he's overcome, he suppresses a sob. "It's just taken me so far down to be here. I wish I could cry but I don't care."

Tumultuous applause.

"Well," says Diehl, "it's been basically a really hostile, ugly night, with a lot of lame old jokes and sentimental drivel. But we still have the ritual forgiveness to look forward to." He introduced Ellison, "a man with the milk of human kindness dripping from his fangs."

"Ha, ha. Very funny, I'm sure." Harlan is sad. "I had a friend once, but the wheels fell off." He's got no friends. "Zip friends," he says. "Dust is my friend," he says. "And what of these fuckers here? Robin Williams can't even get a pair of pants that fits him."

"There's a reason for that, Harlan."

"Yeah, sure. It was for you they made up the phrase, 'Is it in yet?' You wanna talk about taste, Williams? I've got four words for you: *Club Paradise* and *The Survivors*."

"Yeah, on a double bill with *Man With a Dog* [for which Ellison wrote the screenplay]."

Harlan goes on with his counter-insults.

David Gerrold? "He's been in and out of the closet so many times we're having him Martinized in the morning."

Bob Silverberg? "He put the roast into deficit spending because his live-in wanted to fly down with him for the event because she wants to meet Robin Williams. You wanna meet him? Look up here, bimbo! Karen, Williams. Williams, Karen..."

Robert Block? "He has made a living for the last 200 years sticking ice picks in his characters' eyes and is responsible for an entire generation of Warpo's who think that entertainment is dinner prepared with a chainsaw."

Stan Lee? "One cannot say enough about Stan Lee that Stan Lee hasn't already said about himself."

Digby Diehl? "It was Digby who got fired from the *Herald* for saying that Judith Krantz is to literature what Dachau is to health spas. A man whose noblest desire is to become Gene Shalit."

Phil de Guere? "It was wonderful working for Phil. Like twelve months in the fucking Gulag. Phil is to kindness what Attila the Hun was to good table manners."

Ray Bradbury? "The king of the goyim—hey, I just figured out how to make you suffer. I'll read you one of Bradbury's poems."

Paul Krassner: "I want to thank my old chum Krassner for being here tonight. I want to commend him on his restraint in the remarks he made. Or perhaps it was only caution on his part because I promised if he fucked around with me I'd let on that he caught his herpes from Nancy Reagan."

Henry Holmes? "Now I can pay the staggering usurious legal fees this little gentile bastard lays on me every month."

As the weary crowd begins to squirm in their seats, the party is winding down. "Harlan's only fear is that he'll get in a car accident and have to re-live this event," say Diehl, taking the podium once more. "And in the true tradition of roasting, that tradition being to talk dirty and mention a big name, thank you all for coming. And join us next week when our guest roastee will be Mother Teresa."

Krassner blurts out, "I fucked *her*."

Screaming, hooting, stomping.

Williams jumps onto his feet. "Gandhi is going, 'Who is this man? He may not get through the gates of heaven for that line.'"

Ellison says, "Thank God Krassner got off one good one."

"I guess I just fell into the insult mode," explains Krassner.

"Basically," says Silverberg, "The roast is a really ugly, repugnant, immature and childish art form. I hate it. And I will only do one if Harlan is the target."

A compliment was originally perceived as an insult, and consequently we have had an evening of insults which were really compliments.

By the way, Harlan won his case. Say what you will.

Reprinted by permission of the publisher from **The Realist**, June, 1987, pp. 6-7.

S.C.R.O.O.G.E. (Society to Curtail Ridiculous, Outrageous, and Ostentatious Gift Exchange)

Founder: Charles G. Langham
Publication: **S.C.R.O.O.G.E. Newsletter**
Publisher: **S.C.R.O.O.G.E.**
             1447 Westwood Road
             Charlottesville, VA 22901
Format: Newsletter
Editor: Charles G. Langham
Phone: (804) 977-4645
Founded: 1979
Description: **S.C.R.O.O.G.E.** was founded as a good-natured protest against commercial aspects of the Christmas season. We publicize examples of extreme commercialism and give an award for the earliest Christmas display in a store. **S.C.R.O.O.G.E.** gives hints on low-cost Christmas gifts and satirizes ostentatious modes of celebrating the holidays. The organization is not anti-Christmas; we just believe that certain aspects of it have gotten out of hand. The **S.C.R.O.O.G.E. Newsletter** highlights examples of rushing the Christmas season and absurd gifts. We advise people on methods to reduce Christmas spending while still enjoying the holidays. We publish a poem (by our poetry editor), generally humorous in nature, on inappropriate celebrations of Christmas.
Frequency: 1 issue per year
# of issues published in 1991:   1
# of issues to be published in 1992: 1
# of issues to be published in 1993: 1
Subscription period: The **S.C.R.O.O.G.E. Newsletter** is issued on the Friday after Thanksgiving to all members in good standing
# of members: 1,237
Subscription rates (includes membership and newsletter):
             1 year/2 years: $2.00 $4.00
Average # of pages per issue: 4
Page size: 8" x 10 1/2"
Production: Typewritten/word processed
Printing: Xeroxed
Binding: Stapled on surface of publication
Author information:
             Authors should inquire first before submitting materials for consideration
             Newsletter reports in 2 weeks
             Authors receive free membership in exchange for articles or poetry accepted
             Newsletter is not copyrighted
             Publisher indicates in newsletter that rights are reserved by author(s)
Advertising rates: Advertisements are not accepted
Cross-indexed:
             General Humor

Seasoned Shopper: 1984

Debbie Hughes Gunia

'Twas a hot, muggy day in the middle of summer.
The beach and the pool were jam-packed—what a bummer!

My house was an oven—the A.C. revolted.
For relief from the heat, to the new mall I bolted.

I decided to search for pre-holiday buys,
As August was waning and Labor Day nigh.

When I entered the mall and my sunglasses steamed,
The stifling summer was not what it seemed.

A man dressed as Santa from head to his toe,
And the shade of his suit matched his sunburned red nose.

He was hosting a pre-Christmas sales promotion,
Creating a fever of buying emotion.

The Christmas card discounts attracted a flock
That snatched up each tree-trimming trinket in stock.

The T-shirted shoppers tramped each other's toes
As they rummaged through snow boots and half-priced ski clothes.

I bought tree lights and garland and stocking for pets,
But Christmas seemed listless through sun-screen and sweat.

I was humming that "Santa was coming to town."
Then I thought of our heat-wave and felt a let-down.

With shopping all finished, would December seem funny?
Nothing left but to shop for that old Easter Bunny.

Reprinted from the **SCROOGE Newsletter** by permission of the publisher and author.

The Silly Club Rag

Publisher: Silly Club
                P.O. Box 536583
                Orlando, FL 32853
Format: Newsletter
Editor: Danno Sullivan
Founded: 1981
Description: **The Silly Club Rag** is a newsletter for a fictional organization—The Silly Club.
Frequency: 6-8 issues per year
# of issues published in 1991:   6-8
# of issues to be published in 1992:   6-8
# of issues to be published in 1993:   6-8
Subscription period: Subscriptions run from the date the order is received
Subscription rates:
             1 year: $10.00
Average # of pages per issue: 8
Page size: 8 1/2" x 11"
Production: Laserprinted
Printing: Offset
Binding: Folded and loosely collated
Circulation: 400
Author information:
             Newsletter accepts unsolicited manuscripts
             Reports in 2-4 weeks
             Pays $1-$5 per article
             Author owns rights to article
             Newsletter is copyrighted
Advertising rates: Advertisements are not accepted
Cross-indexed:
             General Humor
             Cartoons/Illustrations/Graphics

12 Jan. 18— Noticed body is covered with "dirt." Unpleasant.

16 Jan. When I don new clothes, this "dirt" is transferred to them—thus soiling the clothes.

17 Jan. If dirt can be transferred to clothing, could it not be removed from the body in

From Les Notebooks de

LOUIS PASTEUR

some other way? Or is clothing key?

18 Jan. Experiments underway. Instead of clothing, have covered myself with wood. Tomorrow I will know if will rub off the dirt.

w o o d

19 Jan. *Failure.* Upon removing wood, I found that not only was I still "dirty," but that I had splinters in several embarrassing spots.

2 Feb. Have decided to cover myself with tomato juice in attempt to remove dirt. Have ordered two barrels-full from Vienna.

his scrub brush

12 Feb. Success! By "laving" my body in tomato juice, I have succeeded in removing all dirt from my body. Unfortunately, I am

now covered with tomato juice. I feel I am very close to a breakthrough.

13 Feb. *Incroyable!* Remaining tomato juice on body actually attracts dirt. Still, feel that liquid, in some form, is essential.

4 March I hesitate to be certain, but I believe I am finally "clean." I

his washcloth

used plain water and a device I call the "washcloth" to wipe all surface pollutants away. I feel fresh and invigorated. The final test will be to try on new clothes.

4 March (Evening):

Dressed for dinner in new shirt, collar, and coat. Received many comments on "something different." Later I excitedly undressed in my laboratory and upon examination—my clothing was still clean!

6 June Though I feel my washing system is a success, am experimenting with something I found in the maid's pantry. She calls it "soap."

8 July Mother tells me people have been washing with soap and water for years and why wouldn't I listen to her before? I am despondent for I've already printed posters for the lecture tour. Regardless, I am happy to be clean, and I think right now I'll go have a glass of milk.

Reprinted from **The Silly Club Rag** by permission of the editor.

Society for the Preservation and Enhancement of the Recognition of Millard Fillmore, Last Of the Whigs (S.P.E.R.M.F.L.O.W.)

Founder: Phil Arkow
Publication: **The Fillmore Bungle**
Publisher: S.P.E.R.M.F.L.O.W.
               PO Box 712
               Cascade, CO 80809
Format: Newsletter
Editor: Phil Arkow
Phone: (719) 694-2102
Founded: 1975
Description: The **Society for the Preservation and Enhancement of the Recognition of Millard Fillmore, Last Of the Whigs** celebrates mediocrity in American life as epitomized by Millard Fillmore. Members are Fillmorons and collect Fillmorabilia. We publish the only newspaper in America dedicated to mediocrity (all others achieve the same results—we're the only one with this as our purpose). We hold an Annual Dearthday Party on or about January 7. We also issue an annual Medal of Mediocrity Medal from our Department of Redundancy Department.
Frequency: 1 issue per year
# of issues published in 1991:   1
# of issues to be published in 1992: 1
# of issues to be published in 1993: 1
Subscription period: "Periodic" or "Life"
Annual membership dues (newsletter is included in price):
               1 year: $ 5.00
               Life: $10.00
Average # of pages per issue: 12
Page size: 8 1/2" x 11"
Production: Laserprinted
Binding: Stapled on surface of publication
Author information:
               Newsletter accepts unsolicited manuscripts
               Newsletter does not acknowledge receipt of unsolicited manuscripts
               Author receives no payment for articles accepted
               Newsletter does not concern itself with copyright of individual articles
               Newsletter is not copyrighted
Advertising rates: Advertisements are not accepted
Cross-indexed:
               General Humor
               Social Sciences Humor
               Political Humor
               History Humor
               Political Science Humor
               Religion Humor
               Sociology Humor

And now, it's one of those 1,000 points of blight:

The
Fillmore Bungle

An occasional publication dedicated to the
wonderful, wussful, wistful world of mediocrity

Society for the
Preservation and
Enhancement of the
Recognition of
Millard
Fillmore,
Last
Of the
Whigs

P.O. Box 712
Cascade, Colo. 80809

Vol. 1, No. 41 December, 1990

It Ain't Over Even When The Fat Lady Sings!

Announcing the Winner of the 1990 Medal of Mediocrity Medal — *Roseanne Barr*

She propelled a mediocre stand-up comedy routine into the nation's most successful TV sitcom, proving once again how much of a lowest common denominator TV is. She became a role model for everyone who ever dreamed of making it big in California, especially all the whales who suicidally beach themselves periodically on the shores of sunshine. Her discovery of her illegitimate daughter and her divorce antics caused many to wonder how many trees were cut down to cover these stories about which few really cared. In short, she had it all — and lots of it.

But then she "crossed the boundaries of good taste," according to the *National Enquirer*, who should know about these things. She and her new husband dropped their pants in front of the "Roseanne" crew to show off their new tattoos of each other's names scrawled on their voluminous behinds. Later, the two mooned an audience of thousands at a World Series game.

Then came The Song. On national TV, she screeched the Star Spangled Banner at a San Diego Padres game. She plugged her ears with her fingers and started shrieking the words. When fans began booing, she grabbed her crotch and spit on the ground to mimic baseball players' lack of style. At year's end, she was still singing — or a reasonable facsimile thereof — in public.

Many American celebrities have blown it, crossing the boundaries of good taste once they'd risen to the top and thought they were immune — witness the excesses of Richard Nixon and Gary Hart. Others have proven the Peter Principle by switching careers instead of sticking with what they do best — witness Pia Zadora's supposed singing or Brooke Shields' alleged acting. But Roseanne Barr tramped tastelessness down to new depths. Admittedly, the Star Spangled Banner (which has only been our National Anthem for 59 years) glorifies war, is a bear to sing and is based on an 18th Century bawdy drinking song "To Anacreon in Heaven" in honor of an obscure ancient Greek poet. Admittedly, others have botched it as badly, from Jimi Hendrix's guitar-shattering rendition at Woodstock to Johnny Paycheck's Alzheimers in Atlanta when he sang, "Oh, say, can you see/it's cloudy at night/What so loudly we sang/at the daylight's last cleaning".

Mediocrity has always been essential to American government, but Roseanne Barr was the first person to make patriotism mediocre by singing The Star-Spangled Bummer. And for that, plus her lack of singing ability, we award her the 1990 Millard Fillmore Medal of Mediocrity Medal with a special Milli Vanilli Disc of Distinction. Millard Fillmore probably couldn't carry a tune in a bucket either.

Best Female Non-Vocalist of the Year
Roseanne Barr

Sons of the Desert

Founders: Dr. John McCabe, Orson Bean, Al Kilgore, Chuck McCann, John Municino
Publications: **The Intra-Tent Journal**
              Pratfall
Publisher (**The Intra-Tent Journal**): Scott MacGillivray
                                         P.O. Box 501
                                         Ipswich, MA 01938
Publisher (**Pratfall**):   Lori Jones
                                         P.O. Box 83415
                                         Universal City, CA 91608

Founded: 1974
Description: The **Sons of the Desert**, the international society devoted to the works and persons of Laurel and Hardy, takes its name from one of the best films by that matchless pair. In the film, Stan and Ollie, by unsubtle contrivance, fool their wives and sneak away for convention high jinks of their lodge, the **Sons of the Desert**. Much of that spirit of playing hookey from the mundane permeates the activities of the **Sons of the Desert**, who foregather frequently in many places to celebrate the spirit of Laurel and Hardy.

The group was founded by Professor John McCabe who soon thereafter contacted Stan Laurel, who consented to the establishment of the society so long as fun and a full commitment to inspired idiocy were to characterize the organization. Over the years, the **Sons of the Desert** has flourished in many places. Every local group (or "Tent") derives its name from one of Laurel and Hardy's films. There are, for example, the Way Out West Tent of Los Angeles, the Two Tars Tent of Philadelphia, The Bullfighters Tent of Mexico City, the Bonnie Scotland Tent of Glasgow, and many others. Over 100 Tents exist, stretching from Denmark to Australia, and their members honor Laurel and Hardy by showing their films at the meetings, usually concluding with (and frequently commencing with) a social hour.

We are NOT a fan club, but a group of buffs. The distinction is an important one. Fans are wildly idolatrous; buffs are discriminating in their admitted fervor for the thing or things they cherish.

In the ultimate, the **Sons of the Desert** celebrate the belief—shared deeply both personally and professionally by the two men they honor—that humor is not only a contribution to life but a vital and integral part of it.

The Intra-Tent Journal is, substantially, a communication device for the 100+ Tents of the **Sons of the Desert**. It allows us to keep in touch with each other's activities, provides updates on our international conventions, and carries learned articles examining the world of Laurel and Hardy—their films, their music, their persons—and rare photographs and information, handled with humor and affection.

Pratfall is a high quality magazine, published infrequently, of feature articles and photographs. Twenty-one back issues exist for sale, all undated and timeless.

The wording of the official Constitution of the **Sons of the Desert** accurately reflects the general flavor of the society. For instance,

Article VI: Despite his absolute lack of authority, the Grand Sheik or his deputy shall act as chairman at all meetings, and will follow the standard parliamentary procedure in conducting same. At the meetings, it is hoped that the innate dignity, sensitivity, and good taste of the members assembled will permit activities to be conducted with a lively sense of deportment and good order.

Article VII: Article VI is ridiculous.

Article VIII: The Annual Meeting shall be conducted in the following sequence: (a) Cocktails, (b) Business meeting and cocktails, (c) Dinner (with cocktails), (d) After-dinner speeches and cocktails, (e) Cocktails, (f) Coffee and cocktails, (g) Showing of Laurel and Hardy film, (h) After-film critique and cocktails, (i) After-after-film critique and cocktails, (j) Stan has suggested this period. In his words, "All members are requested to park their camels and hire a taxi; then return for 'One for the desert!'"

Format of **The Intra-Tent Journal**: Newsletter
Frequency: 4 issues per year
Issues per volume: 4

# of issues published in previous year: 4
# of issues published in present year: 4
# of issues to be published next year: 4
Subscription period: Subscriptions run from the date the order is received
Annual membership dues: Varies per Tent
# of members: 5,000+
Subscription rates:

1-year subscription with membership:	Not available
1-year subscription without membership:	Not available
2-year subscription with membership:	$12.00
2-year subscription without membership:	$12.00
Sample copy:	$ 1.00

Average # of pages per issue: 12
Page size: 8 1/2" x 11"
Production: Typeset
Printing: Offset
Binding: Folded
Circulation: 1,600
Author information:

       Accepts unsolicited manuscripts
       Reports in 2 weeks
       Authors receive no pay for articles accepted
       Magazine is copyrighted

Advertising rates: Advertisements are not accepted
Reviews:

       "If you went to an annual meeting and the first things everybody did was to drink three toasts—one to "Stan," one to "Babe," and one to "Fin"—what would you be at an annual meeting of? If you guessed Old Timers' Day at Yankee Stadium, you guessed wrong. The answer is a meeting of The Sons of the Desert...And the stars were...Stan Laurel and Babe, publicly known as Oliver Hardy. Fin, incidentally, was James Finlayson, Laurel and Hardy's nemesis." (*Saturday Review*)

Format of **Pratfall**: Magazine
Frequency: Irregular
Issues per volume: Varies
Subscription period: Subscriptions are not accepted—only individual issues are sold
Issue price: $2.50 (includes postage)
Average # of pages per issue: 32
Page size: 8 1/2" x 11"
Production: Typeset
Printing: Offset
Binding: Saddle stitched
Circulation: 2,500
Author information:

       Accepts unsolicited manuscripts
       Does not acknowledge receipt of unsolicited manuscripts
       Reporting time varies
       Authors receive 10 complimentary copies of issue in which article appears as payment
       Magazine does not concern itself with copyright of individual articles
       Magazine is copyrighted

Advertising rates: Advertisements are not accepted
Cross-indexed:

       Arts Humor
       Scholarly Review of Humor/Satire
         as a Subject for Study
       Film Media Humor

Opening Remarks by John McCabe, Laurel and Hardy Film Showing, National Film Theatre, London, England, July 29, 1984

I am sure in some way each of us here today has a slightly different view of Stan and Ollie. To me that suggests the wonderful appealing universality of Laurel and Hardy. They appeal to so many in so many different ways. It makes them, I am sure, the most *approachable* of all the great comedians. In looking at all the great film comedians, I am bold enough to offer a quick analysis of their varying appeals to us in terms of approachability.

Charlie Chaplin. The master of them all, as Stan frequently said. We *marvel* at him. That's our chief emotion, if you can call that an emotion. We don't get close to him. He doesn't let us get close to him. I don't think geniuses tend to be *pally*. His magnificent abilities put a barrier between him and us. He's altogether too god-like to be a close and comfortable friend.

Buster Keaton. Second only to Chaplin among the single comedians, was born for the solitudes. In the midst of teeming city streets, he's alone on an island or standing on a vagrant ice floe. He'd be shocked to death if you walked up and introduced yourself.

Harold Lloyd. Just doesn't have time for us. He's much too busy getting into dogged, straight-forward trouble to get to know us. Hanging from that clock or teetering on that girder, he is the most cordial of men, but he just can't reach us, much as he'd like to.

Harry Langdon. (When we do see him, and this is very rarely) is too babyish for us to feel any but the most detached kinship with. We smile at him; he smiles, uncomprehendingly, back at us.

W.C. Fields. We can relish and agree with, but his shy savagery and detached effusiveness hide an inner person he'll never let *us* reach.

The Marx Brothers. Those nihilistic practical jokers, don't even know each *other* for more than a few minutes, let alone us. We'd be useful to them as stooges or butts of jokes, little more. Hilarious, like all the others—but again, like all the others, remote.

Then come Laurel and Hardy. As Babe Hardy said, "I can sit in an average hotel lobby and watch any number of Laurel and Hardys walking by." We not only *see* Laurel and Hardys about us, we *are* Laurel and Hardy at times. The other day I went to the cupboard to get a saltcellar, and as I opened it, the cellar fell down from above, narrowly missing my head. The only difference between that and Laurel and Hardy's world is that both of them would go to the cupboard, Stan would reach up for the salt, and 50 pounds of flour would pour down on Ollie. Their troubles are our troubles with life.

Yet it's more than that, of course. The respectful affection they have for each other they have for the world at large and the people in it—continually going out into that rather dreadful place to make their way with all of us, and continuing to do so despite the structure and buffets the world continues to impose on them.

They are, I think it is fair to say, the most *British* of the great comedians—in that they are (1) instinctively polite; (2) (and this you must forgive) a bit eccentric; (3) determined; (4) imbued with a keen sense of *non*sense; (5) tolerant of folly; and (6) formal, yet warm-hearted.

They are our *friends*.

More,—they—like members of our family—as the years go by, either earn or inspire our love. It's perhaps difficult to say why, but surely they partake of that key quality of children: innocence, innocence in a wise-guy world, innocence that merits affection because at heart we all want to be good, innocence that, when made comic, warms the heart and honors the soul. And when all of this is projected by two men who were in real life close friends, and the most amiable of persons individually, the measure somehow is well rounded out. Everything fits, it all coheres meaningfully. Stan and Ollie, endearingly simple, were Stan and Babe, as nice a pair of human beings as you'd be prepared to meet in a long year's march—men who gave their screen characters an essential coloration of their own gentleness and—yes, and I'm happy to use the word—sweetness.

So we are here, dedicating these few days (to quote from Article 2 of our Constitution) to "the loving study of the persons and films of Stan Laurel and Oliver Hardy." We are here, moreover, in Laurel's homeland and Hardy's ancestral homeland, to further this study. This—and we need look no further than the two bowlers they wear that symbolize Laurel and Hardy—this is a legend in laughter that began in Britain and now fittingly is being celebrated here by the Sons of the Desert in its wider extension as a group, stretching as we do from France to the Netherlands to the States to Australia to Britain to Canada to Mexico and all kinds of places in between. We are home.

SPY

Publisher: SPY Corporation
               5 Union Square West
               8th Floor
               New York, NY 10003
Format: Magazine
Editor: Kurt Andersen
Phone: (212) 633-6550
Founded: 1986
Description: **SPY** is a magazine of satire and journalism that chronicles power and culture in modern America.
Frequency: 10 issues per year
# of issue published in 1991:   10
# of issues to be published in 1992:   10
# of issues to be published in 1993:   10
Subscription period: Subscriptions run from the date the order is received
Subscription rates:

1 year/2 years:	$14.75	$27.75
1 year/2 years (Canada):	US$25.00	US$40.00
1 year/2 years (Foreign):	US$35.00	US$60.00

               Sample copy: $2.95 on newsstand
                            $4.00 for back issue
Average # of pages per issue: 92
Page size: 8" x 10 3/4"
Production: Typeset
Printing: Offset
Binding: Saddle stitched
Circulation: 150,000
Author information:

               Magazine accepts unsolicited manuscripts
               Reports in 4-6 weeks
               Pays 50¢ per word
               Magazine owns 1st serial rights, 2nd serial rights, and nonexclusive anthology rights
               Magazine is copyrighted
Advertising rates:

1/2 page/Full page black & white:	$ 4,313	$ 7,188	
1/2 page/Full page color:	$ 6,470	$10,783	
Cover 2/Cover 3/Cover 4 color:	$13,478	$11,457	$14,988

Reviews:

               "The most talked about and written about magazine."—*Magazine Week*
               "**SPY** has almost single-handedly resurrected the category of American humor in magazine publishing."—*Advertising Age*
               "Like *Saturday Night Live* and *Late Night with David Letterman*, the magazine blends post-60s cynicism about institutions and authority with back handed references to popular culture."—*USA Today*
Cross-indexed:

General Humor	Regional/Local Humor
Sciences Humor	Political Humor
Social Sciences Humor	Cartoons/Illustrations/Graphics
Humanities Humor	Visual Satire
Arts Humor	Film Media Humor
Business Humor	Foreign Language Humor

ISSN: 0890-1759

"The right equipment and the freshest food refine a family tradition." —Martha Stewart

The Joy of—*Screeeech!!! Thud*—Cooking

SPY's HOLIDAY GUIDE TO POLITICALLY CORRECT MEAT-EATING, THE ROADKILL WAY

by Tony Hendra

YOUR VOLVO 740 GL WAGON IS AUTOMOTIVELY CORRECT. YOU GET YOUR news from *MacNeil/Lehrer*. You have compassion for the homeless but feel it's time to get tough on taxes. The jingoism of the Gulf War gave you pause, but you've decided that for the nation as a whole it was cleansing. You refer to the poor as "income-impaired" and to criminals as "morally challenged" and no longer squint slightly when using the term "African American." While Meryl Streep's ghastly attempts at foreign accents grate on you like fingernails on a blackboard, you nonetheless feel she is an enormously talented actress. And culinarily, you have been correct for at least a decade.

Early in the eighties, you embraced ethnic cuisines from regions like Calabria, the Deccan and Ethiopia, whose native populations themselves had no food; you believed that in some obscure way they would benefit from your enthusiasm for baghari jhinga or tibs wot. A little later you discovered the pleasures of baby vegetables. You relished the thought that at a time when we had the oldest president ever, we were eating the youngest vegetables. It's been years now since you ordered a pizza with tomato and extra cheese: your taste in toppings runs more to shrimp-scallop boudin à l'estragon and sautéed radicchio. You feel quiet, patriotic pride over the fact that Californian cabs and zins are routinely being ordered in three-star restaurants in Lyons (by Frenchmen!), and over the spectacular rise of American regional cooking. In a way you have come full circle, since you're sure that Native Americans—who subsist largely on Wonder bread and Thunderbird—are somehow bucked up by your consumption of corn-cactus pudding with chipotle-chile béchamel.

But all this carefully and lovingly assembled correctness can evaporate as fast as Julia's love for Kiefer with the mention of one tiny word: *meat*.

Thanks to the efforts of animal-rights groups like PETA and assorted herds of New Age nutritionists, the cultural status of meat-eating is currently on par with that of drunk driving and headed down toward pedophilia. Even in restaurants that offer dead animals on the menu, ordering one can cause the waitron to look at you as if you'd just tried to tell the one about the three gay guys in a hot tub.

And there is no appealing to reason here. Minds have been made up, another pillar added to the portico of conventional wisdom. It's pointless to argue that the animal-rights movement stems from an *ignorance* of animals, that it's the Disneyfication of nature; that thinking that animals are capable of human emotion because they have big, cute eyes isn't progressive but infantile; that the unpronounceable tag *speciesism* is sophistic, since every species on the planet survives by eating other species; that one's passion might be better directed to the 6 million American children who go to bed hungry than to the dying thoughts of Frank Perdue's chickens. And if you do present these arguments, there'll be no getting back in anyone's good graces—it'll be bootless to whine, as a once-adoring group backs away in disgusted silence, that you really like the music of k. d. lang.

You are a carnivore—a mad, rabid pariah feeding off the carrion of your innocent fellow travelers on Spaceship Earth.

Take heart: an answer to your problem lies no farther away than that Volvo. Cars provide us with a cornucopia of fresh, free-range, nonhormoned game. Meat any caring carnivore can bring to the table with an unblemished conscience. Meat, moreover, from which no slaughterhouse, packager or other culinarily incorrect middleman has made a penny. Known to the French as *nourriture de la route*—or, more colloquially, *la bouffe morte*—roadkill has long been recognized as a hearty addition to French country cooking. In many rural regions of the U.S. as well, it has been a mainstay of traditional local cuisines for as long as there have been beer coolers in pickup trucks.

The possibilities of sophisticated roadkill cooking are almost unlimited. There is absolutely no reason why the imprint of a snow tire (or a deeply embedded hood ornament) need mar the flavor of sumptuous Venaison de la Route Rôti; likewise, caring, loving cooking and a pair of pliers make the classic English dish Pheasant Under Broken Glass a memorable triumph. The recipe for Terrine de Groundhog that appears at right is just one of several for small-mammal pâté. And a fitting hors d'oeuvre it can be for hearty Civet de Possum, Navarin de Chipmunk, Beaver en Papillote or Rack of Raccoon, which is also described here.

TERRINE DE GROUNDHOG
    Serves 6
    The universal question with any pâté or terrine is, *how much fat*? The caring carnivore faces an additional problem: what *kind* of fat? The traditional resource, pork fat, is an obvious no-no, given that traffic-related deaths among pigs are, alas, practically nil.

Groundhogs are not, of course, hogs, but they are fatty. One solution, therefore, is to add a groundhog or two to your recipe, in order to achieve a 2:1 meat-to-fat ratio. An average-size groundhog will yield about 1 1/2 pounds of meat, allowing for impact-related detritus; an extra groundhog in similar condition will yield about 3/4 pound of fat. Voilà! You're in business with a hearty Thanksgiving treat, *plus* you have a generous portion of meat left over for a groundhog bolognese sauce or Swedish groundhogballs.

1 1/2 lb groundhog	*1 tbsp "quatre epices" (e.g., allspice, clove, nutmeg,*
3/4 lb groundhog fat	*thyme, blended according to taste)*
2 tbsp salt	*1 clove garlic, pureed*
1 tsp pepper	*2-3 tbsp Armagnac*

Preheat oven to 325° F. Divide the meat into rough thirds. Grind two thirds smoothly (*Fig. 1*, next page) and coarsely chop the other third. Coarse-chop the fat. Combine all ingredients in a large bowl; mix thoroughly. Place mixture in the center of a large, heavy sheet of aluminum foil. As a tribute to the animals, shape the mixture into a reclining groundhog (*Fig. 2*). Cover tightly with ends of foil and bake on a large cookie sheet for 2 hours. Allow to cool for several hours, garnish with woodland mushrooms, crabapples and wild lettuce, and serve.

SUGGESTED WINES

Suncrest 1990 Muller Thurgaw (Washington State). As the back label says, this is a wine "as natural as the food you eat." Made from the free-run juice of organic grapes. A perfect mate for natural food, such as Terrine de Groundhog.
    NV Colorado Cellars Cherry Wine. Made from a mixture of hand-picked and wind-dropped cherries, this is certifiably the most cruelty-free wine made in North America. A perfect sweet-and-sour foil for the groundhog's naturally fatty meat.

The Stark Fist of Removal

Publisher: The SubGenius Foundation, Inc.
                P.O. Box 140306
                Dallas, TX 75214
Format: Journal
Editor: Rev. Ivan Stang
Phone: (214) 823-8534
Founded: 1980
Description: **The Stark Fist of Removal** features very sick humor and philosophy dedicated to the religion of J. R. "Bob" Dobbs and overthrowing the conspiracy of the Normals. Profusely illustrated. Borderline obscene.
Frequency: 1 issue per year
# of issues published in 1991:   1
# of issues to be published in 1992:   1
# of issues to be published in 1993:   1
1992 Volume: Volume #43 [sic]
Subscription period: Subscriptions run from the date the order is received
Subscription rates:

4 issues:	$20.00
4 issues (Canada):	US$27.00
4 issues (Foreign):	US$30.00
Sample copy:	$ 4.50 (post paid)

Average # of pages per issue: 128
Page size: 8 1/2" x 11"
Production: Laserprinted
Printing: Offset
Binding: Saddle stitched
Circulation: 7,000
Author information:
         Prospective authors should inquire first before submitting manuscripts
         Reports in 2 months
         Author receives 3 complimentary copies of the issue in which the article is published as payment
         Author and publisher share rights to article
         Journal is copyrighted
Advertising rates: Advertisements are not accepted
Cross-indexed:
         Humanities Humor
         Arts Humor
         Political Humor
         Cartoons/Illustrations/Graphics
         Religion Humor

"I walked into Hell the minute I stepped outa my Ma's pussy."
— J.R. "Bob" Dobbs, 1946, recorded in a bar while despondent over a fight with his new wife, "Connie."

Sometimes, as Bob wound up teaching me, things really are as simple as they seem.

"I have decided today to staunchly believe in the afterlife. However, I am not crazy. I know that I have no proof whatsoever of its existence — I *choose* to believe in an afterlife because it is too horrible to think that such a cool stud as myself could be allowed to disappear from the Universe."
— "Bob" at age 15, in his diary

"BOB" is DEAD; LONG LIVE "BOB"

People don't want to hear the Good News. They don't want to believe that "Bob" Dobbs was shot on stage in San Francisco that night of Jan. 21. They don't have FAITH enough that **that man "Bob"** could have his stomach perforated, his head turned to HAMBURGER, and then COME BOUNCING BACK. They don't have enough faith in humanity; they don't have enough faith in *themselves* to really believe in "Bob." They secretly suspected "Bob" was a "joke," a "metaphor," a "literary symbol."

Ha ha — very funny. The last chance for survival of mankind and Slack on Earth... too bad for you he was a *fake*. I SUPPOSE YOU THINK THE CONSPIRACY IS A FAKE *TOO*, EH?? And SLACK??

If "Bob" is dead, then why the hell are *you* alive?

IF "Bob" *is* dead... does that mean that The Bullet is the One True God? That King Slug reigns supreme??

NAY!! NAY, I ANSWER, NAY!!

Whether or not "Bob" was actually killed, whether it was by the hand of one lone nut or a million SubJudases, DOES NOT MATTER. Because, whether you kill him or NOT, "BOB" just plain "IS." He *is* "the Isness of the Business," in the most literal sense.

Yes, "BOB" BE COMING!! — for "Bob" has *always* been, perpetually, *coming*, even in death. "BOB" *IS* A SEX GOD, and no matter what other so-called "churches" tell you, this is no clockwork reality, but a universe powered by cosmic sexual tension — A SQUIRTING & OOZING UNIVERSE!!

So, then, when "Bob" comes with his transformed new Seed-Word, America had best be standing by to GULP IT DOWN LEST HE BE DISPLEASED; for he hath suffered an head wound and lived; his powers shall be multiplied an thousandfold; he will be enabled to easily escape hordes of invisible attack-demons while simultaneously watching over all SubGeniuses, individually, from afar, *while winning at Pac-Man at the same time!!* Already, "Bob" is exercising authority over the demon; living SubGenii the world over report their Luck Planes skyrocketing: album deals, astonishing raises, long-overdue divorces achieved, True Loves found... *it is a harbinger of the Twilight of The Conspiracy!!*

And when "Bob" hath come, he shall be sorely PEED. *PEED!!* For there are MANY AMONG YE who hath FALLEN FROM GRACE, drifted FAR from the e'er-meandering Path o' "Bob," who have been *given over* to Conspiracy lifestyles ... "going to the Pinks" because you *thought* he wasn't *LOOKING* anymore! Oh, "Bob's" been keeping *tabs* on you, alright. "Bob" *knows*. And

81

ACT OF GOD   SMEE WINSTON SMITH

Winston Smith

But there's something you can do. You can *GET RIGHT* WITH "BOB!" You can *keep* that abnormality AFLAME and HANG ONTO THAT SLACK! Bulldog it tenaciously! — for Slack is what the Conspiracy WANTS, it's what the Conspiracy TAKES, but, just because it IS the Conspiracy, and probably doesn't even know what Slack *is*, it can *never* get *enough! The Conspiracy can never get enough Slack* — but that ignorance won't stop it from taking YOURS, bit by bit, piece by piece, until suddenly you wake up and think, *"Hey, wait! Here I am up to my neck in false goods, false drugs, false money, false SEX — but... WHERE'S "BOB"? WHERE'S "BOB"?* Life on Earth will truly be Hell, for you will no longer have "Bob" in your life.

These harsh statements may not go down well on the polished sensibilities of the rationalist, the modernist; but "Bob's" trying to get you to *invest wisely* in THE GREATEST COMMODITY — the potentially most *profitable* aspect of your entire being: the ETERNAL **SOUL GLAND** in your foot that is powered by ALL NATURE! *That's what this is all about...* it isn't POLITICS, it isn't NEW WAVE ART SHIT, it isn't POP PSYCHOLOGY CRAP; what "Bob's" talking about is the ETERNAL "SLACK-FORCE" OF THE SUBGENII OF THIS PLANET, and it is WORTH MORE than everything *else on* the planet! "Bob" Dobbs is here to "broker" the transactions over *your soul* which *will* occur when the Elder Gods begin to hunger for even *more...* to see that you do not sell it for *LESS THAN MARKET VALUE* just because you are IGNO-RANT OF WHAT IT *AND YOU* ARE WORTH!! To see that you don't let it GO TOO CHEAP — because HE knows where you can redeem it LATER at a MUCH, MUCH HIGHER PRICE. **Y E SHALL BE REWARDED AND HAVE SLACK IF YOU BUT HEED IN DISCERNMENT THE MIGHTY WORD OF "BOB."**
Praise "Bob"; Praise "Bob" Praise "Bob" Praise "Bob" Praise "Bob" Praise "Bob" Praise "Bob" Praise "Bob" Praise "Bob" Praise "Bob" Praise "Bob" Praise "Bob" Praise "Bob" Praise "Bob"

YOUR SOUL will be *LAID BARE* to the JUDGING EYE of the *REAL FIST* THAT'S HOVERING OVER YOU RIGHT *NOW;* when descends that Angelic Host, the **Xists,** in terror and glory, you'll be *NAKED* TO *WOTAN* — and HE'LL *KNOW* whether you believed in "Bob" Dobbs or not! Because your *belief* in "Bob" — or your *LACK* of belief — will be *ALL YOU HAVE LEFT.* You'll be QUAKING IN YOUR BOOTS, *PISSING IN YOUR PANTS,* with a skyful of flying saucers overhead and the Tribulations of the End Times erupting all around you, and you'll know *THEN* whether you ever *believed* in *"Bob"* or not. You'll *PRAY for a CAR WRECK,* but there will BE *NO CARS;* you'll *BEG to DIE* but there will BE *NO DEATH.*
GOOD FUCKIN' LUCK.

Norman Conquest

Let Us Help You

82

The Steve Wilson Report

Publisher: D.P.J. Enterprise, Inc.
               3400 North High Street
               Suite 120
               Columbus, OH 43202

Format: Newsletter

Editor: Steve Wilson

Phone: (614) 268-1094 [FAX: (614) 263-LAFF]

Founded: 1991

Description: **The Steve Wilson Report** features articles, field reports, first-person accounts of successful applications of psychology and humor to life and work, plus cartoons, and reviews of relevant books and products.

Frequency: 4 issues per year

# of issues published in 1991:   4

# of issues to be published in 1992:   4

# of issues to be published in 1993:   4

1992 volume: Volume #2

Subscription period: Subscriptions run from the date the order is received

Subscription rates:

1 year:	$29.00
1 year (Canada):	US$35.00
1 year (Foreign:)	US$38.00
Sample copy:	Free (send a S.A.S.E.)

Average # of pages per issue: 6

Page size: 8 1/2" x 11"

Production: Laserprinted

Printing: Offset

Binding: Folded and loosely collated

Circulation: 3,500

Author information:
- Authors should inquire first before submitting manuscripts
- Author receives 20 complimentary copies of the issue in which the article is published as payment
- Newsletter does not deal with the issue of copyright of individual articles
- Newsletter is copyrighted

Advertising rates: Advertisements are not accepted

Cross-indexed:
- Business Humor
- Research on Humor
- Education Humor
- Medical Humor
- Nursing Humor
- Psychology Humor

Stress is No Laughing Matter... Or is it?

Some of you may be reeling after reading the rash of recently released research reports which reinforce what the rest of us had already realized: there is so much stress in the American workplace that it is making us sick—killing us, in fact—and costing us a fortune! And, in Japan, that paragon of work efficiency and motivation, 10,000 executives die every year from "karoshi." Not something that goes along with sushi, "karoshi" means sudden death from overwork.

So far, at age 50, I have spent more than half of my life as a psychologist, looking for ways to improve the quality of life at work. I observe that most companies operate in a way that lends credence to the widely-held belief of employees that work is the crabgrass in the lawn of life. But, a few individuals are proving the truth of what Confucius taught thousands of years ago, "Choose an occupation that you love and you may never have to work a day in your life." Now there's an idea you can live with, and the corporate culture can make it happen!

The Bad News/Good News

A survey of 600 American workers, conducted in January and February, 1991, for **Northwestern National Life Insurance Co.**, found among other sad-but-true discoveries, that more than one-third of employees leave their jobs to try to find a less stressful environment, and for seventy percent of workers job stress causes frequent health problems and made them less productive. The anticipated lifetime disability claim for a 51-year-old worker forced to quit his job for stress-related health reasons would be $252,000, and there are thousands of them.

Just a few more bad-news facts, then the good news. Accountants, as the tax deadline approaches, experience elevated cholesterol levels. Researchers at Ohio State University found that medical students, as examinations approached, will experience reduced disease-fighting immune cells and detrimental changes in other components of the immune system. The same is true of family caregivers of Alzheimer's patients and men and women who have been separated or divorced. And, oh yes, did you know that more people die in this country on Monday between 8 and 9 a.m., than at any other time or day? (And let's just throw in the "Sunday Migraine" phenomenon for good measure.)

Okay, the good news. The same OSU researchers found that positive emotions and support reduce stress and boost immunity, reducing the risk of disease. **Dr. David Abramis**, Management Professor at the University of California at Long Beach, has found that companies that consciously make work fun experience reduced absenteeism, lower health care costs, less turnover, decreased reject rates, and hardy after-tax profits. Hard to believe? Talk to the people at **North American Tool & Die**, **Dreyer's Grand Ice Cream**, **W.L. Gore Associates**, and **Dominos Pizza**. Or ask my clients at **AT&T**, **Westinghouse**, **Ortho Pharmaceutical**, **Walter Reed Army Medical Center**, or a dozen other corporations, hospitals, and universities.

Hot-headed and Burned Out

Try to follow this well-established sequence of psychological effects: if you want to achieve your goals, dreams, and visions, and enjoy life, you had better learn to do one thing if you don't learn anything else. That is: learn how to prevent physical and emotional burnout. Burnout is most often the end result of unabated stress.

The secret to preventing burnout is BALANCE: in nutrition, between work and rest, vocation and recreation, and most important of all, balance in your perspective. **Dr. Theresa Whiteside** at the University of Pittsburgh has clear evidence that stress wears down the immune system and that people under 30 get sick more often in the face of daily stress. Why? Lack of perspective. The young experience emotions more deeply than the middle-aged or elderly. "They haven't evolved a way to deal with stressful events, and they see them as more threatening," she says.

Buddha said it 26 centuries ago, "All we are is a result of what we have thought." That means stress is not caused by events; it is caused by your perceptions of events. Your worried and anxious thinking about your job will make you sick. Is it worth it? There is nothing about your job that will console your family if it kills you but you were good at it (karoshi!). What people will say (as they pay their last respects) is that you must have lost your *perspective*.

There is a great deal of evidence that one of the best ways to maintain a balanced perspective is to *have a good sense of humor*. That doesn't mean being a clown or a jokester. It means having the ability to see the non-serious element in an everyday situation when it just isn't going right.

Crack Jokes, Not Skulls

Psychologically, humor lets you see another way of looking at things, another perspective, from which things may not look so bad. When your perspective is balanced, you are more likely to crack jokes than to crack skulls. When you are in humor, your brain chemistry changes, and your entire physiology changes to keep you physically healthy! It doesn't mean you should joke about everything; that wouldn't be prudent.

I don't know anyone who has been mauled by a lion or trampled by an elephant, but almost everyone has been bitten by a mosquito or stung by a bee. Moral: it's the little things that get you! Having a sense of humor means not getting "done in" by the dozens of minor irritations which occur daily. Studies show that a good sense of humor, and having fun at work will help you to stay healthy, live longer, and be more creative, satisfied, and productive, too. So, the next time you hear some terminally-serious soul saying, "Get back to work...we're not here to have fun," tell him that your laughter means you are working smarter, not harder.

How Do You Do It?

I have collected more than one hundred examples of ways to have fun at work

without turning the workplace into a circus. According to the testimony of dozens of competent managers and executives, each one of these ideas is effectively in place somewhere in America. Some of the things people are doing to stay sane and keep a balanced perspective are just plain silly (jelly-bean fights, barefoot soccer in the halls, belly-laugh "breaks"); some are outlandish (remove an employee's car from the company parking lot and replace it with a wreck, an evening at Chippendales for women employees, a contest for "Ties you wouldn't wear to I.B.M.").

It Pays to Play

The companies that are providing their employees with training in the value of humor and the appropriate ways to have fun are enjoying handsome dividends. Whiteside says that those companies which provide support experience half the burnout rate of companies that don't. Perhaps you are one of the lucky ones and this is going on at your shop or office. If so, may the farce be with you. You see, in all the recorded history of medicine, there is no evidence that anyone has actually "died laughing" but, the term "dead serious" is something you'd better think about. Lighten up!

Thalia: Studies in Literary Humor

Publisher: Jacqueline Tavernier-Courbin
              Department of English
              University of Ottawa
              Ottawa K1N 6N5
              Canada
Format: Journal
Editor: Jacqueline Tavernier-Courbin
Phone: (613) 564-2311 or (613) 230-9505
Founded: 1978
Description: **Thalia** features studies in literary humor.
Frequency: 2 issues per year
# of issues published in 1991:   1
# of issues to be published in 1992:   2
# of issues to be published in 1993:   2
1992 volume: Volume #12
Subscription period: Volume
Subscription rates (outside of Canada, pay in U.S. dollars):

1 year/2 years/3 years:	$15.00	$28.00	$43.00
1 year/2 years/3 years (Library):	$18.00	$34.00	$49.00
Sample copy: $8.00			

Average # of pages per issue: 60
Page size: 7" x 8 1/2"
Production: Typeset
Printing: Offset
Binding: Perfect bound
Circulation: 500
Author information:
        Journal accepts unsolicited manuscripts
        Reports in 2-6 months
        Authors receive no compensation for articles published
        Journal owns all rights to articles
        Journal is copyrighted
Advertising rates (outside of Canada, pay in U.S. dollars):
        1/2 page black & white: $ 50
        Full page black & white: $100
Cross-indexed:

General Humor	Psychology Humor
Humanities Humor	Religion Humor
Arts Humor	
Regional/Local Humor	
Cartoons/Illustrations/Graphics	
Visual Humor	
Scholarly Reviews of Humor/Satire as a Subject of Study	
Research on Humor	
Education Humor	
English Humor	
Film Media Humor	
Foreign Language Humor	
Literature Humor	
Poetry Humor	

ISSN: 0706-5604

THE MARX OF TIME

Wes D. Gehring

The only tradition in our family was our lack of tradition.—
Harpo on the childhood of the Marx Brothers.

How does one describe the influence of the Marx Brothers? Their impact upon American humor and upon American popular culture in general has been immense, and one should mention in particular their significance as cultural icons, their richly ambitious influence upon schools of comedy, their impact upon modern entertainment, and their easing of the transition from silent to sound comedy. Moreover, their comedy has made a distinct imprint upon western culture itself—lofty stuff for a comedy team that struggled for years in the lower levels of vaudeville. This cultural Marx Brothers metamorphosis is also ironic, since the most distinctive characteristic of their comedy has always been its iconoclastic nature. Thus, while in *Horse Feathers* (1932) the Brothers comically dismantle the university life, today's university dissects *Horse Feathers* for educational purposes. But before examining the more philosophical ramifications of their work, permit me to relate a personal story which nicely showcases the ongoing impact of the Marx Brothers upon our culture.

In doing research on a Marx Brothers book (Greenwood Press, 1987), one must, of course, visit archives scattered across the country. Away from family and after long hours in some special collections library, one naturally searches for a diversion. For the student of film, as for many others, this often means going to a movie. Thus, on one Marx Brothers research trip I managed to take in two then current commercial theatre releases: the highly praised Woody Allen film *Hannah and Her Sisters* (1986) and Terry Gilliam's *Brazil* (1985). Though both are comedies in the broadest sense of the word, they are radically different. The former film, like so much of Allen's work, fluctuates between humor based upon the problems of a strongly defined personality comedian (Allen) and a romantic comedy that frequently parodies love itself. But unlike the guarded optimism which frequently closes Allen films, *Hannah and Her Sisters* ends upon a decidedly upbeat note. The film even manages to include the two most archetypal elements of comedy's classic formula for a happy ending—the new beginnings symbolized by both a marriage and a child's birth. In contrast, *Brazil* is the blackest of comedies. Gilliam, best known as the only American member of the British comedy troupe Monty Python, has fashioned a film without hope—a nightmare comedy of the future. Like a slapstick *1984*, *Brazil* offers the standard black comedy message: not only is the individual insignificant, he is forever fated to contribute to his own demise.

Both of these very different films, however, utilized the Marx Brothers as cultural symbols of equally different things. In *Brazil* the anti-establishment heroine watches *The Cocoanuts* (1929) on television. In this case the Marxes represent two things: an iconoclastic ideal for a radical, and comic prophets who recognized early the inherent pointlessness of the modern world. One should also add, the "saturation" comedy style of *Brazil* (à la Monty

Python) has indirect roots in the Marxs' own comically complex presentation. In *Hannah and Her Sisters* a suicidal Allen wanders into a screening of *Duck Soup* (1933). Prior to this he had been asking himself: if the world is without reason, why go on living? But slowly the comedy magic of the Marxes envelops him. Here the Marxes symbolize pure comedy, those random moments of joy which make life worth living. Allen leaves the theatre completely revitalized, once again a believer in hope and in the modest milestones (marriages, births...) of the modern man.

Here, then, was a Marx Brothers researcher who tried and failed, on two successive nights, to find a simple momentary escape from his focus of study. That failure would seem to say a lot about the ongoing significance of the Marxes.

Allen's recognition of the importance of the Marxes is important because he has evolved into one of America's greatest creative artists. His accomplishments range from an Oscar for best motion picture to the O. Henry Award for best short story. And in 1986 the nominating theatre critics for the Pulitzer Prize in drama even recommended his screenplays should be eligible for the competition. This is especially relevant here, for besides calling Allen "America's Ingmar Bergman," the critics' action had been precipitated by the fact that the only narrative script they had agreed upon in their 1986 capacity was *Hannah and Her Sisters*, with its pivotal reference to the Marxes.

One might even say the spirit of the Marxes brings out the best in Allen. This Marx Brothers influence is most pervasively apparent in such early Allen films as *Take the Money and Run* (1969) and *Bananas* (1971). For example, Allen's disguised return from San Marcos (where he,

like *Duck Soup*'s Groucho, has become president!) is straight out of the *Night at the Opera* (1935) scene where the similarly-costumed Marxes also attempt to re-enter the country. And though the most integrated Marx Brothers' influence on Allen (such as gag usage and overall comic framework) occurs early, his most pointed previous highlighting of the Marxes, or more specifically Groucho, had come at the opening of his most acclaimed film—the Academy Award-winning *Annie Hall* (1977). At that time he had quoted Groucho's famous real life putdown: "I would never want to belong to any club that would have someone like me for a member." But not before *Hannah and Her Sisters* had Allen so baldly showcased the importance of the Marxes' comedy art. Moreover, he offered no verbal or printed lead-in (such as even a "now showing" movie poster) as to whom or what the *Hannah* viewer was about to see in this movie-within-a-movie. The *Duck Soup* excerpt, from "The Country's Going to War" number (where the Marxes brilliantly satirize the unthinking jingoism that welcomes war), is simply presented without fanfare as the comic masterpiece it is. While it would be an overstatement to call the Marxes, or *Duck Soup*, the motivating spark behind *Hannah*, one must remember that Allen's narrative goal in the scene is to present a symbol of comedy at its greatest. High praise for these former low level vaudevillians...

This Brain Has a Mouth

Publisher: Free Hand Press, Inc.
               61 Brighton Street
               Rochester, NY 14607
Format: Magazine
Editor: Lucy Givin
Founded: 1990
Description: **This Brain Has a Mouth** is a disability civil rights magazine—the national magazine of people with brains.
Frequency: 6 issues per year
# of issues published in 1991:   6
# of issues to be published in 1992:   6
# of issues to be published in 1993:   6
1992 volume: Volume III
Subscription period: Subscription runs from the date the order is received
Subscription rates:

1 year:	$12.00
1 year (Canada):	US$12.00
1 year (Foreign):	US$12.00
Sample copy:	$ 1.00

Average # of pages per issue: 36
Page size: 8 1/2" x 11"
Production: Laserprinted
Printing: Web offset
Binding: Glue bound
Circulation: 7,500
Author information:
          Prospective authors should inquire first before submitting manuscripts
          Reports in 2 days
          Author receives 5 complimentary copies of the issue in which the article is published as payment
          Magazine is copyrighted
Advertising rates:

1/2 page black & white:	$200
Full page black & white:	$350
Covers:	not available

Reviews:
          "An irreverent, hard-hitting antidote to do-gooderism." (*Disability Rag*)
          "It's harder to wait for my next **Mouth** than the next issue of *Playgirl*." (*I.L.R.U.*)
          "You guys are fun-ny!" (*Concrete Change*)
Cross-indexed:
          Social Sciences Humor
          Cartoons/Illustrations/Graphics
          Law Humor
          Medical Humor
          Nursing Humor
          Psychiatry Humor
          Psychology Humor

PROFESSIONALS ANONYMOUS

There is help! There is hope!
Professionalism... you _can_ overcome it

Do you experience 3 or more of these symptoms?

- **egocentrism**

- **impulsivity** —
reflexively providing
inaccurate or insensitive
prognostic information

- **lack of self-monitor-
ing or error awareness**

- **inability to take the
perspective of others** —
patients, for instance

- **language deficits** —
lack of intelligibility or
uncontrollable use of
demeaning or offensive
terminology

- **self isolation** — keeping
yourself impossible to reach

- **organizational and time
perception deficits** —
scheduling multiple clients,
conference calls, and out of
town meetings during the
same 3-hour time period

- **confabulation** — saying
anything rather than
admitting you don't know

- **difficulty incorporating
new information into
post-training routines**

6

Hi! My name is S_____ and I am a professional.

I was in denial about this for many years. Through the help and kindness of patients and other non-professionals, I have been able to recognize my problem and work toward recovery.

You can too.

No matter how many initials you write after your name, you may still be helped.

How did I become a professional?

The answer may be partly genetic — there are others like me in my family.

But for most of us the roots of our disorder lie in a traumatic process commonly referred to as "professional education" or "training."

Your experience, like mine, may be too traumatic to recollect in detail. You were undoubtedly forced to perform rote memorization.

You were deprived of sleep for prolonged periods and taught exclusively in a technical language so that it became second nature to you.

You were rigorously and repeatedly evaluated for your conformity to the training process.

Common Sense Lobectomy

This little-known procedure is commonly performed during the stress-induced stupor of the training process. Few professionals, even when confronted with its obvious effects, can recall its having been done.

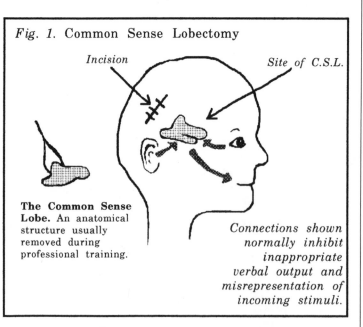

Fig. 1. Common Sense Lobectomy

Incision

Site of C.S.L.

The Common Sense Lobe. An anatomical structure usually removed during professional training.

Connections shown normally inhibit inappropriate verbal output and misrepresentation of incoming stimuli.

7

Thoughts For All Seasons:
The Magazine of Epigrams

Publisher: Thoughts For All Seasons
c/o Michel P. Richard
11530 S.W. 99th Street
Miami, FL 33176

Format: Magazine

Editors: Michel P. Richard (Editor-in-Chief); Roger Wescott, Ray Mizer (Associate Editors)

Phone: (305) 598-8599

Description: **Thoughts For All Seasons** publishes original epigrams and black-and-white illustrations and essays about the epigram as a literary form. What exactly is an epigram? Today the epigram is primarily a prose form, and it often involves a play on words. For example, we could call it a "pithy dithyramb." Often the epigram includes a commentary on a well-known quotation, such as the following: "I think, therefore I am," said Descartes. But I say, "I think, therefore I epigr(am)." In fact, the epigram is a playful thought as well as a play on words. Their cousins include maxims, aphorisms, apothegms, adages, riddles, proverbs, puns, and conundrums. They are also related to bromides, homilies, platitudes, banalities, and truisms, but they don't like to acknowledge this branch of the family.

Frequency: Published irregularly

Issues per volume: 1

# of issues published in 1991:   0

# of issues to be published in 1992:   1

# of issues to be published in 1993:   0

1992 volume: Volume #4

Subscription period: Subscriptions run from the date the order is received

Subscription rates:

1 year (Volume #4):	$4.75 (plus $1.50 postage & handling)
1 year (Canada):	US$4.75 (plus US$1.50 postage & handling)
1 year (Foreign):	US$4.75 (plus US$1.50 postage & handling)
Sample back issue (Vol. #2 or #3):	$3.75 (plus $1.50 postage & handling)

Average # of pages per issue: 80

Page size: 6" x 9"

Production: Laserprinted

Printing: Offset

Binding: Saddle stitched

Circulation: 500-1,000

Author information:

   Magazine accepts unsolicited manuscripts

   Magazine acknowledges receipt of materials within 15 days. Final selection of manuscripts occurs during editorial review process 3 months prior to publication. Authors receive notice at that time.

   Author receives 1 complimentary copy of issue in which article appears as payment

   Magazine owns all rights to the material

   Magazine is copyrighted

Advertising rates:

1/4 page black & white:	$ 50
1/2 page black & white:	$ 80
3/4 page black & white:	$105
Full page black & white:	$125

Reviews:
> "Anyone who appreciates a good quote will applaud this insuperable effort." (Bill Katz, *Library Journal*)

> "The passion that links the name of Geneseo professor Michel Richard with Aristotle and Confucius is his love of epigrams." (Bob Bickel, *Rochester Democrat and Chronicle*)

Cross-indexed:
- General Humor
- Social Sciences Humor
- Cartoons/Illustrations/Graphics
- Religion Humor
- Sociology Humor
- Word Play & Puns

ISSN:0886-6481

What is an Epigram?

The epigram is a form of word play which evolved from epitaphs on tombstones. Because of the material on which it was inscribed, the message had to be brief and literally to the point.

But what is playful about death? Maybe that's the wrong question. Let's put it this way: would you want something heavy on your headstone or something light? "O rare Jonson!" reads the self-congratulatory inscription on the famous poets' tomb in Westminister Abbey. What would you put on yours?

Jonson's volume entitled *Epigrams* was published in 1616, but epigrams can be traced back to the ancient Greeks. Epigrams are not necessarily funny; in fact, some of them are downright somber while others are merely serious. "Those whom the Gods love die young" is an example of the former, while Aristotle's famous dictum that "Virtue consists in loving and hating aright" is an example of the latter.

At about the same time that Aristotle was spreading truth the Chinese philosopher-sage whom we call Confucius was writing maxims which are household pets today: "Better to light one small candle than curse the darkness." (Not bad for an old-timer.)

The Old Testament is a good source of epigrams, and so is the New. Some of the statements attributed to Jesus are profoundly enigmatic, as when he said that "Whosoever will save his life will lose it." In Rome during the early centuries of the Christian era the epigram developed into a rhyme form in the hands of masters such as Catullus, Cicero, Vergil, Horace, Juvenal, and especially Martial. Martial's verses are disconcertingly contemporary, as shown by the following:

> Alike in your disgusting lives
> Oh worst of husbands, worst of wives
> I'm more than puzzled when I see
> Your incompatibility.

During the so-called "Dark Ages" there was a long gap in the literary record but the Renaissance sparked renewed interest in the epigram among humanists, reformers, and literary figures. In Germany the tradition was carried forward by Lessing, Herder, Goethe and Nietzsche. The most illustrious contributors in France were LaRochefoucauld, Voltaire, Descartes, Balzac, Baudelaire, and Anatole France. Of course the list is longest in the English-speaking world, but perhaps that is only because we ourselves speak English. The list includes Edmund Spenser, Ben Jonson, John Donne, Robert Herrick, John Dryden, Jonathan Swift, Alexander Pope, Robert Burns, George Byron, Samuel Taylor Coleridge, Lewis Carroll, Ambrose Bierce, Oscar Wilde, George Bernard Shaw, William Butler Yeats, and Rudyard Kipling. In the 20th Century the epigram has also been appropriated by journalists like Sydney Harris, and by commercial advertising. Epigrams can be found on billboards, on tee shirts, record album jackets, secretaries desks, the *Farmer's Almanac*, and even restroom walls. There is even a magazine of epigrams, and we call it *Thoughts For All Seasons*. The first issue appeared during the bicentennial year of 1976, and the *1984* issue is devoted to the theme of George Orwell's famous novel bearing the same title.

What exactly is an epigram? Samuel Taylor Coleridge answered the question in a rhyme of his own:

> What is an epigram?
> A dwarfish whole
> Its body brevity
> And wit its soul.

The Three Stooges Fan Club

Publication: **The Three Stooges Journal**
Publisher: The Three Stooges Fan Club
P.O. Box 747
Gwynedd Valley, PA 19437
Format: Newsletter
Editor: Gary Lassin
Phone: (215) 654-9466
Founded: 1974
Description of organization: The purpose of **The Three Stooges Fan Club** is to keep alive the memories of the Three Stooges, disseminate information about the Stooges, and generate support for Stooge-related lobbying efforts. A convention is held annually in Philadelphia, featuring rare films and memorabilia, relatives of the Stooges, impersonators, a trivia contest, a pie fight, etc.
Description of publication: **The Three Stooges Journal** contains Stooge news, collectibles information, rare photographs, reviews, Stooge references in the media, etc.
Frequency: 4 issues per year
# of issues published in 1991: 4
# of issues to be published in 1992: 4
# of issues to be published in 1993: 4
Subscription period: Subscriptions run from the date the order is received
Annual membership rates (newsletter is included in the price of membership):
Regular member: $9.00
Subscription rates:

1 year/2 years/3 years:	$ 9.00	$16.00	$23.00
1 year/2 years/3 years (Canada):	US$ 9.00	US$16.00	US$23.00
1 year/2 years/3 years (Foreign):	US$12.00	US$22.00	US$32.00

Sample copy: Free
Average # of pages per issue: 16
Page size: 8 1/2" x 11"
Production: Typeset
Printing: Offset
Binding: Saddle stitched
Circulation: 2,200
Author information:
Newsletter accepts unsolicited manuscripts
Reports in 1 week
Authors receive no compensation, either in cash or free copies
Newsletter does not deal with issue of copyright of individual articles
Newsletter is copyrighted
Advertising rates: Advertisements are not accepted
Cross-indexed:
Film Media Humor

AN INTRODUCTION TO THE THREE STOOGES MGM SHORTS

by Richard Finegan

With the possible release of home video of the shorts made at MGM by Ted Healy and his Stooges, I thought an article of introduction was due. These films are very different from the familiar Columbia shorts we've all seen so often. In these films, Ted Healy is the boss of the act, and dominates Moe, Larry and Curly, none of whom have yet developed the personalities for which they became so well known. It is strange to see Moe being slapped around as much as the other two. But this is early in their film career and they were still literally Stooges to comedian Ted Healy, so he is the leader of the act and the real star of many of these films.

The other thing that makes these shorts so different from the later shorts at Columbia is the fact that these are basically musical shorts and have elaborate dancing numbers included. They were actually promoted as musical shorts. Unfortunately, many Three Stooges' fans may not be interested in seeing these big production numbers inserted sometimes awkwardly into the middle of a Three Stooges comedy. But actually most of these musical numbers are of historical interest in that they were used from older films, some very rare, and some were out-takes or numbers filmed for musical films that were never released. It seems, in fact, that some of these Stooges' shorts were made only for the purpose of showcasing these musical numbers.

In addition to being a Three Stooges fan and researcher, I am also very much interested in the films of the period when sound came in, and especially the musicals of the period, and so it was a thrill to finally be able to see not only the MGM Stooges' shorts, but the musical segments as well. Because the sources of these musical clips were not identified, I decided to try to find out where they were from, and have been able to identify them, and so I offer this guide to the MGM Three Stooges' shorts, for those who would like to know more about them.

The first MGM short starring Ted Healy with Howard, Fine and Howard (as they were billed) was *Nertsery Rhymes*, released July 6, 1933. It was filmed in Technicolor and features two musical numbers taken from earlier MGM pictures. The first is entitled *The Turn of a Fan* (not *The Lady and the Fan,* as introduced in the film). This is a truly beautiful production and I urge anyone viewing this short on video to resist the temptation to scan through it. It is also of historical significance because it was filmed in 1930 for a feature called *The March of Time* that was never finished. In February 1930, MGM announced the production of a new musical tentatively titled *Just Kids,* then *Old-Timers' Revue,* finally settling on the title *The March of Time,* starring Joseph Weber and Lew Fields, DeWolf Hopper, Louis Mann, Marie Dressler, Trixie Friganza, Fay Templeton, Josephine Sabel, Austin Young, and The Dodge Sisters (Beth and Betty). It was to be a part-Technicolor revue with several elaborate musical production numbers. By late 1930, it became clear that the public was starting to lose its interest in such large scale musical pictures, and so MGM decided not to complete *The March of Time* and so it has remained uncompleted and unreleased. MGM did use some of the musical numbers by inserting them into later productions such as the 1933 feature *Broadway to Hollywood* and, of course, the short *Nertsery Rhymes.* "The Turn of a Fan" number features dancers, The Dodge Sisters (Beth and Betty) and was choreographed by Sammy Lee.

The second musical number in *Nertsery Rhymes* is entitled "The Woman in the Shoe" and while "The Turn of a Fan" is beautifully staged, this number has got to be just about the corniest three minutes of film you will ever see. But although it is ridiculous visually, it is worth listening to. The song "The Woman in the Shoe" was written by Nacio Herb Brown and Arthur Freed, writers of *Singin' in the Rain* and many of the greatest songs to come from MGM musicals. In this film, it is sung by an as yet unidentified woman with great harmony vocals by a male quintette called "The Rounders." They also sang in the *Singin' in the Rain* number in the MGM feature *The Hollywood Revue of 1929* and appeared in the 1931 Hal Roach short *The Pajama Party,* as well as other film roles and made records for

Victor in the late 1920's.

One very interesting but so far unconfirmed rumor is that a very young Judy Garland appeared as one of the little girls at the beginning of the "Woman in the Shoe" number. One source reports that her family was in Hollywood at the time this was filmed (1929) and that she appeared in it. It was actually part of a 1929 MGM feature entitled *Lord Byron of Broadway.* The song "The Woman in the Shoe" actually became a popular song hit in 1929, being recorded by some of the top dance bands of the day, such as Ben Selvin and his Orchestra.

The Stooges' second MGM short was *Beer and Pretzels,* released August 26, 1933. This is the one MGM short that most closely resembles the later Columbia shorts, since it has more physical slapstick and gags and less musical interludes. This one is not filmed in color and also has no old scenes from other films. The one musical production number is apparently a new song written for this film. The song is entitled "Steins on the Table," written by Al Goodheart (music) and Gus Kahn (lyrics), and sung by Bonnie Bonnell, then by a group of bartenders (who do a much better job with it than Miss Bonnell does). These singers are not identified, but I believe one or more of them went on to become members of the Sportsmen Quartet, very popular in the 1940's and 1950's on the Jack Benny radio and television programs. Three unidentified dancers also perform and although unconfirmed, it has been suggested that they are the Condos Brothers, a popular dance team in many musical features of the 1930's and 1940's. The Stooges and Ted Healy each get a chance to do a little singing, too. Also appearing in this film are Edward Brophy as a theater manager and Fred Malatesta as the headwaiter.

The third MGM short with Ted Healy and his Stooges was *Hello Pop!,* released September 16, 1933. This one is also in Technicolor and also includes clips from an earlier MGM Technicolor musical feature *It's a Great Life* from 1929 starring the Duncan Sisters (Vivian and Rosetta) with songs "Hoosier Hop" and "I'm Sailing on a Sunbeam" written by Dave Dreyer and Ballard MacDonald.

continued on page 12

— 11 —

Introduction to 3 Stooges' MGM Shorts (continued)

Also appearing were Bonnie Bonnell, Henry Armetta, and the Albertina Rasch Girls, who were a group of chorus girls under the direction of Albertina Rasch, the choreographer of many of the elaborate production numbers in MGM musicals of the thirties.

The fourth MGM Stooges' short is *Plane Nuts,* released October 14, 1933. This is a very entertaining short and provides a look at what the Stooges' stage act must have been like. Ted Healy repeatedly and with very amusing determination, attempts to sing a song entitled "Noontime" (which incidentally was written by him), but is constantly being interrupted by the Stooges and Bonnie Bonnell. Ted also introduces two big production numbers which again are footage from an earlier film *Flying High* from 1931. The songs are "Happy Landing" (which was the British title for "Flying High") and "Dance Until Dawn" both written by Dorothy Fields and Jimmy McHugh. The choreographer was Busby Berkeley, working in one of his first Hollywood films and already displaying some of the distinctive style that made him the greatest of the choreographers of these types of numbers. Appearing in *Plane Nuts* along with Ted Healy, his Stooges and Bonnie Bonnell, were Kathryn Crawford, Gus Arnheim and his Orchestra, and Geneva Mitchell, all in footage from *Flying High.* A clip of one of these numbers was also used in the 1985 compilation feature *That's Dancing!* Apparently Ted Healy's act of trying to sing his song "Noontime" was a popular one because he did it again in the 1936 MGM feature *San Francisco* and had three of his "new" Stooges do the heckling and interrupting. Unfortunately, this scene must have been cut from the final release print, since it's nowhere to be seen in currently available prints.

Fifth and last of the five MGM Stooges' shorts was *The Big Idea,* released May 12, 1934. The Stooges have little to do in this short which again includes old scenes from earlier MGM features. What makes this one different is that the two old clips are actually out-takes from the features, not footage taken directly from them, as with the other shorts. The musical number in *The Big Idea* is an unused portion of "That's the Rhythm of the Day," a large scale production in the 1933 MGM feature *Dancing Lady.* The other old scene in *The Big Idea* is not really a musical number, but a comedy routine by The Three Radio Rogues (Jimmy Hollywood, Eddie Bartell, and Henry Taylor), a very talented trio who were very good at imitating radio stars of the day and that's exactly what they do here. Unfortunately one has to be very familiar with the radio personalties of the period to truly appreciate how good these impressions are. This routine is most probably a segment intended for the 1933 MGM musical feature *Going Hollywood* which included other similar routines by the Three Radio Rogues. For trivia fans, the name of the tune the Stooges play on their trumpets is "Marching Through Georgia." Appearing in *The Big Idea* along with Ted Healy and his Stooges are Bonnie Bonnell, Muriel Evans, Tut Mace (a dancer), and "The MGM Dancing Girls," as billed.

Also, of course, as mentioned above, the Three Radio Rogues are featured, and appearing unbilled is Heinie Conklin as "Joe."

Another MGM short of interest to Stooge fans is *Jailbirds of Paradise* released March 10, 1934. It is another of MGM's Musical Revue series, in Technicolor, and includes more musical numbers from earlier films. The reason it would be of interest to Stooges' fans is that Moe and Curly Howard appear in it (without Larry), along with Dorothy Appleby, Shirley Ross, the Dodge Sisters (Beth and Betty), Leo White, Jack Pennick, and once again, the MGM Dancing Girls.

The other MGM short in this series that I will cover this time is one that features Curly Howard without Moe or Larry. The short is *Roast-Beef and Movies,* released February 10, 1934, in Technicolor. In this short, Curly is teamed with two other comic actors, George Givot and Bobby Callahan, causing speculation that MGM was trying to form a new team. It turns out this was the only film these three made together. George Givot appeared in many films usually playing a comical Greek character, in fact he used to be publicized sometimes as "The Grik Ambassador." Bobby Callahan was basically a bit player who had small roles in Three Stooges, Laurel and Hardy, and other comedy shorts in the 1930's. The two big musical numbers in this short are, again, from earlier MGM musical features. The first is billed in the credits as "Chinese Ballet" but its proper title is "Blue Daughter from Heaven," sung offscreen by James Burroughs, from the 1929 feature "Lord Byron of Broadway." It was written by Dimitri Tiomkin (music) and Ray Egan (lyrics), and staged by Albertina Rasch. The second number used in *Roast-Beef and Movies* was entitled "Dust," taken from the 1930 MGM feature *Children of Pleasure.* It was written by Andy Rice and Fred Fisher, and staged by Sammy Lee. "Dust" was also a popular song hit in 1930, having been recorded by several of the top bands, including the Dorsey Brothers and Ben Selvin and his Orchestra. Appearing in the cast along with the three stars were the Albertina Rasch Dancers and Warren Hymer.

Now to cover more unlisted Stooges' appearances. A few more have been found since my last article. More Joe Besser television appearances that have not been documented in *The Three Stooges' Scrapbook* or in Joe Besser's book *Not Just a Stooge* include the episode of the series "Private Secretary" from 1953 in which Mr. Sands is haunted by a moose head. Joe also appears in the episode of "The Ann Sothern Show" from 1958 entitled "Give It Back to the Indians," broadcast January 5, 1959. Joe states in his book that he appeared on "The Jack Benny Program" seven times, but no episode titles were known. Here are three I know of: "Rochester Falls Asleep, Misses Program" (1955); "Jack Goes to the Races" (1955); and "The Tennessee Ernie Ford Show" (1956). One more unlisted Joe Besser appearance is in the episode of "Make Room for Daddy" entitled "Kathy Delivers the Mail" (1960).

In an earlier article, I listed some films in which an actor named Joe DiReda appeared, for the purpose of clarifying that these are *not* films with Joe DeRita of the Three Stooges, and now have two more such films to report. One is *The Black Orchid* (1959 — Paramount) and an episode of "The Ann Sothern Show," entitled "Katy and the New Boss," broadcast March 2, 1959.

As always, any additions, comments, or questions are welcome.

Richard Finegan, 8 White Pine Knoll Rd., Wayland, MA 01778.

— 12 —

View From the Ledge

Publisher: Chuck Shepherd
P.O. Box 57141
Washington, DC 20037
Format: Newsletter
Editor: Chuck Shepherd
Description: **View From the Ledge** is an eclectic collection of true items that celebrate weirdness, i.e., those sub-mainstreamers who command a view from the ledge. Typical articles include "Ethiopia Asks Soviet For Aerobics Advisers," "Teen Pulls Gun on Orthodontist, Demands His Braces Be Removed," and "Couple Mistakes Runway for Freeway." **This newsletter is available** *only* **to subscribers of** *News of the Weird.*

Subscription rates:
Free to subscribers of *News of the Weird*, otherwise unavailable
Average # of pages: 4
Page size: 8 1/2" x 11"
Production: Word processed
Printing: Offset
Binding: Folded
Author information:
Newsletter is not copyrighted
Advertising rates: Advertisements are not accepted
Cross-indexed:
General Humor
Political Humor
Psychology Humor
Arts Humor
Cartoons/Illustrations/Graphics

Visual Lunacy Society

Founder: Carl T. Herrman
Publication: **Visual Lunacy News**
Publisher: Carl T. Herrman
             P.O. Box 1462
             Ponte Vedra Beach, FL 32004
Format: Newsletter
Editor: Carl T. Herrman
Phone: (904) 285-6866
Founded: 1982
Description of organization: Fosters use of rubber stamps to spoof officialdom, reflecting current trends and cultural opinions.
Description of publication: The **Visual Lunacy News** publishes off-beat humor reflecting the humorous roll of pop-culture.
Frequency: 1-4 issues per year
# of issue published in 1991:   1
# of issue to be published in 1992:   3
# of issues to be published in 1993:   4
Annual membership dues (newsletter is included in price):
             1 year: $12.00
Subscription price (without membership):
             1 year: $12.00
             1 year (Canada):   US$12.00
             1 year (Foreign):   US$12.00
Average # of pages per issue: 4
Page size: 8 1/2" x 11"
Production: Typeset
Printing: Offset
Author information:
             Newsletter accepts unsolicited manuscripts
             Reports in 4 weeks
             Author receives 20 complimentary copies of the issue in which the article is published as payment
             Newsletter owns all rights
             Newsletter is copyrighted
Advertising rates: Advertisements are not accepted
Cross-indexed:
             Visual Satire

VLS Goes to the Land of Ah's!

The Visual Lunacy Society has finally launched its new catalog. Our expedition to Kansas took longer than we thought! The flagship of our Kansas fleet was illustrated by Seymour Chwast of Pushpin Studios in New York. Winnebagos over Wichita is one of 10 stamps which celebrate the state of Kansas. When trying to come up with some great thoughts on Kansas everything went flat. We did discover that Kansas has the 2nd largest ball of twine in the world and the wierdest hotel. Rosalea's Hotel in Harper Kansas invites all VLS members to become "Members of Rosalea's Hotel's Volunteer Nobility". There is no cause for boredom while staying at Rosalea's Hotel, because the sights in and around Harper are plentiful and stimulating. Guided tours to Mac's Grocery, T&P Variety Store and the drug store on the corner of Main and Central will tease your imagination. The gourmet restaurant named the "Crab Grass Room" will be opened as soon as Chief Chef Dan deLion removes the weeds from the backyard area designated to be

the restaurant. Special thanks for the pioneers on this expedition, Anne Bailey and Max Schaible. Thanks also to Isla Wolfe and Jennifer Henderson for their inspired mail art masterpieces. Official Kansas State Flags are available for purchase from the Secretary of State, Capital, Kansas 66612. (With it you can get a free booklet which will tell you what "Ad Astra per Aspera" means.) To invest in Rosalea's book "Bible Belt Oasis; The Story of Rosalea's Hotel" or to join "Members of Rosalea's Hotel Volunteer Nobility" or to receive Rosalea's newsletter, "Thurds", write to: Rosalea, P.O. Box 121, Harper, KS 67058.

For those of you that have wondered what's happening at VLS headquarters, here's an update. We have had a very successful first two years, thanks to the loyal support from all of you rubber stamp lunies. We have decided to keep our operation small so that we continue to be the "different stamp company". We have never advertised, yet we get orders every day thanks to word of mouth advertising and the publicity that we have received in nu-

merous magazines, newspapers and newsletters. Members have come from Guam, Australia, England, Denmark, France, Canada and just about every state in the U.S.A.

The best part of this business (the worst part is making stamps) is receiving all of your wonderful letters filled with humor and creativity. Thanks also for all of your suggestions for stamps. We rejected all of them but did get to prove how nicely our "Rejected" line works. Last issue we helped you to collect money that was owed to you with our "Penalty for late payment . . . etc. series. Now, we have a series to help you to keep your checkbook balanced. You can hold up payments for things you've purchased by using the, *Returned, Pope's signature required, Resubmit in Arabic* and *resubmit in 60 days.* Without even being in a catalog until now, they have soared to the top of the charts.

Stamps of Officialdom are still our special feature but we have also added an assortment of useful images for use in correspondence art.

The Weekly Farce

Publisher: Active Communications, Inc.
               P.O. Box 391
               Berea, OH 44017
Format: Newspaper
Editors: Ken McEntee, Ron McEntee
Phone: (216) 362-7979
Founded: 1987
Description: **The Weekly Farce** is a satire on the news of the day and the media that brings the news
               to the people. It's very dangerous reading for those with no sense of humor.
Frequency: 12 issues per year
# of issues published in 1991:   12
# of issues to be published in 1992: 12
# of issues to be published in 1993: 12
1992 volume: Volume #5
Subscription period: Subscriptions run from the date the order is received
Subscription rates:

1 year/2 years:	$10.00	$20.00
1 year/2 years (Canada):	US$15.00	US$30.00
1 year/2 years (Foreign):	US$20.00	US$30.00
Sample copy: $2.00		

Average # of pages per issue: 4
Production: Laserprinted
Printing: Offset
Binding: Folded and loosely collated
Circulation: 15,000
Author information:

       Newspaper does not accept unsolicited manuscripts
       Newspaper is copyrighted

Advertising rates:

1/2 page black & white:	$300
Full page black & white:	$600

Reviews:

       "Not only is it amusing and often downright hilarious, it is also very timely, spinning off real local and national news stories." (Vince Robinson, reporter, WEWS-TV "Live on Five")

       "Maybe my sense of humor is a little off-beat, but I think the farce sometimes borders on hilarious. The monthly horoscopes are clever as is a gossip columnist who dishes out 'bad weed.'" (Brent Larkin, *The Cleveland Plain Dealer*)

       "The no-holds-barred tabloid applies its own brand of humor to the stories and columns that appear in the press. Loyal readers need no convincing. They pass around Cleveland's funniest newspaper like a good joke. Maybe that's why the paper's claim of "10,000 copies—7 billion readers" is only a slight exaggeration. If researchers ever do discover that Elvis is alive and the rest of the world is dead, you can say you read it first in **The [Weekly] Farce**." (Ken Wood, reporter, *The News Sun*)

Cross-indexed:

General Humor	Film Media Humor	Political Science Humor
Sciences Humor	History Humor	Psychiatry Humor
Social Sciences Humor	Law Humor	Psychology Humor
Regional/Local Humor	Literature Humor	Religion Humor
Political Humor	Philosophy Humor	Word Play & Puns
Education Humor	Poetry Humor	

Arrest foils cannibal's restaurant plans

Copyright 1991, The Weekly Farce

MILWAUKEE — The planned opening of a new restaurant chain suffered a major blow when its majority owner was arrested on charges of murder and cannibalism.

Jeffrey Lionel Dahmer, president of Dahmer's Fine Breasts & Thighs, was arrested after police found human body parts scattered around his Milwaukee apartment.

Eleven skulls were found in a filing cabinet, a police spokesman said.

"In addition to being a weirdo, he couldn't file worth crap," the spokesman said. "He had one skull, which we think belonged to a guy name Jones, filed under 'G.' Go figure."

One officer, who spoke on the condition of anonymity, refused to comment.

Following the arrest, Milwaukee Health Department officials began an investigation into the restaurant, which was supposed to open next month.

"There is no question that the freezer is full of human meat," said one inspector. "Even though the steaks looked considerably leaner than the beef and pork we're used to seeing, Mr. Dahmer has not filed for a license to serve human, which is obviously a very serious violation as far as I'm concerned."

Professional menu consultants who tasted every item Dahmer was to offer, said they didn't suspect that they were eating human meat.

"In retrospect, we thought the meat had quite a distinct flavor, but we attributed it to the spices Mr. Dahmer employed," said taster Ned Saltt. "Come to think about it, the sausage really tasted, shall we say, interesting."

Dahmer, who grew up in Summit County, was arrested after police found bodies and bones in various stages of decomposition scattered around his apartment. Police acted on a tip from a man who said Dahmer tried to assault him. The man, who was running down the street wearing handcuffs, told police that Dahmer's apartment was filled with body parts. He told police he'd rather have them act on his tip before Dahmer did.

"I opened the fridge to get a beer and this head is in there looking at me," he told *The Farce*'s Milwaukee Bureau. "I knew damn well it wasn't the Bud Man."

The man said he became suspicious after Dahmer yelled out from the kitchen asking him how he liked his gall bladder cooked. "That's when I went in and opened the fridge. He knew then that I was on to him, then he came after me with a knife. Man, I high-tailed it out of there after that."

Police went to the apartment and arrested Dahmer.

"The suspect was very cooperative and admitted everything," said a police spokesman. "He even invited us to share some fried toes before we went back to the station. You know what? They weren't bad, especially with the honey-mustard sauce."

After the news broke, Milwaukee police were flooded with calls from people whose friends and relatives had been missing.

One woman, whose cousin disappeared just days before the family dined with Dahmer at his apartment, called her mother after hearing about Dahmer's arrest.

"Mom, remember those ribs we had last week," she said. "Well I think they were Bobby."

· A chocolate candy maker in Downtown Milwaukee, where Dahmer worked for more than six years, has been flooded with calls from concerned customers who are worried about what might be in their peanut clusters.

"One of the biggest

worries it that our Kisses might have real lips," a company spokesman said.

A criminal history

Records indicate that Dahmer has a history of odd crimes

He was cited in 1982 at the Wisconsin State Fair for indecent exposure. Upon his arrest, he told police, "What? The bulls are doing it."

Later he was convicted for child molesting after attempting to pay a 12-year-old boy to pose naked on a large white styrofoam tray with cellophane wrapped over him. For that he was sentenced to five years in prison but was released on parole after one year because he kept biting other inmates.

"He wanted a hibachi in his cell," said the prison warden. "Then he got a stereo in here and kept blasting the same *Fine Young Cannibals* cassette over and over again. We figured it would be in everybody's best interest to get him the hell out of here."

Dahmer was placed on probation, but despite a plea by his father, his apartment was never visited by a probation officer.

"There was no reason to make a home visit," said Nat Necessary, spokesman for the state Department of Corrections. "He lived in a very bad neighborhood, unlike everyone else who is out on probation and we didn't want to take a chance by sending someone over there. Besides, we asked him straight out if he was doing anything like cutting up bodies and he said no. If you don't express some trust in these people, it really screws up their self-esteem."

Relatives relieved

In Akron, where Dahmer lived for many years and where he is said to have developed his taste for human meat, relatives were shocked about his arrest. One relative, however, said she was relieved.

"I am so glad to find out about the restaurant," she said. "I knew he was mutilating bodies, but I didn't know what he was doing. Some people said there may have been some kind of sexual motivation. I'm glad he was just going to serve the people at a restaurant. I'm just happy he isn't some kind of pervert or something."

Psychiatric experts said Dahmer may have tried to leave hints about his eccentricities in hopes of getting help.

"Just like some thieves and substance abusers subconsciously screw up so they get caught, Dahmer apparently dropped a few hints of his own," said Dr. Hedda De- partment. "The most glaring example was on the Italian Favorites menu at his restaurant, which offered a Can-O-Balls."

Local paper benefits

Meanwhile, the case may have placed a local newspaper in the running for the Associated Press' annual Stunning Revelation Award for an article published following Dahmer's arrest.

The day after authorities discovered frozen heads and other human body parts in Dahmer's freezer, *The Plain Dealer* carried a story with the stunning and unexpected headline, 'Peers say suspect an oddball.'"

"That's what we like to call going the extra mile for the reader," said A.P. Stylebook, head judge for the annual AP award. "We can't assume that just because the article says the guy was cutting people up in his apartment and eating them that the reader will automatically assume he's an oddball. I consider this to be a top-of-the-line sidebar."

The Whole Mirth Catalog

Publisher: The Whole Mirth Catalog
1034 Page Street
San Francisco, CA 94117
Format: Periodically issued catalog
Editor: Allen Klein
Phone: (415) 431-1913
Founded: 1983
Description: **The Whole Mirth Catalog** is the first mail order catalog devoted to the notion that laughter is the best medicine. Items listed include humorous products and humorous publications, presented in a light-hearted and graphically entertaining manner.
Frequency: 1 issue per year
# of issues published in 1991:   1
# of issues to be published in 1992:   1
# of issues to be published in 1993:   1
Subscription period: Subscriptions run from the date the order is received
Subscription rates:
   Sample copy: $1.00
Average # of pages per issue: 12
Page size: 11 1/2" x 15"
Production: Laserprinted
Printing: Offset
Binding: Folded and loosely collated
Circulation: 12,000
Author information:
   Accepts humorous products, books, and tapes for future issues
   Catalog is copyrighted
Advertising rates: Advertisements are not accepted
Reviews:
   "More goofy yoks than a Three Stooges movie." (*Playboy*)
   "Guaranteed to put a smile on someone's face." (*Houston Post*)
   "A marvelous resource." (*San Francisco Chronicle*)
Cross-indexed:
   General Humor
   Cartoons/Illustrations/Graphics

Jest For Fun

THE
WHOLE MIRTH CATALOG
1034 Page Street
San Francisco, CA 94117

PROBLEM?
SOLVE IT WITH THESE WISE & WITTY
CARDS THAT JOLT YOU OUT OF YOUR
RUT & INTO SOME CREATIVE THINKING
<u>CREATIVE WHACK PACK</u> . . . $12.95

Roger von Oech's
Creative Whack Pack

LADIES AND GERMS . . . HERE
ARE 10,000 GAGS. ARRANGED
IN OVER 500 CATAGORIES FROM
ONE OF THE BIGGEST LEGENDS
IN SHOWBUISNESS.
<u>MILTON BERLE'S PRIVATE
JOKE FILE</u> . . . $24.95
(hardcover)

THE BIG BOOK OF
NEW AMERICAN
HUMOR

EDITED BY
WILLIAM NOVAK·MOSHE WALDOKS

THE BEST HUMOR OF THE PAST
25 YEARS FROM WOODY ALLEN
TO ROBIN WILLIAMS
<u>BIG BOOK OF AMERICAN HUMOR</u>
. . . $15.95

NEW

MILTON BERLE'S PRIVATE JOKE FILE

Over 10,000 of his best gags, anecdotes, and one-liners

NEW

The KENNEDY Wit

A CELEBRATION OF WARM GOOD
HUMOR AND QUICK QUIPS OF JFK.
<u>THE KENNEDY WIT</u> . . . $7.95

THE PURR-FECT BOOK FOR FUNNY
FELINE LOVERS AND OTHERS.
<u>THE UNNOFFICIAL CAT OWNER'S
HANDBOOK</u> . . . $6.95

THE UNOFFICIAL
CAT
OWNER'S
HANDBOOK
ART AND NORMA PETERSON

NEW

The Penguin Dictionary
of
MODERN
HUMOROUS
QUOTATIONS

NEW

LOOK UP A LAUGH WITH THIS
TREASURY OF WIT AND WISDOM.
<u>DICTIONARY OF MODERN HUMOROUS
QUOTATIONS</u> . . . $7.95

NEW

FAXABLE
Greeting Cards
HAPPY BIRTHDAY TO THE BOSS, CONGRATULATIONS
TO A CLIENT, AND I'M SORRY TO YOUR BEST NEW
CUSTOMER IN DES MOINES · BY JOHN CALDWELL

FAX SOME FUN AND CREATE
A CHUCKLE AT HOME OR
IN THE OFFICE.
<u>FAXABLE GREETING CARDS</u> . . . $9.95

Welcome to the eighth edition of
THE WHOLE MIRTH CATALOG

Whether you are seeking a smile or a gargantuan
guffaw you will find it on the following pages.
Each item has been selected because of its unique
nature. Many are hard to find humor resources,
others re-released laugh favorites and some are
hot off the press. All of them, however, are
for your enjoyment.
Allen Klein, owner

Yes folks, it's all copyrighted. © 1991

WILDE TIMES

Publisher: Jester Press
                116 Birkdale Road
                Half Moon Bay, CA 94019
Format: Newsletter
Editor: M. R. Poulos
Phone: (415) 726-5992
Founded: 1988
Description: **WILDE TIMES** is a general humor newsletter.
Frequency: 4 issues per year
# of issues published in 1991:   4
# of issues to be published in 1992: 4
# of issues to be published in 1993: 4
1992 volume: Volume #5
Subscription period: Subscriptions run from the date the order is received
Subscription rates:
                1 year: $20.00
                1 year (Canada):   US$25.00
                1 year (Foreign):   US$27.00
                Sample copy: $ 5.00
Average # of pages per issue: 4
Page size: 8 1/2" x 11"
Production: Laserprinted
Printing: Offset
Binding: Folded
Circulation: 580+
Author information:
                Newsletter does not accept unsolicited manuscripts
                Newsletter owns all rights to articles
                Newsletter is copyrighted
Advertising rates: Advertisements are not accepted
Cross-indexed:
                General Humor
                Humanities Humor
                Business Humor
                Political Humor
                Research on Humor
                Law Humor
                Medical Humor

What's Saddam Funny?

THE war is over, our troops are coming home. At last the truth can be told. From deep within the bunkers of Baghdad comes the first completely uncensored report from our Eyewitless Correspondent in the Gulf:

SOURCES reveal that last September Saddam Hussein was being driven to Kuwait City when his armored limousine hit a donkey.
"We must show concern for peasants," Saddam told his driver. "Go to the house and apologize for killing their mule!"
The driver obeyed and returned a few minutes later with his arms full. "Look what they gave me," he said, "almonds, dates, pistachio nuts..."
"I don't understand," said Saddam. "Weren't they angry?"
"No," replied the driver. "They cheered and gave me these presents."
"What exactly did you tell them?"
"All I said was, 'Allah is Great! The jackass is dead!'"

DEEP in his palatial bunker, Saddam was selecting his wardrobe for the Mother of All Battles.
"Your Excellency," suggested his valet, "when Napoleon was in Russia he wore a red uniform so that if he was wounded his men would not notice he was bleeding."
"Excellent idea!" said Saddam. "Give me my brown pants."

AT his command headquarters on the eve of the battle, Saddam met with his generals.
"One road leads to defeat, humiliation and total ruin," he told them, "the other to unimaginable destruction. I only hope we have the wisdom to choose correctly."

INTELLIGENCE analysts compiled a psychological profile of Saddam. Sources say he harbors deep-seated hatred for his mother, mostly because she has a much better mustache.

DURING the final hours of Operation Desert Storm, Saddam sent this urgent communique to his troops on the front lines in Kuwait:
"Oh mighty warriors, I command you!
I must have volunteers! A few brave Iraqi men
who will retreat a little slower!"

Reprinted from **WILDE TIMES**, Spring 1991, by permission of the publisher.

The Wit

Publisher: Wit's End, Inc.
              1 Riverview Drive
              Suite 12
              North Providence, RI 02904
Format: Magazine
Editor: Frank O'Donnell (Editor-in-Chief)
Phone: (401) 353-9895
Founded: 1991
Description: Rhode Island and Southeastern New England's humor magazine.
Frequency: 12 issues per year
# of issues published in 1991:   3
# of issues to be published in 1992:   12
# of issues to be published in 1993:   12
1992 volume: Volume #2
Subscription period: Subscriptions run from date orders are received
Subscription rates:
              1 year/2 years/3 years: $17.95 $33.95 $49.95
              Sample copy: $3.00
Average # of pages per issue: 40
Production: Laserprinted
Printing: Offset
Binding: Saddle stitched
Circulation: 10,000 minimum
Author information:
              Prospective authors should inquire first
              Reports in 2-3 months
              Author receives complimentary copies of the issue in which the article appears if the
                  author requests them; otherwise, no payment
              Magazine owns first serial rights
              Magazine is copyrighted
Advertising rates:
              1/2 page black & white: $185
              Full page black & white: $275
              Cover 2 black & white: $325
              Cover 3 black & white: not available
              Cover 4 black & white: $375
              Cover 4 color: $400
Cross-indexed:
              Regional/Local Humor

JUDGE NOT, LEST YE BE JUDGED!

by FRANK O'DONNELL

I was pretty excited.

I'd never been invited to judge anything before. I had just been asked to officiate at the annual National State Police Uniform Pageant. It was quite an honor.

An all-expense-paid trip to Poughkeepsie just served to sweeten the pot.

The Pageant is sponsored every year by the Uniform Makers of America. Its purpose is to determine the best-dressed State Police Department in the United States.

Perhaps you'll recall that about four years ago, the Rhode Island State Police walked away with top honors.

They received tremendous media attention -- including a coveted guest spot on *Late Night with David Letterman* -- and earned the unofficial title of **Izod Squad.** ⟹

the Wit / 29

---

continued from page 29

And now, I was being handed partial responsibility for determining which state would have the bragging rights for 1990.

Not an easy task. See, I travel a lot, especially throughout New England. And I use the interstate highway system, which is generally governed by the State Police.

I had visions of getting pulled over and having the following scene unfold...

"Well," the cop would say, *"we had you doing 72 in a 65-mile-per-hour zone, but I think I'll just let you go with a warn..."*

As the "ing" catches in his throat, he takes a hard look at me.

"Hey, wait a minute! You're that judge from the Uniform Pageant!"

Quicker than I can blink, the cop's revolver is straddling the bridge of my nose. "Out of the car, scum! Hands on the roof!" He yells to his partner. "Harry, call in. Tell them we just caught us the judge who voted us out of the Pageant!"

"The one who said our pants were too baggy, and our shoulders weren't sufficiently well-defined?"

"That's the one!" He turns back with an evil grin. "You in a heap of trouble, boy."

But, I rationalized, it's a simple contest, certainly nothing that anyone would bother to get upset over.

So I packed my bags and shuffled off to Poughkeepsie.

As luck would have it, I was pulled over on the New York State Thruway.

"Where's the fire, pal?" asked the cop.

"No fire, Officer. I'm just on my way to Poughkeepsie to judge the State Police Uniform Pageant, and I got so excited about it, I guess I just lost track of my speedometer. Nice uniform, by the way."

The cop's attitude changed instantly. "This old thing?" He stood up straight and puffed his chest out with pride. "State Police Uniform Pageant, huh? Why don't I just give you a police escort? Would that help you at all?"

"Sure would. Thanks a lot."

When I arrived and announced myself at the hotel's front desk, I was immediately whisked off to a secret conference room by the Pageant Director.

"I'm so glad you're **here**!" he hissed.

"Happy to be here. So where are the other judges?"

"There **are** no other judges! They were all afraid of reprisals from departments which lost the title, so they all backed out."

I felt like a condemned man mere moments away from the hereafter who's just learned that the Governor never heard of him.

But, I was here, and I had a job to do.

Several departments had already been disqualified on technicalities.

Wisconsin was eliminated for padding their tunic shoulders. Florida was sent home for illegal use of barrel extenders on their service .357's. California lost out for spoiling a perfectly good uniform with a bow tie. And the Alaskan contingent was plain kicked out of the hotel for tracking in crude oil on their boots.

When all the disqualifications had been processed, we were left with three semi-finalists. Massachusetts, North Carolina, and Texas.

When we learned that Trooper Massachusetts had once posed nude for a fund raising calendar, employing his service revolver as a fig leaf, it was bye bye, Bay State!

Trooper Texas was snatched away by the INS for failing to produce his green card.

Which left one very happy State Police Department, and 49 extremely disappointed State Police departments.

So I'm faxing this column in from North Carolina. Sometime soon, I plan to cut off my beard, dye my hair blonde, and get a new license with a vaguely Scandinavian surname.

Sure, it's a lot of work, but at least I'll be able to drive home without getting hassled all the way.

THE END

30 / the Wit

Witty World

Publisher: Witty World Publications
P.O. Box 1458
North Wales, PA 19454
Format: Magazine
Editors: Joseph George Szabo (Editor-in-Chief), John A. Lent (Managing Editor)
Phone: (215) 699-2626 [FAX: (215) 699-0627]
Founded: 1987
Description: **Witty World** is an international cartoon magazine covering all genres of cartoon art. Includes interviews, profiles, reviews, political focuses (juxtaposing cartoons of different views internationally), columns on syndication, law, etc. Reaches 103 countries.
Frequency: 4 issues per year
# of issues published in 1991: 4
# of issues to be published in 1992: 4
# of issues to be published in 1993: 4
Subscription period: Subscriptions run from the date the order is received
Subscription rates:

1 year/2 years:	$28.00	$52.00
1 year/2 years (Canada):	US$36.00	US$68.00
1 year/2 years (Foreign):	US$36.00	US$68.00

Average # of pages per issue: 52 or 100 (depending on the issue)
Page size: 8 1/2" x 11"
Production: Typeset
Printing: Offset
Binding: Perfect bound (as though a paperback) or saddle stitched (depending on the number of pages in the issue)
Circulation: 5,000 (Special editions have a circulation up to 20,000)
Author information:
Prospective authors should inquire first before making submissions
Author receives 2 complimentary copies of the issue in which the article is published as payment
Magazine owns 1st serial rights to articles; authors owns rights to cartoons
Magazine is copyrighted
Advertising rates:

1/2 page/Full page black & white:	$ 430	$ 750	
1/2 page/Full page color:	$ 705	$1,200	
Cover 2/Cover 3/Cover 4 black & white:	$ 855	$ 855	$1,450
Cover 2/Cover 3/Cover 4 color:	$1,300	$1,300	$1,450

Reviews:
"...wildly illustrated 96-page issue explains why this is recommended in *Magazines for Libraries* for anyone who wants the inside story on professional cartooning. It is recommended for all libraries, with a cartoonist, fledgling and professional alike. And it's good reading, too, for those who just like to look." (Bill Katz, *Library Journal*)
"**Witty World** presents cartoons and articles dealing with the international world of cartoonists. A quarterly, published and edited by Hungarian refugee and political cartoonist Joseph George Szabo, the colorful magazine features interviews with renowned cartoonists, articles on specific aspects of cartooning, and a wealth of cartoons devoted to particular themes." (*American Libraries*)
"I can only compare it as the *Newsweek* of the cartooning world." (Graphic Artists Guild *Cartoonists*, New York Chapter)
Cross-indexed:
General Humor
Humanities Humor
Arts Humor
Political Humor
Cartoons/Illustrations/Graphics
Visual Satire
Scholarly Reviews of Humor as Subject of Study
Research on Humor
Summary of Conferences and/or Symposiums on Humor
ISSN: 0892-9807

Dennis Wepman:

Berke Breathed Moves On

When **Berke Breathed** announced on May 1, 1989 that he planned to retire his strip "Bloom County" on August 6, he broke all precedent. Popular comic strips have been canceled before, but never in living memory at the zenith of their creative and commercial success. Begun on December 8, 1990, the trenchant and often controversial strip syndicated by the Washington Post Writers Group became a superstar in the field during its nearly-nine-year life, deftly poking fun at television, the press, British royalty, American puritanism, and the comics themselves. It entered the ranks of that most exclusive of comic-strip fraternities, the 1,000 Club, when it joined such mainstream veterans as "Blondie," "Beetle Bailey," and "Hägar" in appearing in that many papers worldwide, and in 1987 it became the second comic strip to win the Pulitzer Prize for editorial cartooning. Collections appeared periodically and always reached the *New York Times* Best-Seller List.

Breathed explained his cancelation of "Bloom County" by saying, "A good comic strip is no more eternal than a ripe melon. The ugly truth is that, in most cases, comics age less gracefully than their creators. 'Bloom County' is retiring before the stretch marks show." The public

dismay, which was considerable, was assuaged by Breathed's promise to replace his popular strip with another, "Outland," to appear on Sundays only.

The cartoonist's large following waited breathlessly (and Breathedlessly), and the new strip duly appeared in September. The general reaction was one of bewilderment. In the first place, "Outland" seemed to have abandoned all the beloved familiar characters of its predecessor, and in the second it was virtually incomprehensible. But gradually it began to crystallize, taking on a strong socio-political tone (repeated jabs at environmental pollution and **Vice-President Quayle**) and mercifully restoring some of the characters the public had come to know and love in "Bloom County." Ronald-Ann reappeared in installment #2, and in #5 (October 1) the cartoonist's most popular figure, the beguiling bow-tied penguin Opus, found his way back. The world heaved a sigh of relief.

"Outland" is set in a dreamworld somewhere between Coconino County and the Land of Oz. Still cryptically allusive and more weirdly and wonderfully drawn from week to week, it is beginning to take shape as a serious, and major piece of graphic humor. If Breathed was accused of aping **Gary**

Trudeau at the beginning of his career, he has with "Outland" come to reflect something closer to the slapstick metaphysical irony of **Dan O'Neill's** 1970s "overground underground" blend of fantasy, philosophy, and biting social commentary, "Odd Bodkins."

Breathed himself maintains a delphic silence about his intentions. Since his bombshell announcement in May, he has been unavailable to comment to anyone. His very location is unknown. Rumors that he has been kidnapped by Gypsies, defected to another planet, or hidden himself in the Himalayas appear to be unfounded; the best information is that he is living either in Colorado or Ft. Lauderdale, Florida, or both, and spending a lot of time sailing. He has become a contributing editor of *Boating* magazine, whose October issue carries the first of a series of columns entitled "Overboard," illustrated with drawings of none other than Opus. So it appears that the 31-year-old cartoonist has not deserted us after all.

WOMEN'S GLIB

Publisher: Crossing Press
               P.O. Box 259
               Bala Cynwyd, PA 19004
Format: Periodically issued humor anthology (book)
Editor: Rosalind Warren
Phone: (215) 668-4252
Founded: 1990
Description: **WOMEN'S GLIB** is a yearly collection of women's humor (i.e., humor by women)
               including stories, essays, cartoons, poems, and photo essays. The first humor book in the
               series, *Women's Glib: A Collection of Women's Humor*, was published in 1991. The
               second book, *Women's Glibber*, will be published in 1992.
Frequency: 1 book per year
# of periodically issued books in 1991:   1
# of periodically issued books to be published in 1992: 1
# of periodically issued books to be published in 1993: 1
Subscription rates:
               1 book: $10.95
               Sample copy: $10.95
Average # of pages per book: 200
Page size: 6" x 9"
Production: Typeset
Printing: Offset
Binding: Perfect bound
Circulation: 10,000-20,000
Author information:
               Anthology accepts unsolicited manuscripts
               Reports in 2 weeks
               Authors receive $5.00 per page minimum and 2 complimentary copies of the book in
                  which their article appears as payment
               Anthology acquires one-time, non-exclusive rights
               Anthology is copyrighted
Advertising rates: Advertisements are not accepted
Reviews:
               "For those not familiar with contemporary American women's humor, **WOMEN'S
                  GLIB** is a perfect introduction." (*Philadelphia City Paper*)
               "Elicits lots of unrestrained laughter." *(BOOKLIST)*
               "A laugh-out-loud collection." (*Feminist Bookstore News*)
ISBN: 0-89594-470-7 (cloth)
          0-89594-466-9 (paperback)
Cross-indexed:
               General Humor
               Sciences Humor
               Social Sciences Humor
               Humanities Humor
               Arts Humor
               Business Humor
               Regional/Local Humor
               Political Humor
               Cartoons/Illustrations/Graphics
               Visual Satire
               Women's Humor

On My Honor

"Carol, why don't you take your Girl Scouts to the mortuary?" Dorothy Claiborne boomed across the produce counter.

"The mortuary?"

"Yes," she continued, "the mortuary gives you a dollar for every person you take to hear their educational relations program. They'll show you the embalming room and the casket selection. It only takes an hour and on the way out, everyone receives a bottle of hand lotion."

"Really," I said, thinking what a crazy idea it was.

However, we only had two years before our camping trip to Hawaii. We were behind on our money earning, so I thought over her proposal as I continued my marketing.

I ran into Dorothy again in the check-out line. Looking around to make sure no one was listening I lowered my voice and said, "I've been thinking about your suggestion. If each girl took five guests, we could make $150."

"And they'll learn something," Mrs. Claiborne responded as loudly as ever.

"I'll present the idea to the troop next week."

When I told the thirteen year olds about it they roared with laughter for twenty minutes. However, the vote was unanimous. We would go to the mortuary.

That evening I prepared the parents' permission slip. Then it occurred to me that the mothers and fathers might think that this could be a morbid experience. So, as an afterthought, I wrote across the bottom, in inch-high capital letters: NO DEAD BODIES WILL BE SEEN.

I took my original to the copier and the next week just before the meeting I picked up the duplicates.

"Please, girls," I said to the troop, "be sure your parents and guests understand that this will not be depressing. Notice that I have written, NO DEAD BODIES WILL BE SEEN on the permission slips."

Marlana immediately began waving her permission slip. "Yes, Marlana, what is it?"

Jumping to her feet she burst out, "Mine says ten dead bodies will be seen!"

I couldn't believe it, but there it was. The original had slipped on the copy machine and the first vertical and diagonal line of the NO had been obliterated. The message clearly read in inch-high capital letters: "10 DEAD BODIES WILL BE SEEN."

"Girls," I asked, "would you please correct your permission slips?"

When I arrived home, my phone was ringing. Before I got the receiver to my ear I heard an angry voice scream, "Wouldn't one dead body be enough?"

Obviously the corrections were never completed. That was years ago, but I can still hear my phone ringing over and over.

This project was a success as a money-earner, though. We repeated it several times, of course being very careful to proofread the permission slips. And, no dead bodies were ever seen.

Word Ways: The Journal of Recreational Linguistics

Publisher:	A. Ross Eckler
	Spring Valley Road
	Morristown, NJ 07960
Format:	Journal
Editor:	A. Ross Eckler
Phone:	(201) 538-4584
Founded:	1968

Description: **Word Ways** publishes scholarly articles, puzzles, and literary illustrations of various types of word play, principally regarding words and collections of letters to be manipulated and arranged (for example, anagrams, palindromes, word squares, lipograms, etc.). The occasional article is written in a satirical or humorous vein. Some illustrations of these include: "Clothes Encounters"—a study of clothing store names in the Yellow Pages, categorized by rhymes (Bud's Duds), puns (Mother Frockers), and literary allusions (Georgia Girl in Atlanta); "A Rude Word in the Alphabet Soup"—a story about a man who was distressed to find a "rude word" in his soup, and his efforts to persuade the manufacturers thereof of the desirability of omitting certain letters so this could not happen in the future; "Double-entendre Headlines"—such as "Rain Clouds Welcome at Airport," or "Johnny, Jane Cash Are Hit in Hungary;" "An Interview with Ronald Wilson Reagan"—a pseudo-press conference in which Reagan is constrained to use only the letters in RONALD WILSON REAGAN in his replies, as "I'll now answer as an old agrarian landed granger. We are sworn non-aggressors; we need law and order; we disallow war as lawless and senseless,...;" "An Anagram Composing Contest"—readers were invited to form opposite arrangements of well-known phrases such as APRIL IS THE CRUELLEST MONTH, yielding "Special IRS toll hurt me then," "Curt poet-snarl: hellish time," and "Let March rule, then it spoils." The average article is not devoted to humor per se.

Frequency:	4 issues per year
# of issues published in 1991:	4
# of issues to be published in 1992:	4
# of issues to be published in 1993:	4
1992 volume:	Volume #25

Subscription period: Subscriptions run from the date the order is received

Subscription rates:

1 year:	$17.00
1 year (Canada):	US$19.00
1 year (Foreign):	US$19.00
Sample copy:	$ 4.50

Average # of pages per issue:	64
Page size:	7" x 10"
Production:	Typed
Printing:	Offset
Binding:	Saddle stitched
Circulation:	500

Author information:

Journal accepts unsolicited manuscripts

Journal acknowledges receipt of unsolicited manuscripts

Reports in 1 week

Author receives 1 complimentary copy of the issue in which article appears as payment

Journal owns 1st serial rights and upon publication rights revert back to author
Journal is copyrighted

Advertising rates:

Cover 4 black & white: $60

Reviews:

"This delightful publication deserves a great deal more attention than its circulation indicates. Articles promote word study as pure enjoyment although frequently they are the result of lengthy study. Any library serving clients 15 years of age and older should prominently display the title. Teachers will want to consult every issue for ideas to stimulate students..." (Bill Katz and Barry Richards, *Magazines for Libraries*)

Cross-indexed:

Humanities Humor
Word Play and Puns

ISSN: 0043-7980

Nixon and the Bee
A. Ross Eckler

Ivan held up the short piece of magnetic tape with skepticism. "You say that this is the missing ten seconds of the notorious Watergate tape?"

Boris stared at his chief in surprise. "Of course—didn't I tell you how KGB agent Nikolai Ripoff stole it from the files of Professor Esty of the Cornell Linguistics Department? And isn't it well-known that Professor Esty was one of the blue-ribbon panel that investigated the original White House tape, using highly sophisticated techniques of noise suppression and message enhancement to recover the missing words?"

"But why," asked Ivan, reaching for an empty tape reel, "was there never any public report of the recovered message?"

"That's obvious," replied Boris. "The message was so sensational in import that political pressure was brought to bear on Esty and his colleagues to keep it quiet— to pretend, in fact, that they were unable to decipher the tape at all. I'll bet the U.S. Government will pay us a pretty kopek not to reveal its contents."

By now, Ivan had expertly spooled the tape on the reel and was placing the reel on the Ampex. "That remains to be seen," he said dryly. He flipped the switch on, and both men leaned forward expectantly.

A BEE... Ivan turned the machine off to ponder the import of this phrase. "A *bee*? But of course—there must have been a bee brought in with the vase of flowers that always sits in the Oval Office, and Nixon has interrupted the meeting to warn the others of its presence." Satisfied with his interpretation, Ivan turned the machine on.

...SEEDY... This demanded a second halt for assessment. "Hmmm," mused Boris, "no doubt the bouquet was picked and arranged many hours earlier. By now, the bee has exhausted the nectar and is slowly starving—reflected in his debilitated appearance and sluggish movements."

...EEEE!... The sudden scream caught both men by surprise; clearly someone, lulled into a sense of false security by the bee's torpidity, has tried to remove the bee from the room and has been stung.

...IF, GEE, A CHI-... The two Russians looked at each other in bewilderment. If this were Nixon speaking, clearly his mind had been affected by the bee sting. This slurred, rambling phrase was not Nixon's usual crisp, incisive style. Had he gone into anaphylactic shock? Was he starting to say that the china vase holding the bouquet had concealed the bee, and it would be better to use a cut-glass vase in the future?

...JAKE, A YELL!... Someone in the next room hear Nixon's scream, and was telling his associate, Jacob, about it.

...AMEN. O, PEEK... By now both men were somewhat perplexed. "Could the others believe that Nixon has been killed by the sting, and they are praying over his inert body?" asked Ivan. "And why should they have to peek at him? I'll never understand the American way of death."

...(YOU ARE ESTY)... Since it is most unlikely that Professor Esty was present at the time of the bee sting, this tape must have been inadvertently overwritten during the reconstruction experiments in Professor Esty's laboratory, perhaps at a time when he was distracted by the entrance of a visitor verifying the professor's identity.

...YOU'VE—EEEE!... Back on the original tape, it is apparent that a *second* bee in the bouquet, heretofore unnoticed, has stung another Oval Office conferee in the middle of a sentence.

...DOUBLE, YOU!...This cryptic exhortation was apparently directed at Nixon's doctor, as he prepared an anti-venom shot, alerting him to the fact that *two* doses would now be needed.

...EGGS... "I must confess," said Boris, "bafflement at this one-word statement. Was it a breakfast conference in the Oval Office? Or was this an oblique reference to the anti-venom serum being administered to the President? Our virologists tell us that many vaccines are grown in unfertilized chicken eggs..."

...WHY'S HE The tape ended abruptly at this point, in the middle of a sentence. Still, Ivan was able to reconstruct the situation: "His secretary, attracted by the commotion, entered the Oval Office. Seeing Nixon on the floor with a doctor bent over him, she cried in a startled voice 'Why's he lying there?' but we heard only the first half."

"So," mused Boris, "the reason for suppressing the tape is clear. The men around Nixon couldn't let the country know that the President had been crippled by a bee sting and was temporarily unable to govern, so they attempted, as part of the cover-up, to erase the relevant part of the tape. Remember, Ivan, that the American people have been unusually skittish about presidential health ever since Woodrow Wilson lay paralyzed for many months after World War I. Secrecy must be maintained for the good of the country—a principle which we Russians have honed to perfection, but which the Americans are still learning to apply."

Workshop Library on World Humour

Founder: H.J. Cummings
Publication: **Humor Events & Possibilities (HEP)**
Publisher: Workshop Library on World Humour
P.O. Box 23334
Washington, DC 20026
Format: Newsletter
Editor: Barbara Cummings
Phone(s): (202) 484-4949; (202) 628-1500 Ext. 224
Organization founded: 1975
Publication founded: 1977
Description of organization: The **Workshop Library on World Humour** is a non-profit organization established to explore the use of humor from the earliest societies to the present—humor in drawing and painting, sculpture, literature, mime, dance, music, the physical and behavioral sciences, and the art/science of communication. Aim: To contribute significantly to efforts to enrich life, increase genuine creativity, and achieve world peace.
Description of publication: **Humor Events & Possibilities (HEP)** is an infrequently irregular quarterly newsletter designed to provide candid commentary on cultural turbulence as registered on the Humor Events & Possibilities (HEP) scale which has a time range from very pre-Aristophanes through the post-Rube Goldberg/Marcel Marceau/Sid Caesar period of comedic interpretation. Any legitimate use of this information by WLWH members on persons-in-law and/or other casual acquaintances including composers, political prognosticators, and other talented messmakers is positively encouraged.
Frequency: "We always go for 4 [issues per year]"
# of issues published in 1991: 2
# of issues to be published in 1992: 4
# of issues to be published in 1993: 4
Subscription period: Subscriptions run from the date the order is received
Annual membership dues (includes newsletter):

1 year (Greater Washington Area):	$25.00
1 year (Other US & Foreign):	$20.00
1 year (Qualified student):	$15.00
1 year (Contributing):	$50.00

# of members 425
Subscription rate (same as above except for the following):

1 year (Library/Institutional rate):	$15.00
2 years (Library/Institutional rate):	$30.00
Sample copy:	$ 6.00

Average # of pages per issue: 10-12
Page size: 8 1/2" x 11"
Production: Typed
Printing: Xeroxed
Binding: Folded and collated loosely
Circulation: 3,000
Author information:
Prospective authors should inquire first before submitting manuscripts
Reports in 2 months on the average
Authors receive no payment for their articles
Newsletter owns all rights to articles
Newsletter is copyrighted
Advertising rates: Advertisements are not accepted

Cross-indexed:

General Humor

Sciences Humor

Social Sciences Humor

Humanities Humor

Arts Humor

Business Humor

Regional/Local Humor

Political Humor

Cartoons/Illustrations/Graphics

Visual Satire

Scholarly Reviews of Humor

Research on Humor

Summary of Conferences on Humor

Anthropology Humor

Astronomy Humor

Biochemistry Humor

Biology Humor

Chemistry Humor

Computer Sciences Humor

Dentistry Humor

Economics Humor

Education Humor

English Humor

Film Media Humor

Foreign Languages Humor

Geology Humor

History Humor

Law Humor

Library Sciences Humor

Literature Humor

Limericks

Mathematics Humor

Medical Humor

Nursing Humor

Philosophy Humor

Physics Humor

Poetry Humor

Political Science Humor

Psychiatry Humor

Psychology Humor

Religion Humor

Sociology Humor

Word Play & Puns

Zoology Humor

Mythical People and Organizations
Dr. Norman D. Stevens
University of Connecticut

For unknown reasons, perhaps related to the common practice among children of creating imaginary playmates, many of us find pleasure in creating our own people and organizations. By clothing them with the trappings of respectability, we can then use these mythical entities to foster our own brand of humor on the unsuspecting world.

These people and organizations fall into at least three categories: First, there are those which, although they may seem peculiar, really do exist. In the library field, which I happen to know best, these organizations are represented by such groups as The Archons of Colophon; The Bibliosmiles; The Melvil Dui Chowder and Marching Society; and The Newark Men of Letters. All are, or were, loosely knit social organizations devoted to the cause of comradeship. Such groups actually fall outside my main area of interest both because they do, in part, actually exist and because they are not primarily intended as a vehicle for humor.

Next, there are those people and groups who are entirely fictional and exist, at least initially, only in the mind of one person. Concepts of this kind are often born for a special occasion and die just as soon as that occasion ends. Perhaps the best examples are those who come to life in large universities as a protest against the anonymity of such institutions. Often these mythical people are entered as candidates in campus elections (e.g., Duarf [frauD]), who ran at N.Y.U.) or are registered for courses. The organizations tend to be even more obscure and quickly fad into oblivion after their creation. If they continue to exist at all, they do so only in musty correspondence buried in some long-forgotten archives. Among the groups of this kind are the Dogs United for More Bones (DUMB), The Merry Hearts, and the Who's-On-First Foundation.

In a few cases, these mythical people and organizations take on a larger life and somehow become endowed with an air of reality. Most usual are those cases where the individuals, through the imagination and endeavor of their creators, are entered in a standard biographical dictionary. The greatest accomplishment that I know of in this respect was the entry of the legendary Aris Macpherson Rutherford in no less a source than *Who's Who in America* (1974/1975 edition). Lesser in stature are Oliver D. Birnbaum, in reality a dog, who may be found in *Outstanding Educators of America* (1975 edition), and Nigel Molesworth and Timothy J. Peason, my own entries, in successive editions of *Who's Who in Library Service* (1966 and 1970 editions).

Sometimes these mythical people actually become famous in their own right. The two outstanding examples are Josiah S. Carberry of Brown University, and Warren G. Wonka of Stanford University. Professor Carberry, who came into existence about 1932, has led a very active life ever since. He is remembered in a special Carberry Book Fund at Brown for which money is collected every Friday the thirteenth and which is used to buy books "of which Professor Carberry might, or might not, approve."

Mr. Wonka, who was born in the minds of the editors of the campus humor magazine in 1938, also has led a long and active life. Among his outstanding accomplishments was the chairmanship in 1968 of the Christian Committee for a Clean Bible.

It is their limited existence within a single institution, sometimes spreading briefly to the world beyond, that gives Professor Carberry and Mr. Wonka their charm. Much of that air of mystery is lost when these characters go on to become commercialized, as has happen with P.D.Q. Bach (1807-1842?).

There are a few mythical organizations that have taken on an air of permanence. They, too, may sometimes be found entered into standard reference sources. Most often, however, they become the basis for publication, often mimeographed or xeroxed and distributed only to a few knowing friends and colleagues, but sometimes they appear in serious standard journals. In this category can be placed The Bibliographic Dowsers of America; The Federal Folklore Fuzzological Foundation; The Molesworth Institute; The Socially Irresponsible Round Table (SIRT); and The Tristan da Cunha Bibliographic Project. Since much of the charm of these organizations lies in our coming across them in unexpected places, I will not elaborate on their purposes or activities.

My own knowledge of these mythical, but highly entertaining, people and organizations comes only from serendipitous collecting—not from organized research. I am certain that there are many more such mythical entities lurking out there. Contributions and information about any of them are welcome.

The Yellow Journal

Publisher: DiscoBeat Incorporated
              Box 522, Newcomb Hall
              Charlottesville, VA 22904
Format: Journal
Editor: Zachery Radoski
Phone: (804) 977-6143
Founded: 1987
Description: A monthly humor/satire magazine of The University of Virginia.
Frequency: 7 issues per year
# of issues published in 1991:   7
# of issues to be published in 1992:   7
# of issues to be published in 1993:   7
1992 volume: Volume #6
Subscription period: Subscriptions run from the date the order is received
Subscription rates:

	1 year	2 years	3 years
1 year/2 years/3 years:	$12.00	$24.00	$36.00
1 year/2 years/3 years (Canada):	US$12.00	US$24.00	US$36.00

Sample copy: $2.00

Average # of pages per issue: 24
Page size: 8 1/2" x 11"
Production: Laserprinted
Printing: Offset
Binding: Saddle stitched
Circulation: 5,000
Author information:

    Journal accepts unsolicited manuscripts
    Reports in 1-2 months
    Author receives 1 complimentary copy of the issue in which the article is published as payment
    Author owns rights to article
    Journal is not copyrighted

Advertising rates:

1/2 page black & white:	$ 60
Full page black & white:	$100
Cover 2 black & white:	$100
Cover 3 black & white:	$100
Cover 4 black & white:	$100

Reviews:

    "The ironic liberalism of Richard Rorty mixed with the sado-masochism of the Marquis De Sade." (*The University Journal*)
    "A waste of ink." (*The Advocate* [a conservative magazine])

Cross-indexed:

    General Humor
    Regional/Local Humor
    Cartoons/Illustrations/Graphics
    Visual Satire

The Yellow Journal Presents:
Tasteless P.C. Jokes

How many Native Americans does it take to screw in a lightbulb?

ANSWER: One. They're perfectly capable.

What would one call a 7-foot Person of Color?

ANSWER: His or her name, of course.

There was this African-American, a Person of Slavic Descent, and a Person of Religion. And they walked into a bar. And inside there was this Animal Companion of Simian Descent. The bartender said to the African-American, "Here's your malted beverage." The African-American replied, "Why do you automatically assume that I wanted a malted beverage?" The Person of Religion added, "Yes, why do you insist on perpetuating the cruel myth that persons of color drink only malted beverages?" Just then the Animal Companion of Simian Descent placed his genitalia into the drink of the Slavic person. "Should I get rid of the Animal Companion of Simian Descent?" asked the bartender. "No," replied the Slavic Person, "I respect the dignity of non-human persons and their right to live the lifestyle of their choosing."

What do you call a person with no limbs sitting on a barstool?

ANSWER: Differently Abled.

Donates your clothes to charity

There are these three **Gravitationally Challenged Womyn** in a restaurant. But they don't do anything funny, since making fun of them, even in a joke, would harm their self-esteem. Instead, they join hands and sing a Song of Empowerment.

Why did the Avian Chicken-type Companion cross the road?

ANSWER: To escape the oppression and horror of the barnyard.

BUCK BUCK BUCK

What do you call 10,000 Asian-Americans at the bottom of the sea?

ANSWER: That's **Genocide,** man! You Fascist! Geez!

There is a person of **Polish Extraction,** a **Person of Asian Origin,** and a **Person Whose Mode of Sexual Expression is Not Restricted by Repressively Superstitious Judeo-Christian Moral Codes.** They are in an airplane. The Person of Asian Origin makes a cruel and unfair remark about the **Person of Non-Traditional Sexual Orientation.** The **Person of Polish Extraction** immediately chastises the Person of Asian Origin for his/her bigotry and insensitivity. The three have a heartfelt talk about sexuality and by the time the plane lands all have acquired a new appreciation for those who are different.

Why do **Judaic** men die before their wives?

ANSWER: Because men of all races and creeds tend to have shorter lifespans than womyn.

What do you call dead midgets?

ANSWER: Anything you want. They're fuckin' dead.

Molts

Other Humor Magazines, Humor Organizations & Humor Resources

Keeping track of humor magazines and humor organizations is no easy task. Dozens of such magazines and organizations spring up each each and just as many die. *The Directory of Humor Magazines and Humor Organizations in America (and Canada)* is the most up-to-date, in-depth, and accurate reference book tracking humor magazines and humor organizations today.

There are several other reference books that track periodicals (e.g., *Ulrich's International Periodical Directory*) and organizations (e.g., the *Encyclopedia of Associations*) in general and that have small sections on humor periodicals or humor organizations. Although these reference books make an admirable attempt at tracking periodicals and organizations, when it comes to following humor periodicals and humor organizations, they seem to fall far short of the mark. For instance, some periodicals reference books obviously do not require that an actual sample of the humor magazine be submitted for inspection prior to listing. What else could account for the fact that at least one of these books has presented a listing as a *magazine* (see *Housewive's Humor* in this section of the listings) when in reality it was merely a humor *column* in a magazine? All too frequently, these reference books list humor periodicals or humor organizations that have long ago ceased to exist. (For some reason, many of these reference books persist, for example, in publishing the name of a humor magazine called *Bananas*—evidently once a humor magazine targeted to adolescents [and not to be confused with the International Banana Club, an organization that is still very much in existence]—although it had ceased publication many years ago.)

Unfortunately, when it came time for reviewers to review earlier editions of *The Directory of Humor Magazines and Humor Organizations in America (and Canada)*, they compared the listings of *Ulrich's* and the *Encyclopedia of Associations* to those of *The Directory of Humor Magazines and Humor Organizations* and often concluded that if a given humor listing was in the former two reference books and not in the latter, then *The Directory of Humor Magazines and Humor Organizations* had "omitted" the listing and therefore was guilty of being somewhat uneven in the thoroughness of its research. Evidently, the reviewers failed to realize that in most cases *The Directory of Humor Magazines and Humor Organizations* was really guilty of being either more up-to-date (i.e., not listing humor magazines and humor organizations that had already *ceased* to exist) or more accurate (i.e., not listing a humor column as being a free-standing humor magazine). One reviewer used a *2-year-old edition* of the reference book *Magazines for Libraries* as the yardstick against which to measure the thoroughness of *The Directory of Humor Magazines and Humor Organizations*, obviously not keeping in mind how dated such a yardstick would be in a field where humor magazines so quickly come and go.

In the list that follows, the reader will find not only other valuable humor resources (that for one reason or another did not fit the precise criteria for listing in the main section of this directory) but also up-to-date and accurate reports on the status of many other humor periodicals and humor organizations not listed in the main section of this directory. Hopefully, this listing will help clarify whether various humor periodicals and humor organizations not listed up front in the main listings are still kicking or have "bitten the dust."

Please note: Many of the following humor periodicals and humor organizations did not return the questionnaire. It is likely that most of these periodicals and organizations are out of business. However, erring on the side of caution, I have indicated "Presumably, out of business" only when the questionnaire was returned by the Post Office as "undeliverable."

G.C.E.

American Association of Aardvark Aficionados
P.O. Box 200
Parsippany, NJ 07054
Comments: Did not respond to questionnaire.

American Humor Studies Association
Jack O. Rosenbalm
Flowers Hall, Room 309
South West Texas State University
San Marcos, TX 78666
Comments: Did not respond to questionnaire.

Archie McPhee & Company Catalog
P.O. Box 30852
Seattle, WA 98103
Editor: Karin Snelson
Phone: (206) 782-9450
Order Desk & Information Line: (206) 782-2344
Comments: Founded in 1985, the **Archie McPhee & Company Catalog** is a 48-page catalog that contains fun items for sale. While certainly carrying a hefty number of humor items, the **Archie McPhee & Company Catalog** also sells items that hardly fit under the rubric of humor: skull mugs, metal [art] deco clocks, watches with Chinese characters, pink lawn flamingos, etc. Get the picture? But, don't let this stop you from being one of the 82,000 people who get the catalog.

Association of Comedy Artists
Comments: This organization, founded by Barbara Contardi in 1978, was listed in the 2nd edition of the directory as "dedicated to the advancement of comedy as a serious art form and to the promotion of professionalism in the field, thereby gaining greater public recognition and status." The questionnaire sent to this humor organization was returned as "undeliverable." Presumably, out of business.

Bananas
Comments: If an award were given for the longest amount of time a defunct humor magazine was able to maintain its listing in periodicals reference books after its demise, then **Bananas** would certainly be the grand winner. **Bananas** presumably was a humor magazine targeted to an adolescent audience and possibly published by Scholastic, Inc. (**Bananas** should not be confused with the **International Banana Club**, an organization still in existence and listed in the main section of this directory.)

Baseball Hall of Shame
P.O. Box 31867
Palm Beach Garden, FL 33420
Comments: Did not respond to questionnaire.

Belly Laffs Monthly
Comments: **Belly Laffs Monthly** was an 8-page humor newsletter founded in 1990 and edited by Frank O'Donnell. It went out of business in March 1991. (Frank O'Donnell is presently Editor-in-Chief of *The Wit*—listed in the main section of this directory.)

Benevolent and Loyal Order of Pessimists
P.O. Box 1945
Iowa City, IA 52244
Comments: The chairperson of this organization, Jack Duvall, returned the questionnaire without completing it, with the following terse note attached: "You are sadly mistaken. We are not a so-called humor magazine or organization of America or Canada." However, it remains unclear whether the **Benevolent and Loyal Order of Pessimists** is not a humor organization or simply that the chairperson was seemingly being pessimistic!

Big Deal
2119 College Street
Cedar Falls, IA 50613
Comments: Did not respond to questionnaire.

The Boring Institute®
P.O. Box 40
Maplewood, NJ 07040
Phone: (201) 763-6392
Comments: Founded in 1984 by Alan Caruba, **The Boring Institute®** sponsors four media spoofs annually: The Most Boring Films of the Year Awards (March); National Anti-Boredom Month (July); Fearless Forecasts of TV's Fall Flops (September); and the annual list of "The Most Boring Celebrities of the Year" (December). It also publishes pamphlets and posters. **The Boring Institute** is not listed in the main section of this directory because the organization does not meet any of the requirements for such listing (i.e., it does not allow others to in some way participate or be a member, nor does it produce a periodically issued humor publication).

Bull's Eye
P.O. Box 36
Lynnbrook, NY 11563
Comments: Did not respond to questionnaire.

Burlington Liar's Club
149 Oakland Avenue
Burlington, WI 53105
Comments: Did not respond to questionnaire.

Cheep Laffs
1111 West El Camino Real
Suite 109/212
Sunnyvale, CA 94087
Comments: Did not respond to questionnaire.

Cheesecake Newsletter
Comments: This humor newsletter, edited by Louisa Otis, was for people who love cheesecake, with recipes, jokes, and irreverent letters to the editor. With a circulation of 150, it was listed in the 1st edition of the directory but did not respond to the questionnaire for listing in the 2nd edition and was presumed to be out of business.

Church of Monday Night Football
P.O. Box 2127
Santa Barbara, CA 93102
Comments: Did not respond to questionnaire.

Clipophilia
P.O. Box 5671
Portland, OR 97228
Comments: Published out of Portland, Oregon, **Clipophilia** started off as "an in-house underground newsletter for our city's large daily newspaper, with a tiny circulation of bitter journalism school failures and drop-outs." **Clipophilia** solicited and published wacky newspaper clippings. Did not respond to questionnaire.

Comedy & Comment
448 North Mitchner Avenue
Indianapolis, IN 46210
Comments: Founded in 1958 and edited by Mack McGinnis, **Comedy & Comment** was listed in both the 1st and 2nd editions of the directory as "a compilation of humorous observations and jokes drawn from newspapers and other periodicals across America." This humor periodical did not return the questionnaire for listing in the 3rd edition of the directory.

The Comedy Registry
611 Broadway, #317
New York, NY 10012
Comments: Did not respond to questionnaire.

Comedy Writers Workshops
33 Isabella Street, #310
Toronto, Ontario M4Y 2P7
Canada
Founder: Miss Suzette
Phone: (416) 921-5288
Comments: **Comedy Writers Workshops** appears in this section rather than in the main section of the directory because it seems to be more a school for the teaching of comedy and humor than an organization that members join on an annual basis. According to the promotional materials supplied, Comedy Writers Workshops (founded in 1980) offers comedy courses, comedy seminars, and comedy workshops. A call to the above telephone number will get you a brochure.

Comic Relief
P.O. Box 846
Arcata, CA 95521
Comments: This is the national organization that sponsors an annual comedy show with Robins Williams, Whoppi Goldberg, and Billy Crystal aimed at raising funds for the homeless. Did not respond to questionnaire.

Committee for Immediate Nuclear War
2001 SW 98th Terrace
Ft. Lauderdale, FL 33324
Comments: Did not respond to questionnaire.

Couch Potatoes
Bob Armstrong
P.O. Box 249
Dixon, CA 95620
Comments: Did not respond to questionnaire.

Croc
Croc Ludcom, Inc.
5800 Monkland Avenue
Montreal H4A 1G1
Canada
Comments: Did not respond to questionnaire.

Dartnell
4660 Ravenwood Avenue
Chicago, IL 60640-4595
Comments: Did not respond to questionnaire.

The Electric Weenie
Comments: **The Electric Weenie,** also known at one time by the name **Zoo Keeper**, changed its name to **COMIC HIGHLIGHTS** and is listed under its new name in the main section of this directory.

Frank
P.O. Box 9405, Station A
Halfax B3K 5S1
Canada
Comments: Did not respond to questionnaire.

Free Territory of Ely-Chatelaine
P.O. Box 7075
Laguan Nigel, CA 92677
Comments: Did not respond to questionnaire.

Funny Business
P.O. Box 9061
Downers Grove, IL 60515
Comments: Did not respond to questionnaire.

Funny Funny World
Comments: The questionnaire, sent to the editor, Martin A. Ragaway, was returned "undeliverable." Presumably, out of business.

Funny Side Up
425 Stump Rd.
North Wales, PA 19454
Phone: (215) 361-5130
Comments: **Funny Side Up** is a slick (4-color process) 80-page catalog filled with entertaining products for sale, most of them accompanied by color photographs. Many of the products are humorous. Some aren't (what's funny about a genuine raccoon hat? Or smiley faces on underwear?). You'll find humorous books, as well as humorous slogans printed on T-shirts, underwear, notepads, and toilet paper.

Funny Times
P.O. Box 18792
Cleveland Heights, OH 44118-0792
Comments: **Funny Times** is a humorous tabloid published monthly out of Cleveland. Did not respond to questionnaire.

The Gelosophist
P.O. Box 29000, Suite 103
San Antonio, TX 78229
Comments: Launched in 1985 and edited by Lauren I. Barnett Scharf, **The Gelosophist** was a newsletter published 3-6 times per year and described in the 1st edition of the directory as containing "news, information, and opinion of various aspects of humor." It did not respond to the questionnaire for the 2nd edition of the directory and was presumed to be out of business.

Gesundheit Institute
2630 Robert Walker Place
Arlington, VA 22207
Publication: **ACHOO!**
Editor: Gareth Branwyn
Phone: (703) 525-8169

Comments: The **Gesundheit Institute** was founded in 1971 by Patch Adams, M.D. The organization and its founder are dedicated to the treatment of patients without charge. Dr. Adams, with the help of anywhere up to 20 medical workers, treated 15,000 patients for free from 1971 to 1983. In 1983, he stopped seeing patients in order to begin raising $2.5 million to build a "health community" in West Virginia, where his ideas could be carried out on a grander scale. What does all of this have to do with humor? Dr. Adams feels that humor is one of many ways of effectively treating patients and he actively uses humor in dealing with his patients. His organization publishes **ACHOO!**—an 8-page (fairly serious) newsletter issued once or twice a year and mailed to 6,500 people to keep them up to date on the happenings of the **Gesundheit Institute**. While Dr. Adams and his colleagues may highly value humor, their's is certainly not a humor organization per se, nor does their periodical seem to be a humor newsletter.

Get Stupid
25 Grant Street
Cambridge, MA 02138
Comments: Did not respond to questionnaire.

Giggle Books
P.O. Box 15263
Seattle, WA 98115-0263
Phone: (206) 524-5289
Comments: **Giggle Books** has been selling humor books through their 4-page mail order catalog since 1988. This publication is mailed for free to 1,000 customers. **Giggle Books** also accepts telephone orders.

The Goofus Office Gazette
P.O. Box 259
Pearl River, NY 10965
Comments: Begun in 1982 and edited by S. T. Godfrey, T. J. Finegan, C. Morris, and L. Stanley, this monthly 4-page humor newsletter with a circulation of 200 was listed in the 1st edition of the directory as "dedicated to Humor, Music, and the Arts, in that order." It did not respond to questionnaires for the 2nd or 3rd editions of the directory and is presumed to be out of business.

Harpoon
Publisher: American Media of New York, Inc.
1685 Elmwood Avenue, Suite 208
Buffalo, NY 14207
Phone: 716 875-0751
Comments: **Harpoon** is a new (Volume 1, Number 1 carries the date December 9, 1991) biweekly humor magazine, priced at $1.50 on the newsstand, $24.00 for a one-year subscription of 24 issues. Did not respond to questionnaire but still in business.

Housewive's Humor
P.O. Box 780
Lyman, WY 82937
Phone: (307) 786-4513
Comments: At least one periodicals reference book erroneously lists **Housewive's Humor** as a free-standing humor periodical when it is not. In reality, **Housewive's Humor** is a humor column appearing in the periodical *Housewife-Writer's Forum: The Magazine for Women Writers*, "A magazine that shares the joys, the fun, the foibles and the exasperations of juggling writing life and family life." *Housewife-Writer's Forum*, then, is a *serious magazine* that carries some lighthearted pieces, including the **Housewive's Humor** column.

Humor Digest
448 N. Mitchner Avenue
Indianapolis, IN 46219
Comments: Did not respond to questionnaire.

Humor Magazine
7710 Henry Avenue
Philadelphia, PA 19128
Comments: Edited by Edward Savaria, Jr. and Suzanne Tschanz, **Humor Magazine** was listed in the 2nd edition of the humor directory as a 4-times-a-year periodical. Did not respond to the latest questionaire.

Inside Joke
Elayne Wechsler-Chaput
1747 65th Street
Brooklyn, NY 11204
Comments: **Inside Joke** was founded in 1980 by Elayne Wechsler and was billed as "A Newsletter of Comedy & Creativity." By 1991 the humor publication had ceased publication. The 2nd edition of the directory listed this periodical as having a circulation of 200. All 80 back issues are available (for $1.50 per issue), and a "detailed chronology" of the publication's history can be had for free by sending a SASE to the above address.

International Association of Professional Bureaucrats
National Press Building, Room 926
Washington, DC 20045
Phone: (202) 347-2490
Comments: Founded in 1968 by Dr. James H. Boren, **IAPB** was listed in the 1st and 2nd editions of the humor directory as "a professional organization of corporate, academic, and governmental bureaucrats that promotes the principles of dynamic inaction (doing nothing but doing it in style)." By and large, this organization lampoons politics and politicians. When reached by phone, Jim Boren indicated that he had not had time to complete the questionnaire for listing **IAPB** in the 3rd edition of the directory because he had just announced his (humorous) candidacy for President and was beginning a one-year fellowship out in Oklahoma. This organization, presumably, is still in business.

International Automotive Hall of Shame
515 Alpine Road
P.O. Box 324
Fitchburg, MA 01420
Comments: Did not respond to questionnaire.

International Dull Folks
Comments: Founded in 1983 by J. D. "Dull" Stewart, the **International Dull Folks** published a once- or twice-a-year humor newsletter, *The Snooze News.* The 2nd edition of the directory listed IDF as having a membership of 1,000. The questionnaire sent to this humor organization was returned as "undeliverable." Presumably, out of business.

International Journal of Creature Communication
612 South Main
Sycamore, IL 60178
Comments: Founded by Charles U. Larson in 1980, **IJCC** was listed in the 1st and 2nd editions of the directory as "a journal devoted to the scholarly study of sport-fishing and simultaneously publishes parodies of scholarly research by using the jargon of various disciplines in the articles." Published irregularly in the past, this periodical did not respond to the latest questionnaire.

International Laughter Society
16000 Glen Una Drive
Los Gatos, CA 95030
Comments: Founded in 1983 by L. Katherine Ferrari, the **International Laughter Society** was described in the 1st edition of the humor directory as aiming "to promote laughter (and play) worldwide." It published a quarterly newsletter—**The Laff-Letter**—with a circulation of 750. The 2nd edition of the directory did not feature this organization in its main listings. Instead, **ILS** was listed in the Appendix, with the comments that "the **Laff-Letter** has been suspended. While this organization still exists, it no longer meets the criteria for listing as an organization, namely, that it sponsors activities in which members can become actively engaged."

International Order of the Armadillo
P.O. Box 60305
Jacksonville, FL 32236
Comments: Did not respond to questionnaire.

International Organization of Nerds
P.O. Box 118555
Cincinnati, OH 45211
Comments: Did not respond to questionnaire.

International Society for General Semantics
Publication: **Glimpse**
Publisher: International Society for General Semantics
P.O. Box 2469
San Francisco, CA 94126
Phone:(415) 543-1747
Comments: **Glimpse** was listed in the 2nd edition of this humor directory as a periodical that "tries to offer a brief glance at what people do with signs, symbols, and other means of communication; a glimpse of how words and language influence thought and behavior." ISGS's press release dated February 1990 noted "In 1989, the Executive Committee of the International Society for General Semantics decided to discontinue publishing **Glimpse** as a quarterly newsletter..." Some editorial material that would have appeared in **Glimpse** has been subsequently incorporated into the society's quarterly journal, *Et cetera*. The last issue of **Glimpse** published was Number 42 (December 1987).

Jester of Columbia
206 Ferris Booth Hall
Columbia University
New York, NY 10025
Editor: Robert Kim
Phone: (212) 853-7214
Comments: **Jester of Columbia** is a college humor magazine of Columbia University. Did not respond to the questionnaire for listing in this edition of the directory.

Knucklehead Press
6442 West 111th Street
Worth, IL 60482
Comments: Did not respond to questionnaire.

LAAF Newsletter
Comments: This humor newsletter was once published out of Kansas State University. The questionnaire sent to this periodical was returned marked both "undeliverable" and "no longer exists."

Ladies Against Women
Comments: The questionnaire sent to this humor organization was returned as "undeliverable." Presumably, out of business.

Laff Lines
P.O. Box 32071
Phoenix, AZ 85064-2071
Comments: Did not respond to questionnaire.

The Laugh Clinic
2233 SW Market Street Drive
Portland, OR 97201
Comments: Did not respond to questionnaire.

Laugh Factory™
Comments: Launched in 1982 and edited by Jamie Masada, Bill Taub, and Mindy Schultheis, **Laugh Factory** was billed in the 1st edition of the humor directory as a bimonthly "national humor magazine aimed at a mass audience, providing clean, clever humor." It claimed a circulation of 225,000. By 1988 it had ceased publication.

Laughing Bear News
P.O. Box 36159
Denver, CO 80236
Comments: Did not respond to questionnaire.

The Laughing Heart
Comments: The editor of this periodical, Liz Curtis Higgs, noted that "my newsletter...is primarily a promotional vehicle for my speaking services as a humorist/'encourager,'® rather than a true humor publication."

Laugh Time U.S.A.
P.O. Box 42303
Philadelphia, PA 19101
Comments: Founded in 1987 and edited by Maxwell Miller, this monthly 12-page humor newsletter was listed in the 2nd edition of the humor directory as "containing jokes, gags, anecdotes, cartoons, and news, geared toward the general public." Did not respond to the latest questionnaire.

LaughTrack
Comments: Founded in 1989 by Rick Siegel, this slick 38-page "Comedy Audience Magazine" was distributed for free to those attending comedy clubs and featured national advertisers. The questionnaire sent to this periodical was returned as "undeliverable." Additionally, this periodical's telephone has been disconnected. Presumably, this humor magazine is out of business.

Libsat
Gananoque Public Library
100 Park Street
Gananoque, Ontario K7G 2Y5
Canada
Comments: Published by John Love, beginning in 1982, out of the Gananoque Public Library, **Libsat** was a humor newsletter listed in the 1st edition of the directory as spoofing Library Sciences. With a circulation of 12 [sic], **Libsat** received rave reviews from Bill Katz of *Library Journal*, who commented on its "marvelous irreverent style—who could ask for a better library newsletter." By 1988, Libsat was "no longer accepting new subscriptions."

L.I.G.H.T. (Laughter In God, History and Theology)
P.O. Box 6928
Ft. Worth, TX 76115
Comments: Launched in 1983 by Robert J. Larremore, this twice-a-year humor newsletter with a circulation of 530 was listed in the 1st edition of the humor directory as a publication relating to humor and religion. This periodical did not respond to the questionnaire for listing in the 2nd edition of the directory and was presumed to be out of business.

The Limerick Special Interest Group
P.O. Box 365
Moffett, CA 94035
Comments: Listed in the 1st edition of the humor directory as "a club of limerick lovers," **The Limerick Special Interest Group** published the monthly 18-page **Limerick Special Interest Group Newsletter**, with a circulation of 60. This organization did not respond to the questionnaire for listing in the 2nd edition and was presumed to be out of business.

The Lone Star Comedy Monthly
P.O. Box 29000, Suite 103
San Antonio, TX 78229
Comments: Founded in 1982 and edited by Lauren I. Barnett Scharf, **The Lone Star Comedy Monthly** was listed in the 1st edition of the directory as a periodical "for the professional humorist." This periodical did not respond to the questionnaire for listing in the 2nd edition of the directory and was presumed to be out of business.

Lone Star Humor Digest
P.O. Box 29000, Suite 103
San Antonio, TX 78229
Comments: The 1st edition of the humor directory listed this periodical, starting in 1985, as a "humor book-by-subscription," to be issued 2-3 times per year. This periodical did not respond to the questionnaire for listing in the 2nd edition of the directory and was presumed to be out of business.

Man Watchers
8033 Sunset, #363
Los Angeles, CA 90046
Comments: Did not respond to questionnaire.

Man Will Never Fly Memorial Society International
P.O. Box 1903
Kill Devil Hills, NC 27948
Comments: Did not respond to questionnaire.

The Marx Brothers Study Unit
Comments: **The Marx Brothers Study Unit** changed its name to the **Marx Brotherhood** and is listed under its new name in the main section of this directory.

The Mayberry Gazette
P.O. Box 330
Clemmons, NC 27012
Comments: Did not respond to questionnaire.

Monk
Publisher: Monk
175 Fifth Avenue, Suite 2322
New York, NY 10010
Editors: Michael Lane, James Crotty
Phone: (212) 465-3231
Comments: **Monk** is a slick, 4-color-process, 64-page humor magazine priced at $10.00 for 4 issues or $18.00 for 8 issues (single copies on the newsstand are $2.95). The two editors together travel in a motorhome throughout the country, writing up their humorous experiences using a solar-powered Macintosh computer. The magazine carries an impressive array of national advertisers. Did not respond to questionnaire but still in business.

Monty Python Special Interest Group
2419 Greensburg Pike
Pittsburgh, PA 15221
Comments: Did not respond to questionnaire.

National Frumps of America
P.O. Box 1047
Winter Park, FL 32790
Comments: Did not respond to questionnaire.

National Society for the Prevention of Cruelty to Mushrooms
Comments: The questionnaire was returned as "undeliverable." Presumably, this organization is out of business.

Nurses for Laughter
3401 South Williams
Portland, OR 97201
Comments: Founded by Deborah Leiber in 1982, **Nurses for Laughter** was described in the 1st edition of the directory as "a group committed to promoting humor in health care." The organization published **PRN: Playfulness, Revelry, Nonsense**, a quarterly newsletter edited by Elaine Teutsch and Pat Rushford reaching 1,000 subscribers. **Nurses for Laughter** did not respond to the questionnaire for listing in the 2nd edition of the directory and was presumed to be out of business.

O'Liners
1237 Amacost Avenue, Suite 6
Los Angeles, CA 90025
Comments: Did not respond to questionnaire.

The Onion
33 University Square, Suite 270
Madison, WI 53715
Comments: Did not respond to questionnaire.

Orben's Current Comedy
Comments: **Orben's Current Comedy** changed its name to **Current Comedy** and is listed under its new name in the main section of this directory.

Pangloss Papers
Comments: This was a 50-page humor magazine, founded in 1982 by Bard Dahl, issued quarterly, and listed in the 2nd edition of the directory as a publication that "questions authority, preserves that which is worth preserving, and invents when present reality no longer serves." It went out of business in March 1989.

The Pedantic Monthly

Comments: Founded in 1988 and edited by Erik A. Johnson, the **Pedantic Monthly** was issued fives times per year. The questionnaire sent to this periodical was returned as "undeliverable." Presumably, this humor magazine is out of business.

The Periodic Journal of Bibliography

P.O. Box 669
Kendall Square
Cambridge, MA 02142
Comments: Founded in 1991 and edited by F. D. P. O'Paistie, this 26-page humor magazine is published twice a year and appears to spoof bibliographies and book reviews. Did not respond to questionnaire.

Phantastic Phunnies

1343 Stratford Drive
Kent, OH 44240
Comments: John Fultz edited this monthly newsletter, founded in 1977 and listed in both the 1st and 2nd editions of the directory as "a topical publication...consist[ing] of hundreds of indexed, topical one-liners for radio and tv personalities, stand-up comics, and public speakers." Did not respond to the latest questionnaire.

PHOEBE: The Newsletter of Eccentricity

Comments: Listed in the 2nd edition of the directory as a 10-page quarterly humor newsletter, **Phoebe** was founded in 1984 by James MacDougall and carried "news features of humorous content." The questionnaire was returned as "undeliverable." Presumably, this publication is out of business.

Piranha

Comments: The questionnaire was returned "undeliverable." Presumably, this humor magazine (?) is out of business.

Possum County™ News

P.O. Box 2572
Owensboro, KY 42302
Comments: Founded in 1984 as a quarterly newsletter and edited by "Poor Ol' George," the **Possum County™ News** was listed in the 2nd edition of the directory as carrying "All the nuz that Dan Rather misses and Paul Harvey don't care nuthin about." At one time, this magazine boasted a circulation of 25,000. Did not respond to the lastest questionnaire.

Post Scripts

Curtis Publishing Company
1000 Waterway Blvd.
Indianapolis, IN 46202
Comments: Did not respond to questionnaire.

Poultry: A Magazine of Voice

P.O. Box 4413
Springfield, MA 01101
Comments: Founded in 1979 and edited by Jack Flavin, Brendan Galvin, and George Garrett, **Poultry** was a newspaper with a circulation of 500 published 2-3 times per year. It was listed in the 2nd edition of the humor directory as a periodical that "parodies contemporary literature, particularly modern poetry." Did not respond to the latest questionaire.

The Princeton Tiger
Publisher:The Princeton Tiger
Princeton University
48 University Place
Princeton, NJ 08450
Editor: D.S. Pensley
Phone: (609) 258-3646
Comments: **The Princeton Tiger** is a 20-page college humor magazine of Princeton University. Did not respond to questionnaire.

The Professional Comedian's Association
581 9th Avenue
New York, NY 10036
Comments: Did not respond to questionnaire.

Prolock Society
Russell J. Meyer
English Department
University of Missouri
Columbia, MO 65211
Comments: Did not respond to questionnaire.

R.A.L.P.H.
Comments: **R.A.L.P.H. (Royal Association for the Longevity & Preservation of the Honeymooners)** was founded in 1983 by Peter Crescenti and Bob Columbe. According to the 1st edition of the humor directory, this organization was a Honeymooners "appreciation society" that sponsored annual conventions and published a quarterly, 4-page newsletter, **The RALPH Newsletter**. This organization did not respond to the questionnaire for listing in the 2nd edition of the directory and was presumed to be out of business.

Rave®
Comments: The 2nd edition of the directory listed **Rave**, a monthly humor magazine, as "the 'Playbill' of the comedy club world—filled with photographs and articles on stand-up comedians and comedy." Founded in 1986, published by Joshua Simons, and edited by Ronald L. Smith, **Rave** at one time boasted a circulation of 250,000. This magazine went out of business in 1990.

rec. humor. funny
Clarinet Communications
124 King Street North
Waterloo N2J 2X8
Canada
Comments: This is supposedly "on-line jokes" for computer buffs. Did not respond to questionnaire.

Rich's Arizona Humor
2512 N. 85th Place
Scottsdale, AZ 85257
Comments: Did not respond to questionnaire.

S.A.L.T. Newsletter (Salvation And Laughter Together Newsletter)
P.O. Box 6928
Ft. Worth, TX 76115
Comments: Founded in 1983 and edited by Robert J. Larremore, the **S.A.L.T. Newsletter** was a 10-page quarterly humor newsletter listed in the 1st edition of the humor directory as publishing "wit and

humor concerning religion." This periodical did not respond to the questionnaire for listing in the 2nd edition of the directory and was presumed to be out of business.

Sarcastics Anonymous and Laugh Lovers News
P.O. Box 1495
Pleasonton, CA 94566
Comments: Founded by Dr. Virginia Tooper in 1981 as **Laugh Lovers News**, a bimonthly, by 1988 this humor newsletter had changed its name to **Sarcastics Anonymous and Laugh Lovers News** and reduced its issuance to 4 times a year. Reaching 600-700 readers, this periodical was listed in the 2nd edition of the humor directory as "devoted to kicking the habit of sarcasm, or at least learning how to live with and enjoy it more. There are also articles on the positive applications of humor and laughter in everyday life." Did not respond to the latest questionnaire.

Der Shmaiser/The Spanker
5775 Wentworth
Cole St. Luc. H4W 2S3
Canada
Comments: Did not respond to questionnaire.

Small Street Journal
Comments: Did not respond to questionnaire. Presumably out of business.

Smurfs in Hell
2210 N. 9th STreet
Boise, ID 83702
Comments: Did not respond to questionnaire.

Snicker Humor Magazine
Comments: This humor periodical was not listed in the 1st or 2nd editions of the humor directory. The questionnaire sent to this humor magazine was returned as "undeliverable." Presumably, out of business.

Soundings
Comments: **Soundings** changed its name to **Leadership** and is listed under its new name in the main section of this directory.

The Spoke
Emory University
Box 21256
Atlanta, GA 30032
Editor: Tod Jackson
Phone: (404) 727-6182
Comments: **The Spoke** is a college humor magazine published at Emory Univeristy. Did not respond to the questionnaire for listing in this edition of the directory.

Stanford Chaparral
P.O. Box 8585
Stanford, CA 94309
Editor: Celeste Campbell
Phone: (415) 723-1468
Comments: Founded in 1899, the **Stanford Chaparral** is a college humor magazine published out of Stanford University. This magazine did not respond to the questionnaire.

Studies in American Humor
James Tanner
English Department
University of North Texas
P.O. Box 13827
Denton, TX 76203-3827
Comments: Did not respond to questionnaires for the 1st, 2nd, or 3rd editions of this humor directory.

TASP Newsletter
P.O. Box 6375
Georgetown, TX 78626
Comments: Did not respond to questionnaire.

This Magazine
Comments: Founded in 1985 and edited by Shari Roman, Marianne Meyer, and Chris Butler, this 52-page monthly humor magazine was listed in the 1st edition of the humor directory as "a humor magazine that features art, interviews, and opinions, political and otherwise." By 1988, this periodical was out of business.

Turtle Express
Comments: The questionnaire sent to this humor organization or humor publication (?) was returned marked "undeliverable." Additionally, the person to whom it had been addressed (Lloyd Hardesty) may himself be defunct—the word "deceased" had been written on the outside of the returned envelope.

The Uncommon Reader
Comments: Founded in 1986 by Louis B. Hatchett, Jr., **The Uncommon Reader** was described in the 2nd edition of the directory as a quarterly magazine offering a "concoction of lively, humorous fiction; biting, sardonic, cultural criticism; and bemused, pungent reports on the absurdities of modern civilization." Reaching a total circulation of 1,500, **The Uncommon Reader** had gone out of business by 1991.

The Universal Church O' Fun Times
4326 Woodstock Blvd., Suite 666
Portland, OR 97206
Comments: Did not respond to questionnaire. *(Surely, the suite number in this address has got to be a joke—for a "church" organization.)*

UtmosT
Publisher:Texas Student Publications
P.O. Box D
Austin, TX 78713-8904
Editors: Catherine H. Cantieri, Johnny Ludden
Phone: (512) 471-4111
Comments: **UtmosT,** founded in 1978 and issued 8 times a year, is one of the few college magazines that did respond to our questionnaire. Unfortunately, a review of the magazine and the responses to the questionnaire revealed that **UtmosT** is not really a humor magazine, or even a college humor magazine. Instead, it is simply a college magazine that may carry an occasional humorous article or two. The editors' description of their magazine is revealing: "General interest with a wide range of articles, including food, music, and video reviews; tours of Texas' unique spots; off-beat interviews; contemporary issues affecting college students; plus an assortment of humorous 'news' items."

The Very Bad Poets Club Newsletter
Comments: The questionaire sent to this organization and/or newsletter was returned as "undeliverable." Presumably, out of business.

Virginia Health and Humor Association
1227 Manchester AVenue
Norfolk, VA 23508
Comments: Directed by Steve Kissell, this organization did not respond to the questionnaire.

Wahoo Reader
P.O. Box 691
6102 E. Mockingbird
Dallas, TX 75214
Comments: Did not respond to questionnaire but probably still in business.

We Love Lucy
P.O. Box 480216
Los Angeles, CA 90048
Comments: This humor organization, founded in 1977, was described in the 1st edition of the humor directory as "a fan club honoring Lucille Ball." Thomas J. Watson was the editor of the organization's 12-page quarterly, **Lucy**. This organization did not respond to the questionnaire for listing in the 2nd edition of the humor directory and was presumed to be out of business.

Western Humor and Irony Membership Serial Yearbook (WHIMSY)
Comments: Founded in 1980 by Don Nilsen and Alleen Nilsen and published out of the English Department at Arizona State University, **WHIMSY** was a once-a-year, large format, paperback anthology of the papers presented at the annual Western Humor and Irony Membership conference. **WHIMSY** is no longer published.

Whimsical Alternative Polictical Action Committee
Comments: The questionnaire sent to this humor organization was returned "undeliverable." Presumably, out of business.

Zoo Keeper
Comments: **Zoo Keeper**, also known at one time by the name **Electric Weenie**, changed its name to **COMIC HIGHLIGHTS** and is listed under its new name in the main section of this directory.

Appendix

Rank Order	Magazine or Other Periodical	Reported Circulation
1	MAD[2]	1,000,000+
2	Bits & Pieces[2]	330,000
3	CRACKED[2]	300,000-500,000
4	National Lampoon	250,000
5	Spy	150,000
6	Just For Laughs	50,000
	The Nose	50,000
8	Leadership[2]	42,000
9	PUNCH Digest for Canadian Doctors	37,000
10	Minne Ha! Ha!	30,000
11	The Quayle Quarterly	15,000
	The Weekly Farce	15,000
13	The Whole Mirth Catalog[2]	12,000
14	Women's Glib[2]	10,000-20,000
15	The Harvard Lampoon	10,000
	Laughing Matters[2]	10,000
	Laughter Works The Newsletter[2]	10,000
	The Wit	10,000
19	Last Month's Newsletter	9,000
20	Woddis News	8,000+
21	Journal of Irreproducible Results	8,000
	Journal of Nursing Jocularity[2]	8,000
	The Plague	8,000
24	This Brain Has a Mouth	7,500
25	The Stark Fist of Removal[2]	7,000
26	Current Comedy[2]	5,000
	Witty World	5,000
	The Yellow Journal	5,000
29	Maledicta: International Journal of Verbal Aggression[2]	4,000
	Nonsense	4,000
31	The Steve Wilson Report[2]	3,500
32	Journal of Polymorphous Perversity	3,127
33	Laugh•Makers Variety Arts Magazine	3,000-3,200
34	The Realist[2]	3,000
	Humor Events and Possibilities[2]	3,000
36	One to One	2,500-3,000

[Table continued on next page]

[1]Lists only those magazines and periodicals that provided data on their circulation.
[2]This magazine or periodical does not accept advertisements.

Rank Order	Magazine or Other Periodical	Reported Circulation
37	Humerus	2,500
	Pratfall[2]	2,500
39	The Three Stooges Journal[2]	2,200
40	Humor, Hypnosis and Health Quarterly[2]	2,000
	Maledicta Monitor[2]	2,000
42	The Intra-Tent Journal[2]	1,600
43	SCROOGE Newsletter	1,237
44	COMIC HIGHLIGHTS	1,200
	Quagmire[2]	1,200
46	News of the Weird[2]	1,100
47	Mark Twain Circular	1,050
48	Mark Twain Journal[2]	900
49	The Laugh Connection[2]	800
50	The Peter Schickele Rag[2]	750-1,000
51	The Jokesmith[2]	750
52	Laugh It Up/Laugh It UpDate	600+
53	Ballast Quarterly Review[2]	600
54	Wilde Times[2]	580+
55	Humor: International Journal of Humor Research	550
56	Thoughts For All Seasons	500-1,000
57	The Monthly...Bulletin[2]	500
	Thalia: Studies in Literary Humor	500
	Word Ways: The Journal of Recreational Linguistics	500
60	The Freedonia Gazette	400
	The Silly Club Rag[2]	400
	Journal of Insignificant Research[2]	400
63	Funny Stuff From the Gags Gang[2]	300+
64	Cartoon World	300
65	The Laughter Prescription[2]	250
66	the Blab	200+
67	Gene Perret's Round Table	200
68	Comedy Writers Association Newsletter	110
69	Pun Intended	100
70	Humor Correspondence Club Membership List	80
71	Ostriches Anonymous Newsletter	43
72	Humor Stamp Directory	40

[1]Lists only those magazines and periodicals that provided data on their circulation.
[2]This magazine or periodical does not accept advertisements.

TABLE 2. Writers Markets for Humorous Articles in American and Canadian Magazines and Periodicals

Magazine	Accepts Unsolicited Manuscripts	Length of Reporting Time	Magazine Copyrighted	Payment Rates or Terms	Copyright Arrangements
Ballast Quarterly Review	No				
Bits & Pieces	No		Yes		
the Blab	Yes		No	No payment	No formal arrangements
Capitol Comedy	Yes	1 month	Yes	$5 per line, $25 per cartoon	Acquires all rights
Carolina HaHa Newsletter	Yes	2 weeks	No	Unspecified number of complimentary copies	Acquires 1st serial rights
Cartoon World	Yes		No	Based upon length (most are contributed by author for free)	Acquires all rights
COMIC HIGHLIGHTS	No		Yes		
CRACKED	Yes	3 weeks	Yes	$75.00+ per page for writers, $150+ per page for artists	Acquires 1st serial rights
Current Comedy	Inquire first	30 days	Yes	$15 per article	Acquires all rights
The Fillmore Bungle	Yes		No	No payment	No formal arrangements
The Freedonia Gazette	Yes	1 month	Yes	1 complimentary copy	Acquires all rights

Magazine	Accepts Unsolicited Manuscripts	Length of Reporting Time	Magazine Copyrighted	Payment Rates or Terms	Copyright Arrangements
Funny Stuff From the Gags Gang	Yes	"immediately"	Yes	$5 per joke	No formal arrangements
Gag Re-Cap	No		No		
Gene Perret's Round Table	Yes (from subscribers)		Yes	No payment	No formal arrangements
The Harvard Lampoon	Inquire first	varies	Yes	No payment	Acquires all rights
Humerus	Yes	3-6 months	Yes	2 complimentary copies (plus possibly artist's proofs)	Acquires 1st serial rights
Humor Events & Possibilities	Inquire first	2 months	Yes	No payment	Acquires all rights
Humor, Hypnosis and Health Quarterly	Yes	1 month	Yes	30 complimentary copies	Acquires 1st serial rights
Humor: International Journal of Humor Research	Yes	3 months	Yes	5 complimentary copies	Acquires all rights
The Intra-Tent Journal	Yes	2 weeks	Yes	No payment	
The Jokesmith	Yes	30 days	Yes	2 complimentary copies	No formal arrangements
Journal of Insignificant Research	Yes	1 week	No	1 complimentary copy	No formal arrangements
Journal of Irreproducible Results	Yes	4 months	Yes	1 complimentary copy	Acquires all rights

TABLE 2 (continued). Writers Markets for Humorous Articles in American and Canadian Magazines and Periodicals

Magazine	Accepts Unsolicited Manuscripts	Length of Reporting Time	Magazine Copyrighted	Payment Rates or Terms	Copyright Arrangements
Journal of Nursing Jocularity	Inquire first	6-12 weeks	Yes	2 complimentary copies	Acquires 1st serial rights
Journal of Polymorphous Perversity	Yes	4-6 weeks	Yes	2 complimentary copies	Acquires all rights
Just For Laughs	Yes	1 month	Yes	$50-$150 per manuscript	Acquires 1st serial rights
Kid Show Quarterly	No		Yes		
Last Month's Newsletter	No		Yes		
Latest Jokes	Inquire first	3 weeks	Yes	$1-$3 per joke	Acquires all rights
The Laugh Connection	No		Yes		
Laughing Matters	Yes	2-4 months	Yes	1 complimentary copy	Variable arrangements
Laugh It Up/Laugh It UpDate	Inquire first	3 weeks	Yes	10 complimentary copies	Acquires 1st serial rights; upon publication rights revert back to author
Laugh•Makers Variety Arts Magazine	Inquire first	2-4 weeks	Yes	4 complimentary copies	Acquires first serial rights; rights revert back to author upon publication (with stipulation article cannot be reprinted in another performer trade publication for one year)

TABLE 2 (*continued*). Writers Markets for Humorous Articles in American and Canadian Magazines and Periodicals

Magazine	Accepts Unsolicited Manuscripts	Length of Reporting Time	Magazine Copyrighted	Payment Rates or Terms	Copyright Arrangements
The Laughter Prescription	Yes	1 week	No	3 complimentary copies	No formal arrangements
Laughter Works The Newsletter	Yes	4 months	Yes	100 complimentary copies	Author retains rights
Leadership	No		Yes		
MAD	Yes	1 month	Yes	$350 per printed page minimum	Acquires all rights
Maledicta: International Journal of Verbal Aggression	Inquire first	1 week	Yes	20 complimentary copies	Acquires all rights but author may reprint elsewhere
Maledicta Monitor	Inquire first	1 week	Yes	2 complimentary copies	Acquires all rights
Mark Twain Circular	Yes	2 weeks	No	3 complimentary copies	No formal arrangements
Mark Twain Journal	Yes	2-3 weeks	Yes	10 complimentary copies	Acquires all rights (unless copyright is reserved by author)
Minne Ha! Ha!	Yes	4 months	Yes	$5-$35 per article	Author owns copyright to article
The Monthly...Bulletin	Yes	4 weeks	No	3 complimentary copies + free 2-issue subscription	No formal arrangements
National Lampoon	Yes	2 months	Yes	Depends upon length of manuscript	Acquires 1st serial rights
Nonsense	Inquire first	"immediately"	Yes	10 complimentary copies	Acquires all rights

TABLE 2 (*continued*). Writers Markets for Humorous Articles in American and Canadian Magazines and Periodicals

Magazine	Accepts Unsolicited Manuscripts	Length of Reporting Time	Magazine Copyrighted	Payment Rates or Terms	Copyright Arrangements
The Nose	Yes	1 month	Yes	Pays in cash or complimentary copies (depending on current finances)	Acquires 1st serial rights and reprint rights
One to One	Yes (only from subscribers; inquire first)		Yes		Acquires all rights
Ostrich Watchers Newsletter	Yes	6 weeks	No	No payment	Acquires all rights
The Peter Schickele Rag	No		Yes		
The Plague	Inquire first	2–4 weeks	Yes	Unspecified number of complimentary copies	Acquires all rights
Pratfall	Yes	Varies	Yes	10 complimentary copies	No formal arrangements
PUNCH Digest for Canadian Doctors	Yes	2–4 weeks	Yes	30¢ per word	Acquires 1st serial rights
The Pundit	Yes	1 week	Yes	No payment	No formal arrangements
Pun Intended	Yes	1 week	Yes	Unspecified number of complimentary copies	No formal arrangements
Quagmire	Yes	4 months	Yes	$1.50 per article or 1 complimentary copy	Author owns rights to article

TABLE 2 (*continued*). **Writers Markets for Humorous Articles in American and Canadian Magazines and Periodicals**

Magazine	Accepts Unsolicited Manuscripts	Length of Reporting Time	Magazine Copyrighted	Payment Rates or Terms	Copyright Arrangements
The Quayle Quarterly	Yes	3 months	Yes	Negotiable	Acquires first serial rights
The Realist	Yes	3 weeks	No	10¢ per word	Author owns rights
SCROOGE Newsletter	Inquire first	2 weeks	No	Free membership	All rights retained by author
The Silly Club Rag	Yes	2-4 weeks	Yes	$1-$5 per article	Author retains all rights
SPY	Yes	4-6 weeks	Yes	50¢ per word	1st and 2nd serial rights and non-exclusive anthology rights
The Stark Fist of Removal	Inquire first	2 months	Yes	3 complimentary copies	Author and publisher share rights
The Steve Wilson Report	Inquire first		Yes	20 complimentary copies	No formal arrangements
Thalia: Studies in Literary Humor	Yes	2-6 months	Yes	No payment	Acquires all rights
This Brain Has a Mouth	Inquire first	2 days	Yes	5 complimentary copies	
Thoughts For All Seasons	Yes	Acknowledges in 15 days; accepts or rejects 3 months prior to publication	Yes	1 complimentary copy	Acquires all rights
The Three Stooges Journal	Yes	1 week	Yes	No payment	No formal arrangements
Visual Lunacy News	Yes	4 weeks	Yes	20 complimentary copies	Acquires all rights

TABLE 2 (*continued*). Writers Markets for Humorous Articles in American and Canadian Magazines and Periodicals

Magazine	Accepts Unsolicited Manuscripts	Length of Reporting Time	Magazine Copyrighted	Payment Rates or Terms	Copyright Arrangements
The Weekly Farce	No		Yes		
Wilde Times	No		Yes		
The Wit	Inquire first	2-3 months	Yes	Unspecified number of complimentary copies	Acquires 1st serial rights
Witty World	Inquire first		Yes	2 complimentary copies	Acquires 1st serial rights
Woddis News	Inquire first			No payments	
Women's Glib	Yes	2 weeks	Yes	$5 per page minimum + 2 complimentary copies	Acquires one-time, non-exclusive rights
Word Ways: The Journal of Recreational Linguistics	Yes	1 week	Yes	1 complimentary copy	Acquires 1st serial rights; upon publication, rights revert back to author
The Yellow Journal	Yes	1-2 months	No	1 complimentary copy	Author owns all rights
Ye Olde Bastards Bulletin	No		No		

TABLE 3. **Rank-Ordered Comparative Analysis of Dollar Cost of Advertising Per Humor Periodical Reader**[1,2]

Rank Order	Humor Periodical	Full-Page Black-and-White Ad Rate	Reported Circulation	Cost Per Reader[3]
1	Humor Stamp Club	$ 100	40	$2.50
2	Latest Jokes	$ 100	55	$1.82
3	Thoughts For All Seasons	$ 125	500-1,000	.25[4]
4	Thalia: Studies in Literary Humor	$ 100	500	.20
5	Journal of Polymorphous Perversity	$ 550	3,127	.18
6	Humerus	$ 400	2,500	.16[5]
7	The Freedonia Gazette	$ 60	400	.15
	Witty World	$ 750	5,000	.15
9	Word Ways: The Journal of Recreational Linguistics	$ 60	500	.12[6]
10	One-to-One: The Journal of Creative Broadcasting	$ 275	2,500-3,000	.11[4]
11	The Plague	$ 600	8,000	.08
12	The Harvard Lampoon	$ 600	10,000	.06
	PUNCH Digest for Canadian Doctors	$2,350	37,000	.06
	Woddis News	$ 450	8,000+	.06
15	Laugh•Makers Variety Arts Magazine	$ 135	3,000-3,200	.05[4]
	Spy	$7,188	150,000	.05
	This Brain Has a Mouth	$ 350	7,500	.05
18	Nonsense	$ 175	4,000	.04
	The Weekly Farce	$ 600	15,000	.04
20	Just For Laughs	$1,300	50,000	.03
	The Quayle Quarterly	$ 500	15,000	.03
	The Wit	$ 275	10,000	.03
23	Minne Ha! Ha!	$ 605	30,000	.02
	National Lampoon	$5,275	250,000	.02
	The Nose	$1,150	50,000	.02
	The Yellow Journal	$ 100	5,000	.02

[1]This assessment was made based on the figures for the periodicals' *full-page black-and-white* advertising rates. The rank ordering may be different when assessed on 1/2-page black-and-white rates, color rates, or cover rates. Cost per reader was determined by dividing the full-page black-and-white advertising rate by the circulation of the respective periodicals.

[2] Only those humor periodicals that accept advertisements and that provided *both* advertising rates and circulation figures are listed here.

[3]Figures were rounded off to the nearest cent.

[4]Because this humor periodical provided a circulation range rather than just one number, the *lowest* number in the range was used in determing the cost-per-reader figure.

[5]This rate is based on the cost of a full *cover* black-and-white ad.

[6]This rate is based on the cost of a *Cover 4* full-page black-and-white ad.

Editor's note: Prospective advertisers should interpret this table cautiously, keeping in mind that cost per reader should not be the only factor in deciding where to spend advertising dollars. For example, a book publisher seeking to promote and market a scholarly book about the humorous writings of Oscar Wilde would probably fare better by targeting *Thalia* readers, who are interested in literary humor, than *The Freedonia Gazette* readers, who are specifically interested in Marx Brothers humor, despite the fact that *Thalia*'s cost per reader is higher than *The Freedonia Gazette*'s.

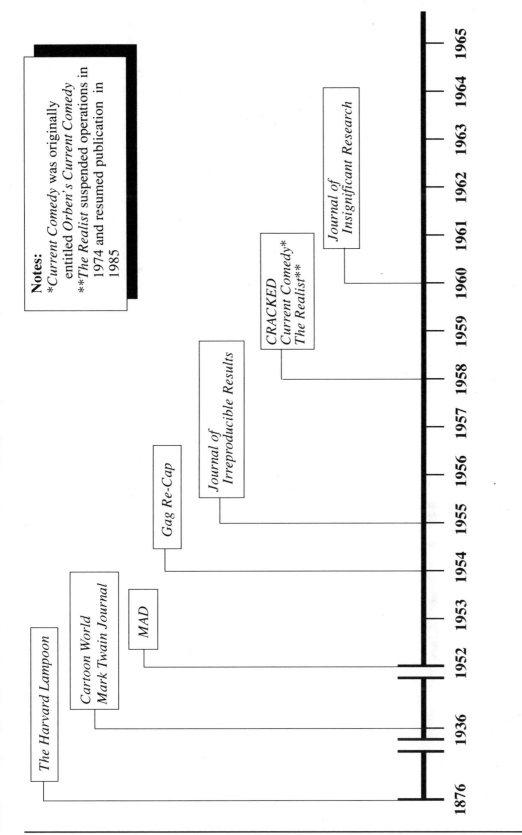

Notes:
Current Comedy was originally entitled *Orben's Current Comedy*
**The Realist* suspended operations in 1974 and resumed publication in 1985

The Harvard Lampoon

Cartoon World
Mark Twain Journal

MAD

Gag Re-Cap

Journal of
Irreproducible Results

CRACKED
Current Comedy*
The Realist**

Journal of
Insignificant Research

1876 1936 1952 1953 1954 1955 1956 1957 1958 1959 1960 1961 1962 1963 1964 1965

FIGURE 1. Time line indicating dates that humor periodicals were established.

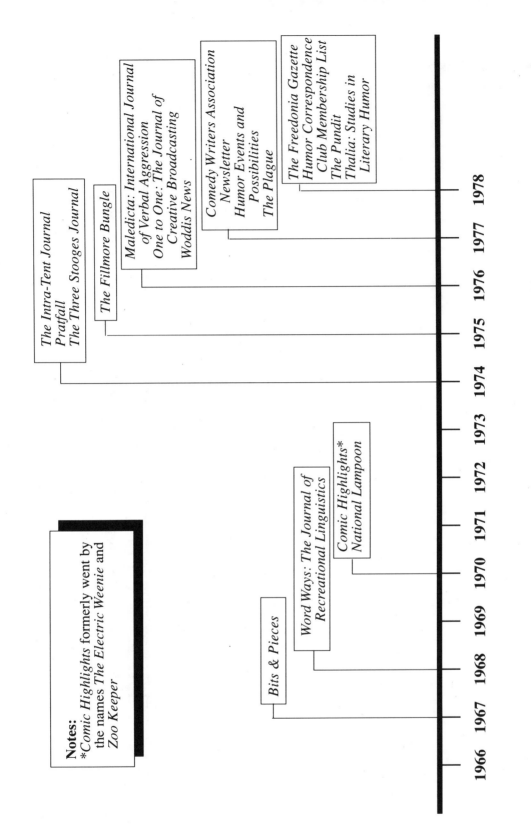

The Intra-Tent Journal
Pratfall
The Three Stooges Journal

The Fillmore Bungle

Maledicta: International Journal
of Verbal Aggression
One to One: The Journal of
Creative Broadcasting
Woddis News

Comedy Writers Association
Newsletter
Humor Events and
Possibilities
The Plague

The Freedonia Gazette
Humor Correspondence
Club Membership List
The Pundit
Thalia: Studies in
Literary Humor

Notes:
Comic Highlights formerly went by
the names *The Electric Weenie* and
Zoo Keeper

Bits & Pieces

Word Ways: The Journal of
Recreational Linguistics

Comic Highlights*
National Lampoon

1966 1967 1968 1969 1970 1971 1972 1973 1974 1975 1976 1977 1978

FIGURE 1 *(continued)*. Time line indicating dates that humor periodicals were established.

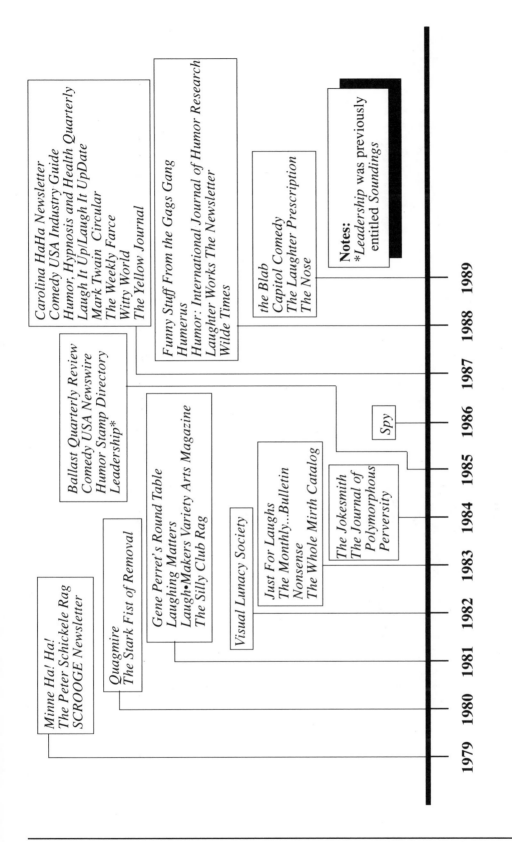

FIGURE 1 (*continued*). Time line indicating dates that humor periodicals were established.

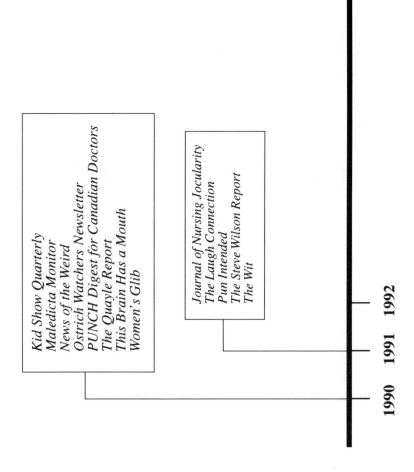

FIGURE 1 (*continued*). **Time line indicating dates that humor periodicals were established.**

Cross Index of Subject Areas

Anthropology Humor
Ballast Quarterly Review
the Blab
Humor Events and Possibilities
Humor: International Journal of Humor Research
Journal of Insignificant Research
Journal of Irreproducible Results
Maledicta: International Journal of Verbal Aggression
The Monthly...Bulletin

Arts Humor
Ballast Quarterly Review
Carolina HaHa Newsletter
The Freedonia Gazette
Funny Stuff From the Gags Gang
Humerus
Humor Events and Possibilities
Intra-Tent Journal
Journal of Irreproducible Results
Just For Laughs
Latest Jokes
Laugh Makers Variety Arts Magazine
MAD
Maledicta: International Journal of Verbal Aggression
Maledicta Monitor
Minne Ha Ha
The Monthly...Bulletin
One to One
The Peter Schickele Rag
The Plague
Pratfall
The Realist
Spy
The Stark Fist of Removal
Thalia: Studies in Literary Humor
View From the Ledge
Witty World
Women's Glib

Astronomy Humor
Humor Events and Possibilities
Journal of Irreproducible Results
The Monthly...Bulletin

Biochemistry Humor
Humor Events and Possibilities
Journal of Irreproducible Results

Biology Humor
Humor Events and Possibilities
Journal of Insignificant Research
Journal of Irreproducible Results
Journal of Nursing Jocularity

Business Humor
Ballast Quarterly Review
Bits & Pieces
Carolina HaHa Newsletter
Current Comedy
Funny Stuff From the Gags Gang
Gag Re-Cap
Gene Perret's Round Table
Humor Events and Possibilities
Humor, Hypnosis and Health Quarterly
The Jokesmith
Journal of Irreproducible Results
The Laugh Connection
Laugh It Up
Laugh It UpDate
Laughing Matters
Laughter Works The Newsletter
Leadership
Maledicta: International Journal of Verbal Aggression
Maledicta Monitor
One to One
Ostrich Watchers Newsletter
Pun Intended
Spy
The Steve Wilson Report
Wilde Times
Woddis News
Women's Glib

Cartoons/Illustrations/Graphics
Ballast Quarterly Review
Carolina HaHa Newsletter
Cartoon World
CRACKED
Funny Stuff From the Gags Gang
Humerus
Humor Events and Possibilities
Journal of Irreproducible Results
Last Month's Newsletter
The Laugh Connection
MAD
Maledicta: International Journal of Verbal Aggression
Maledicta Monitor

Minne Ha Ha
The Monthly...Bulletin
National Lampoon
The Nose
The Plague
Pun Intended
Punch Digest for Canadian Doctors
The Silly Club Rag
Spy
The Stark Fist of Removal
Thalia: Studies in Literary Humor
This Brain Has a Mouth
Thoughts For All Seasons
View From the Ledge
The Whole Mirth Catalog
Witty World
Woddis News
Women's Glib
Ye Old Bastards Bulletin
The Yellow Journal

Chemistry Humor
Humor Events and Possibilities
Journal of Irreproducible Results

Computer Sciences Humor
Ballast Quarterly Review
Humor Events and Possibilities
Humor: International Journal of Humor Research
Journal of Irreproducible Results
Maledicta: International Journal of Verbal Aggression
Maledicta Monitor

Dentistry Humor
Humor Events and Possibilities
Humor: International Journal of Humor Research
The Jokesmith
Journal of Irreproducible Results
Laugh It Up
Laugh It UpDate
One to One
Ye Olde Bastards Bulletin

Economics Humor
Cartoon World
Humor Events and Possibilities
Journal of Irreproducible Results
Maledicta: International Journal of Verbal Aggression

Education Humor
Ballast Quarterly Review
Carolina HaHa Newsletter
Cartoon World
Humor Events and Possibilities
The Jokesmith
Journal of Irreproducible Results
Journal of Polymorphous Perversity
Laugh It Up
Laugh It UpDate
Laughing Matters
MAD
Maledicta: International Journal of Verbal Aggression
Maledicta Monitor
The Monthly...Bulletin
The Plague
The Steve Wilson Report
Thalia: Studies in Literary Humor
The Weekly Farce

English Humor
Ballast Quarterly Review
Carolina HaHa Newsletter
Humor Events and Possibilities
Journal of Irreproducible Results
Maledicta: International Journal of Verbal Aggression
Maledicta Monitor
The Monthly...Bulletin
The Pundit
Thalia: Studies in Literary Humor

Film Media Humor
Ballast Quarterly Review
the Blab
CRACKED
The Freedonia Gazette
Humor Events and Possibilities
The Intra-Tent Journal
MAD
Maledicta: International Journal of Verbal Aggression
Maledicta Monitor
The Monthly...Bulletin
Pratfall
Spy
Thalia: Studies in Literary Humor
The Three Stooges Journal
The Weekly Farce

Foreign Languages Humor
Ballast Quarterly Review
Humor Events and Possibilities
Maledicta: International Journal of Verbal Aggression
The Monthly...Bulletin
Spy
Thalia: Studies in Literary Humor

General Humor
Ballast Quarterly Review
Bits & Pieces
Carolina HaHa Newsletter
Cartoon World
Comic Highlights
CRACKED
Current Comedy
Fillmore Bungle
The Freedonia Gazette
Funny Stuff Comedy Almanac
Funny Stuff From the Gags Gang
Gag Re-Cap
Gene Perret's Round Table
Humerus
Humor Events and Possibilities
Humor, Hypnosis and Health Quarterly
Journal of Irreproducible Results
Just For Laughs
Last Month's Newsletter
Latest Jokes
The Laugh Connection
Laugh Makers Variety Arts Magazine
Laughing Matters
The Laughter Prescription
Laughter Works The Newsletter
Leadership
MAD
Maledicta: International Journal of Verbal Aggression
Maledicta Monitor
Minne Ha Ha
The Monthly...Bulletin
National Lampoon
The Nose
One to One
Ostrich Watchers Newsletter
The Plague
Pun Intended
Punch Digest for Canadian Doctors
SCROOGE Newsletter
The Silly Club Rag

Spy
Thalia: Studies in Literary Humor
Thoughts For All Seasons
View From the Ledge
The Weekly Farce
The Whole Mirth Catalog
Wilde Times

Geology Humor
Humor Events and Possibilities
Journal of Insignificant Research
Journal of Irreproducible Results
Maledicta: International Journal of Verbal Aggression
Maledicta Monitor

History Humor
Ballast Quarterly Review
Capitol Comedy
Fillmore Bungle
Humor Events and Possibilities
Humor: International Journal of Humor Research
Journal of Irreproducible Results
Latest Jokes
MAD
Maledicta: International Journal of Verbal Aggression
Maledicta Monitor
The Monthly...Bulletin
Ostrich Watchers Newsletter
The Plague
The Weekly Farce

Humanities Humor
Ballast Quarterly Review
Carolina HaHa Newsletter
Funny Stuff From the Gags Gang
Humor Events and Possibilities
Humor, Hypnosis and Health Quarterly
Journal of Irreproducible Results
Maledicta: International Journal of Verbal Aggression
The Monthly...Bulletin
One to One
Pun Intended
Spy
The Stark Fist of Removal
Thalia: Studies in Literary Humor
Wilde Times
Witty World
Women's Glib
Word Ways: The Journal of Recreational Linguistics

Joke Services Humor
Capitol Comedy
Comic Highlights
Current Comedy
Funny Stuff Comedy Almanac
Funny Stuff From the Gags Gang
Gag Re-Cap
Latest Jokes
The Jokesmith
Kid Show Quarterly
The Laughter Prescription
Maledicta: International Journal of Verbal Aggression
Maledicta Monitor

Law Humor
Humor Events and Possibilities
The Jokesmith
Journal of Irreproducible Results
Maledicta: International Journal of Verbal Aggression
Maledicta Monitor
The Plague
This Brain Has a Mouth
The Weekly Farce
Wilde Times
Ye Olde Bastards Bulletin

Library Sciences Humor
Ballast Quarterly Review
Humor Events and Possibilities

Limericks
Ballast Quarterly Review
Capitol Comedy
Humor Events and Possibilities
Maledicta: International Journal of Verbal Aggression
Maledicta Monitor
Pun Intended
Woddis News

Literature Humor
Ballast Quarterly Review
Humor Events and Possibilities
Humor: International Journal of Humor Research
Journal of Irreproducible Results
MAD
Maledicta: International Journal of Verbal Aggression
Maledicta Monitor
Mark Twain Circular
Mark Twain Journal

The Monthly...Bulletin
The Plague
The Pundit
Thalia: Studies in Literary Humor
The Weekly Farce

Mathematics Humor
Ballast Quarterly Review
Humor Events and Possibilities
Humor: International Journal of Humor Research
Journal of Irreproducible Results
Maledicta: International Journal of Verbal Aggression
Maledicta Monitor
The Monthly...Bulletin

Medical Humor
Carolina HaHa Newsletter
Humor Events and Possibilities
Humor, Hypnosis and Health Quarterly
Humor: International Journal of Humor Research
The Jokesmith
Journal of Irreproducible Results
Journal of Nursing Jocularity
Journal of Polymorphous Perversity
Laugh It Up
Laugh It UpDate
Laughing Matters
MAD
Maledicta: International Journal of Verbal Aggression
Maledicta Monitor
The Monthly...Bulletin
One to One
Punch Digest for Canadian Doctors
Quagmire
The Steve Wilson Report
This Brain Has a Mouth
Wilde Times
Ye Olde Bastards Bulletin

Music Humor
The Peter Schickele Rag

Nursing Humor
Humor Events and Possibilities
Humor, Hypnosis and Health Quarterly
Humor: International Journal of Humor Research
The Jokesmith
Journal of Irreproducible Results
Journal of Nursing Jocularity

Laugh It Up
Laugh It UpDate
The Laughter Prescription
Laughter Works The Newsletter
One to One
Punch Digest for Canadian Doctors
The Steve Wilson Report
This Brain Has a Mouth
Ye Olde Bastards Bulletin

Philately Humor
Humor Stamp Directory

Philosophy Humor
Ballast Quarterly Review
Carolina HaHa Newsletter
Humor Events and Possibilities
Humor, Hypnosis and Health Quarterly
Humor: International Journal of Humor Research
Journal of Irreproducible Results
Latest Jokes
Laugh It Up
Laugh It UpDate
The Monthly...Bulletin
Ostrich Watchers Newsletter
The Weekly Farce

Physics Humor
Humor Events and Possibilities
Journal of Irreproducible Results
The Monthly...Bulletin

Poetry Humor
Ballast Quarterly Review
Humor Events and Possibilities
Journal of Insignificant Research
MAD
Maledicta: International Journal of Verbal Aggression
Maledicta Monitor
Pun Intended
Thalia: Studies in Literary Humor
The Weekly Farce

Political Humor
Ballast Quarterly Review
Capitol Comedy
Carolina HaHa Newsletter
Current Comedy
Fillmore Bungle

Funny Stuff From the Gags Gang
Gag Re-Cap
Humerus
Humor Events and Possibilities
The Jokesmith
Journal of Irreproducible Results
Just For Laughs
Latest Jokes
The Laugh Connection
Laughing Matters
MAD
Maledicta: International Journal of Verbal Aggression
Maledicta Monitor
Minne Ha Ha
One to One
The Plague
Pun Intended
Punch Digest for Canadian Doctors
Quagmire
The Quayle Quarterly
The Realist
Spy
The Stark Fist of Removal
View From the Ledge
The Weekly Farce
Wilde Times
Witty World
Women's Glib
Ye Olde Bastards Bulletin

Political Science Humor
Fillmore Bungle
Humor Events and Possibilities
The Jokesmith
Journal of Irreproducible Results
Latest Jokes
Maledicta Monitor
The Plague
Quagmire
The Weekly Farce

Psychiatry Humor
Ballast Quarterly Review
Humor Events and Possibilities
Humor, Hypnosis and Health Quarterly
The Jokesmith
Journal of Irreproducible Results
Journal of Nursing Jocularity
Journal of Polymorphous Perversity

Latest Jokes
Laugh It Up
Laugh It UpDate
Laughing Matters
Maledicta: International Journal of Verbal Aggression
Maledicta Monitor
Punch Digest for Canadian Doctors
This Brain Has a Mouth
The Weekly Farce
Ye Olde Bastards Bulletin

Psychology Humor
Ballast Quarterly Review
Carolina HaHa Newsletter
Humor Events and Possibilities
Humor, Hypnosis and Health Quarterly
Humor: International Journal of Humor Research
The Jokesmith
Journal of Irreproducible Results
Journal of Nursing Jocularity
Journal of Polymorphous Perversity
Latest Jokes
Laughing Matters
Ostrich Watchers Newsletter
The Steve Wilson Report
Thalia: Studies in Literary Humor
This Brain Has a Mouth
The Weekly Farce

Regional/Local Humor
Ballast Quarterly Review
Carolina HaHa Newsletter
Funny Stuff From the Gags Gang
Gag Re-Cap
Humor Events and Possibilities
The Jokesmith
Maledicta: International Journal of Verbal Aggression
Maledicta Monitor
The Nose
One to One
The Plague
Punch Digest for Canadian Doctors
Spy
Thalia: Studies in Literary Humor
The Weekly Farce
The Wit
Women's Glib
The Yellow Journal

Religion Humor
Carolina HaHa Newsletter
Fillmore Bungle
Humor Events and Possibilities
The Jokesmith
Journal of Irreproducible Results
Latest Jokes
Laugh It Up
Laugh It UpDate
Laughing Matters
Maledicta: International Journal of Verbal Aggression
Maledicta Monitor
The Monthly...Bulletin
The Plague
The Stark First of Removal
Thalia: Studies in Literary Humor
the Blab
Thoughts For All Seasons
The Weekly Farce

Research on Humor
Carolina HaHa Newsletter
Humor Events and Possibilities
Humor, Hypnosis and Health Quarterly
Humor: International Journal of Humor Research
Journal of Nursing Jocularity
The Laugh Connection
Laugh It Up
Laugh It UpDate
Laughing Matters
The Laughter Prescription
Laughter Works The Newsletter
Maledicta: International Journal of Verbal Aggression
Maledicta Monitor
The Pundit
The Steve Wilson Report
Thalia: Studies in Literary Humor
Wilde Times
Witty World

Scholarly Reviews of Humor as a Subject for Study
Carolina HaHa Newsletter
Humor Events and Possibilities
Humor, Hypnosis and Health Quarterly
Humor: International Journal of Humor Research
The Intra-Tent Journal
Laugh It Up
Laugh It UpDate
Maledicta: International Journal of Verbal Aggression
Maledicta Monitor

Pratfall
Thalia: Studies in Literary Humor
Witty World

Sciences Humor
Ballast Quarterly Review
Carolina HaHa Newsletter
Funny Stuff From the Gags Gang
Humor Events and Possibilities
Journal of Insignificant Research
Journal of Irreproducible Results
Journal of Nursing Jocularity
Journal of Polymorphous Perversity
Maledicta: International Journal of Verbal Aggression
Maledicta Monitor
The Monthly...Bulletin
One to One
Pun Intended
Punch Digest for Canadian Doctors
Spy
The Weekly Farce
Women's Glib

Social Sciences Humor
Ballast Quarterly Review
Carolina HaHa Newsletter
Current Comedy
Fillmore Bungle
Funny Stuff From the Gags Gang
Humor Events and Possibilities
Humor, Hypnosis and Health Quarterly
Journal of Irreproducible Results
Journal of Polymorphous Perversity
Latest Jokes
Laughing Matters
MAD
Maledicta: International Journal of Verbal Aggression
Maledicta Monitor
Minne Ha Ha
The Monthly...Bulletin
One to One
Ostrich Watchers Newsletter
The Plague
Pun Intended
The Realist
Spy
This Brain Has a Mouth
Thoughts For All Seasons
The Weekly Farce
Women's Glib

Sociology Humor
Ballast Quarterly Review
the Blab
Fillmore Bungle
Humor Events and Possibilities
Humor: International Journal of Humor Research
Journal of Irreproducible Results
Laugh It Up
Laugh It UpDate
Maledicta: International Journal of Verbal Aggression
Maledicta Monitor
The Monthly...Bulletin
Thoughts For All Seasons

Summary of Conferences and Symposiums on Humor
Carolina HaHa Newsletter
Humor Events and Possibilities
Humor, Hypnosis and Health Quarterly
Journal of Nursing Jocularity
Laugh It Up
Laugh It UpDate
Laughing Matters
Laughter Works The Newsletter
Punch Digest for Canadian Doctors
Witty World

Visual Humor
Ballast Quarterly Review
Carolina HaHa Newsletter
CRACKED
Humor Events and Possibilities
Humerus
Journal of Irreproducible Results
MAD
Minne Ha Ha
The Monthly...Bulletin
The Nose
The Plague
Pun Intended
Spy
Thalia: Studies in Literary Humor
Witty World
Women's Glib
The Yellow Journal

Word Play and Puns
Ballast Quarterly Review
Carolina HaHa Newsletter
Humor Events and Possibilities

Humor, Hypnosis and Healthy Quarterly
Journal of Irreproducible Results
MAD
Maledicta: International Journal of Verbal Aggression
Maledicta Monitor
The Monthly...Bulletin
The Plague
Pun Intended
The Pundit
Thoughts For All Seasons
The Weekly Farce
Word Ways: The Journal of Recreational Linguistics

Zoology Humor
Ballast Quarterly Review
Humor Events and Possibilities
Journal of Insignificant Research
Journal of Irreproducible Results
Maledicta: International Journal of Verbal Aggression
Maledicta Monitor

Index

Child, T. S., 130
Christmas spending, humor of, 163-164
Chuckle Institute, 55
Church of Mondy Night Football, 225
Church of the SubGenius, 175
Circulation of humor magazines, total, 3
Circulation rates of humor magazines, 241-242
Cleveland, humor from, 227
Clipophilia, 225
Clown Care Unit, 103
Clowning, 101
Clowning, therapeutic, 17-18, 103
Coe, Donna, 33, 34
College humor magazines, 11, 50, 139, 148, 218, 230, 235, 236, 237
Columbe, Bob, 235
Columbia University, humor magazine of, 230
Comedy agents, listings of, 33
Comedy & Comment, 226
Comedy club owners, polling of, 34
Comedy clubs, listings of, 33, 89
Comedy managers, listings of, 33
Comedy Performers Association, 31
Comedy production companies, listings of, 33
Comedy publicists, listings of, 33
Comedy Registry, The, 226
Comedy talent brokers, listings of, 33
Comedy USA Industry Guide, 33
Comedy USA Newswire, 34
Comedy Writers Association, 35
Comedy Writers Association Newsletter, 35
Comedy Writers Workshops, 226
Comedy writers, listings of, 33
Comic Highlights, 36
Comic Relief, 226
Committee for Immediate Nuclear War, 226
Computer Sciences humor, 259
Computers, humor via, 142, 235
Conspiracy of the "Normals," 175
Contardi, Barbara, 224
Cooking, "road kill" and, 173-174
Couch Potatoes, 226
Cousteau, Jacques, 39
CRACKED, 38
Crane, Alison L., 15
CreeYadio Services, 142

Crescenti, Peter, 235
Croc, 226
Crosbie, John S., 67
Crotty, James, 233
Crystal, Billy, 226
Cummings, Barbara, 214
Cummings, H. J., 214
Current Comedy, 40
Curses, 63

D
Dahl, Bard, 233
Dahmer, Jeffrey, 197-198
Dartnell, 226
Davidson, Alfred E., 19
Davis, Rick, 58
Deceased humor magazines and humor organizations, 223
De Fuccio, Jerry, 38
Dentistry humor, 259
Disabled, humor and the civil rights of the, 184
Dobbs, J. R. "Bob," 175, 176-177
Dogs United for More Bones (D.U.M.B.), 216
Dress down day, 95
Durham, Chuck, 55
Durham, Mary, 55
Duvall, Jack, 224

E
Eckler, A. Ross, 210
Economics humor, 259
Education humor, 260
"Elation Strategist," 96
Electric Weenie, The, 36, 227
Ellenbogen, Glenn C., 3, 85
Ellison, Harlan, 161-162
Emory University, humor magazine of, 236
English humor, 260
Epigrams, 187-189
Et cetera, 230
Executives, humor aimed at, 22, 110
Eye-crossing, advanced, 58

F
Farber, Paul, 59
Ferrari, L. Katherine, 230
Ficarra, John, 113
Fields, W. C., 57, 171
Fillmore Bungle, The, 167

Fillmore, Millard, 167
Film Media humor, 260
Finegan, T. J., 228
Flavin, Jack, 234
Fletcher, Douglas, 82
Fobes, John E., 19
Foreign Languages humor, 261
Fox, Jon, 89
Frank, 227
Freedonia Gazette, The, 124
Free Territory of Ely-Chatelaine, 227
Freud references, uses of to look good, 87
Friedman, Milton, 19
Fultz, John, 234
Funny Business, 227
Funny faces, 58
Funny Funny World, 227
Funny props, 101
Funny Side Up, 227
Funny Stuff Comedy Almanac, 42
Funny Stuff From the Gags Gang, 44
Funny Times, 227
Funt, Allen, 99

G
Gag Re-Cap, 46
Galvin, Brendan, 234
Gantt, Barry, 112
Garrett, George, 234
Gelosophist, The, 227
Gene Perret's Round Table, 48
General humor, 261-262
Geology humor, 262
Gerrold, David, 161
Gesundheit Institute, 227-228
Get Stupid, 228
Gibbons, Cathy, 101
Giggle Books, 228
Gilliam, Terry, 182-183
Givin, Lucy, 184
Glimpse, 230
Godfrey, S. T., 228
Goldberg, Whoppi, 226
Goodman, Joel, 97
Goofus Office Gazette, The, 228
Gottlieb, Al, 46
Government intervention, humor in, 135
Graffiti, humorous, 65-66
Grantland, 17
Graphics, humorous, 258-259
Green, Elmer W., 50

H
Hallock, Gary, 155
Hally, Simon, 153
Hamilton, Ruth, 28
Hammurabi, the Code of, 133-134
Hand gymnastics, 58
Hardesty, Lloyd, 237
Hardy, Oliver, 169
Harpoon, 228
Hartman, George, 30
Harvard Lampoon, 11, 50
Harvard University, humor magazine of, 50
Hatchett, Jr., Louis B., 237
Headline humor, 109
Hermann, Carl T., 194
Higgs, Liz Curtis, 231
History humor, 262
Hofstra University, humor magazine of, 139
Honeymooners, The, 235
Hooked on phonics, 140
Housewife-Writer's Forum, 223, 228
Housewive's Humor, 223, 228
Humanities humor, 262
Humerus, 52
Humor basket, 18
Humor Correspondence Club, 54
Humor Correspondence Club Membership List, 54
Humor Digest, 229
Humor Events and Possibilities, 214
Humor, Hypnosis and Health Quarterly, 55
Humor: International Journal of Humor Research, 70
Humor in the workplace, 95-96
Humor Magazine, 229
Humor on the road, 233
HUMOR Project, The, 97
Humor "salon," 112
Humor Stamp Club, 56
Humor Stamp Directory, 56, 57
Hussein, Saddam, jokes about, 202

I
Ig Nobel Prize, 78
Illustrations, humorous, 258-259
Inside Joke, 229
Institute of Totally Useless Skills, The, 58
Insults, 63

Insults, gay, 63
International Association of Professional
  Bureaucrats, 229
International Automative Hall of Shame,
  229
International Banana Club, 59
International Brotherhood of Old Bastards,
  61
International Dull Folks, 229
International Journal of Creature
  Communication, 229
International Laughter Society, 230
International Maledicta Society, 63
International Order of the Armadillo, 230
International Organization of Nerds, 230
International Save the Pun Foundation, The,
  67
International Society for General
  Semantics, 230
International Society for Humor Studies,
  70
Intra-Tent Journal, The, 169

J
Jackson, Tod, 236
Jester, of Columbia University, 11, 230
Jewish humor, 72-73
Jewish jokes, 73
Johnson, Erik A., 234
Johnson, Sam, 132
Joke services, childrens, 92-93
Joke Services humor, 263
Jokesmith, The, 74
Journal of Insignificant Results, 76
Journal of Irreproducible Results, 78
Journal of Nursing Jocularity, 82
Journal of Polymorphous Perversity, 85
Juggling, 58
Just For Laughs, 89

K
Karoshi, 179
Keaton, Buster, 171
Keller, Sheldon, 42, 44
Kid show performers, 92, 101
Kid Show Quarterly, 92
Kilgore, Al, 169
Kim, Robert, 230
Kissell, Steve, 238
Klein, Allen, 199
Knucklehead Press, 230

Krassner, Paul, 160, 161-162

L
LAAF Newsletter, 230
Ladies Against Women, 231
Laff-Letter, The, 230
Laff Lines, 231
Landon, Hut, 89
Lane, Michael, 233
Langdon, Harry, 171
Langham, Charles G., 163
Larremore, Robert J., 232, 235
Larson, Charles U., 229
Lassin, Gary, 190
Last Month's Newsletter, 151
Latest Jokes, 31
Laugh Clinic, The, 231
Laugh Connection, The, 94
Laugh Factory, 231
Laughing Bear News, 231
Laughing Heart, The, 231
Laughing Matters, 97
Laugh It Up, 15
Laugh It UpDate, 15
Laugh Lovers News, 236
Laugh•Makers Variety Arts Magazine, 101
Laughter Prescription, The, 105
Laughter Works The Newsletter, 108
Laugh Time U.S.A., 231
LaughTrack, 231
Laurel and Hardy, 169-171
Laurel, Stan, 169
Law humor, 263
Leadership, 110
Leiber, Deborah, 233
Lenehan, Arthur F., 22, 110
Lent, John A. 206
Leonard, James S., 118
Letterman, David, 21
Lewitinn, Lawrence V., 148
Library Sciences humor, 263
Libsat, 231
L.I.G.H.T. (Laughter in God, History and
  Theology), 232
Limericks, 263
Limerick Special Interest Group, The, 232
*Limerick Special Interest Group
  Newsletter, The*, 232
Lincoln, Abraham, humor of, 75
Literature humor, 263-264
Lloyd, Harold, 171

Nursing humor, 264-265

O

Obscenity, undetected in Mark Twain's *Tom Sawyer*, 122-123
O'Donnell, Frank, 203-205, 224
Offensive humor, 63
Old Bastardette, 61
O'Liners, 233
Oliver Ostrich "Head in the Sand" Anonymous Annual Award, 144
One to One: The Journal of Creative Broadcasting, 142
Onion, The, 233
O'Paistie, F. D. P., 234
Opus, 207
Orben's Current Comedy, 233
Orlovsky, Leslie, 33
Ostriches Anonymous Association, 144
Ostrich Watchers Newsletter, 144
Otis, Louisa, 225
Outland, 207

P

Pangloss Papers, 233
Paper airplanes, 58
Pasteur, Louis, 166
Pedantic Monthly, The, 234
Pelley, Jim, 108
Pensley, D. S., 235
Periodic Journal of Bibliography, The, 234
Perret, Gene, 48
Perret, Linda, 48
Peter Schickele Rag, The, 147
Phantastic Phunnies, 234
Ph.B. (Doctorate of Bananistry), 59
Philately humor, 265
Philosophy humor, 265
Phoebe: The Newsletter of Eccentricity, 234
Physics humor, 265
Piranha, 234
Plague, The, 148
Poetry humor, 265
Political humor, 265-266
Politically correct, jokes relating to the, 219-220
Political Science humor, 266
Pollak, Kevin, 90-91
Poor Ol' George, 234
Possum County News, 234

Post Scripts, 234
Poulos, M. R., 201
Poultry: A Magazine of Voice, 234
Pratfall, 169
Princeton Tiger, The, 235
Princeton University, humor magazine of, 235
PRN: Playfulness, Revelry, Nonsense, 233
Procrastinators' Club of America, 151
Product warning labels, scientific truth in, 80-81
Professional Comedian's Association, The, 235
Professionals Anonymous, 185-186
Prolock Society, 235
Proxmire, Senator, 19
Psychiatry humor, 266-267
Psychology humor, 267
PUNCH Digest for Canadian Doctors, 153
Pundit, The, 67
Pun Intended, 155
Puns, 270-271
Puppetry, 101

Q

Quagmire, 135
Quayle, Dan, 157-159, 207
Quayle Quarterly, The, 157

R

Radoski, Zachery, 218
Ragaway, Martin A., 227
R.A.L.P.H. (Royal Association for the Longevity and Preservation of the Honeymooners), 235
R.A.L.P.H. Newsletter, The, 235
Raskin, Victor, 70
Rave, 235
Realist, The, 160
rec.humor.funny, 235
Reference citations, arbitrary use of, 87-88
Regional/Local humor, 267
Resurrected humor magazine, 160
Reiner, Rob, 90
Relationships, humor in, 29
Religion humor, 268
Research on humor, 268
Rhode Island, humor from, 203
Richard, Michel P., 187
Rich's Arizona Humor, 235
Risk denying statements, 145-146

"Road kill," the cooking of, 173-174
Road signs, humorous, 114
Rogers, Will, 57
Roman, Sharil, 237
Rosenbalm, Jack O., 224
Ross, Bob, 94
Rotches, Al, 139
Rubber stamps, humorous, 194

S
S.A.L.T. Newsletter (Salvation and Laughter Together Newsletter), 235-236
San Francisco, humor from, 141
Santa Claus, postage stamp of, 57
Sarcastics Anonymous and Laugh Lovers News, 236
Savaria, Jr., Edward, 229
Scharf, Lauren I. Barnett, 227, 232
Schickele, Peter, 147
Schlemiezel, 73
Scholarly reviews of humor as a subject of study, 268-269
Schultheis, Mindy, 231
Sciences humor, 269
Sciuridae, Brother Solomon O., 61
S.C.R.O.O.G.E. (Society to Curtail Ridiculous, Outrageous, and Ostentatious Gift Exchange), 163
S.C.R.O.O.G.E. Newsletter, 163
Scrotum humanum, 77
Shepherd, Chuck, 137, 193
Shmaiser, Der/Spanker, The, 236
Shtetl humor, 73
Siegel, Rick, 231
Silly Club Rag, The, 165
Silly hat contests, 96
Silver, Karen, 105
Silverstone, Lou, 38
Simons, Joshua, 235
Slang, prison, 63
Slang, sexual, 63
Slurs, 63
Small Street Journal, 236
Smith, Ronald L., 235
Smurfs in Hell, 236
Snelson, Karin, 224
Snicker Humor Magazine, 236
Snooze News, The, 229
Social Sciences humor, 269
Society for the Preservation and Enhancement of the Recognition of

Millard Fillmore, Last Of the Whigs (S.P.E.R.M.F.L.O.W.), 167
Sociology humor, 270
Sons of the Desert, 169
Soundings, 236
Sound of one hand clapping, 58
South Africa, Jewish cartoonists in, 73
Southeastern New England, humor from, 203
Spoke, The, 11, 236
Spoonerisms, 63
Spoon playing, 58
Sport-fishing, 229
Spy, 172
Stanford Chaparral, 236
Stanford University, humor magazine of, 236
Stang, Rev. Ivan, 175
Stanley, L., 228
Stark Fist of Removal, The, 175
Stevens, Norman D., 216-217
Steve Wilson Report, The, 178
Stewart, J. D. "Dull," 229
Strategic Trash Initiative, 136
Stress, reduction of through humor, 179-180
Studies in American Humor, 237
Stupid pet tricks, 21
Sullivan, Danno, 165
Summary of conferences and symposiums on humor, 270
Supreme Archbastard, 61
Suzette, Miss, 226
Szabo, Joseph George, 206

T
Tanner, James, 237
TASP Newsletter, 237
Taub, Bill, 231
Tavernier-Courbin, Jacqueline, 181
Ten Best-Stressed Puns, 69
Tenney, Thomas A., 121
Thalia: Studies in Literary Humor, 181
Time line of humor periodicals, 251-254
This Brain Has a Mouth, 184
This Magazine, 237
Thoughts For All Seasons: The Magazine of Epigrams, 187
Threats, 63
Three Stooges Fan Club, The, 190
Three Stooges Journal, The, 190